If the Kids are United

2015 Remastered edition: revised, added to, updated*

*Also available in red vinyl

Tony Hill

Tony Hill hails from Jacksdale, an old mining village on the Nottinghamshire/Derbyshire border, deep in D.H. Lawrence country. The world famous writer used to come dancing in Tony's village, where he had a great time, until, allegedly, getting knocked out for not supporting a local team. This is mentioned in Tony's books *If the Kids are United* and *The Palace and the Punks*. One of the last authors to be published by Victor Gollancz (before the Orion takeover), his - *Kes* evoking - book *If the Kids are United* was called 'the working-class Fever Pitch,' and received 5 and 4 star reviews. A punk writer, his style is fast paced and spontaneous.

If the Kids are United

'A witty insight into the loneliness of the long-distance red. Like Hill's life, the book is balanced between two worlds – the very real world of Jacksdale, and the almost mythical world of Old Trafford, which haunts the young Hill's mind much in the same way as Atlantis must have menaced the infant Captain Nemo. And while it's hard to describe villages like Jacksdale without straying into parody, Hill describes his village and his family with wit and pathos.'
★★★★★ *Four Four Two*

'This story of a Red growing up in a pit village during the 70's and 80's is both funny and sad at times...A great read.'
4/5 Glory Glory Man United (MUFC official magazine)

'For younger fans, there is an intoxicating account of the run-in to Fergie's first title triumph in 1993, while older fans will relish exhilarating memories of United in the 70's, a decade of Cup finals and cock-ups. Equally entertaining is Hill's witty and often poignant portrayal of a youth spent in a declining mining community...Impassioned and bleak but also hilarious.'
Manchester UNITED (the official MUFC magazine)

'Hill can be funny, but really finds his voice in harrowing recollections of the Hillsborough tragedy.'
Daily Mail

'A laddish feast of music, football and autobiography. Hill's passion for the game shines out like floodlights at a night-time match.'
Nottingham Evening Post

'A veritable collection of football stories from Hillsborough to Busby, Scargill to flares. It's a refreshing perspective from a non-Manc Red and it has poignant recollections from 70's Cup finals and 80's hoolie days.'
United We Stand

'A days-of-our-lives view of Man United from the wilderness years of the 70's to the rattling rise of Fergie's Red army.'
★★★★ *Total Football*

'Tony Hill made his momentous decision to become a Red Devils supporter in the 1970's and for the next twenty-two years lived and breathed to bag a Cup Final ticket. In this hilarious debut, Hill describes his consistently thwarted attempts to get his hands on the elusive voucher.'
EGO

'An East Midlands *Fever Pitch* without the middle-class guilt complex. It also points out that D.H. Lawrence got panned in a local pub for not supporting a Nottingham team.'
Left Lion

2015 – REVISED, ADDED TO AND UPDATED.

Also by Tony Hill
The Palace and the Punks

'It was as likely as finding a diamond in your dustbin. There it was in the heart of a scruffy, coal-scarred mining village whose narrow, terraced streets had no-nonsense names like Edward and Albert. Inside an old converted cinema, beneath a nicotine-stained ceiling, a local entrepreneur named Alf Hyslop opened a music venue called the Grey Topper. Somehow this nondescript, unvarnished venue managed to become part of music history. Tony Hill's book is a must-read for any muso who boogied, rocked or pogo-ed at anytime from '69 to '81.'
Nottingham Evening Post

'A very good and interesting perspective of those times.'
Andy Scott, Glam Rock band Sweet

'You can see the sweat dripping off the ceiling, sense the globule of spit skimming past your cheek, feel the poke in the eye of a spiky mohican or hear the rattling of bondage straps on pogoing punks. Tony Hill's book paints such a vivid picture of the Grey Topper that you're in there, sharing the hopes of the bands on the threshold of stardom or the despair of those on their way down. A compelling read.'
Derbyshire Times

'Endlessly gobsmacking...piss yourself laughing...like music books? Buy this.'
Left Lion magazine

New (major chapter in Tony Hill's life)

Even Everest Shook

Caught in the Nepal Earthquake 2015

Looking for adventure Tony Hill made the spontaneous decision to trek to Everest Base Camp in April 2015. After visiting the ancient temples and squares of Kathmandu, he flew into 'the most dangerous airport in the world,' Lukla, and with a group of fellow travellers from around the world set off up the Himalayan valleys Everest bound. Only 3 days into the trek they were in a mountain village when the devastating Nepal Earthquake struck. Lucky to escape uninjured - buildings crumbled at their side, boulders crashed through the ceiling of their teahouse - they find themselves stranded. Journey with Tony Hill, before, during and in the aftermath of the earthquake (and many aftershocks), and through his writing and eyes (via a series of stunning and haunting photographs) experience breathtaking beauty, the bonding and humour of a diverse set of characters, then overwhelming tragedy, and the fragility, resilience and spirituality of the human condition, as he slowly makes his way out of a disaster zone and home.

If the Kids are United
The Palace and the Punks
Even Everest Shook: caught in the Nepal earthquake 2015
Skye-Walker's Landscapes of Legends Quest
The Curse of the Crooked Spire and other fairytales
The Glastonbury Spirit and other tales of the supernatural
The Flowers of Romance
Glastonbury Tour

www.manutdbooks.com

If the Kids are United

Tony Hill

Northern Lights Lit

First published in Great Britain by Victor Gollancz in 1999.
Published in 2000 by Phoenix,
an imprint of Orion Books Ltd.
This edition published in 2015 by Northern Lights Lit.

Copyright © Tony Hill 2015.

ISBN: 978-0-9568409-5-0

For Mam and Dad

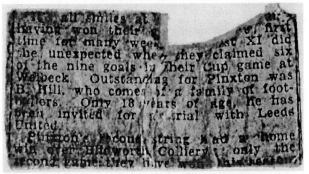

*Local press 1950's - 'Outstanding for Pinxton was B. Hill.
Only 18 years of age he's been invited for a trial with Leeds
United.' Man City were also showing interest in Dad. My life
could have turned out so differently.*

1970's

1970s

It's Living Inside Me

'No! No, no, yuh had enough time t'tek lace out on it...wing...there's a man free on yuh left...pass it...Gi'e it him....Tek him on...Shoot! Shoot...Gggooooaaalll...offside! Yuh must be bloody joking, linesman.'

'Dad's shouting was drifting up from downstairs again. I must have been about three or four. I climbed out of bed and quietly walked across the bedroom and out on to the landing, carefully avoiding the floorboards that creaked when stepped on. Slowly I began to descend the stairs. I'd reached the fifth step down. . .

'Useless! Bloody useless,' Dad's voice raged.

I turned and bolted back upstairs across the landing into my bedroom and dived under my bedsheets. Who was Dad mad at? Mam? I wondered. But she'd gone to bed early after tucking me in. Again I climbed out of bed and made my way to my parents' room. There was Mam, also awake.

'What's up, Tony?' asked Mam.

'Who's Dad shouting at?'

'Oh, that's just football on the telly. Go back to bed.'

I was thinking football must be important to make Dad so mad, but sometimes so happy. I like to think now that my first memory of hearing Dad shouting at football on the television was him watching Manchester United beat Benfica in the 1968 European Cup Final.

Our minds can be selective in what we remember from childhood. My memory has chosen George Best playing for Man United as the first time I saw football on the television. In the same way it has selected the gripping coverage of the Apollo space missions as my earliest television memories instead of *Gardeners' World*.

It had been snowing heavily and I was standing on my tiptoes looking out of the front-room window as a snow plough worked its way through the estate.

'Tony! Tony! Look, look. George Best,' said Dad.

I turned around, and there on the telly was this football player who looked like Jesus in a Red Devil shirt, dancing past defenders before putting the goalkeeper on his backside with a body swerve and side-footing the ball into the net. I don't know if it was then that I decided that Man United were my team or because my older brother (who never really liked football) said he supported them. Anyway, I decided that Man United were my team, setting myself up for a life-time of verbal abuse from the locals in the mining village (now ex-mining village) of Jacksdale, where I live, on the Nottinghamshire-Derbyshire border.

When I was a kid in the 1970s, Jacksdale was still typical of many northern working-class villages: terraced houses, a 1950's council estate, back-street spit-and-sawdust pubs with darts, dominoes and skittle teams, a miners' welfare club. And, although on the decline, there was still many a flat cap and demob suit to be seen. So many, in fact, that me and my friends had devised a game. We had to make it from one end of the village to the other without being spotted by a capper (our name for men who wore flat caps). Each of us started with five lives; if a capper looked at you then a life was lost. We'd be halfway through the village when an old man wearing a flat cap would be spotted staggering down the road between pubs.

'Capper,' I'd shout. And we'd all dive over a wall or hedge into someone's garden and lie there laughing until he passed by.

'Aah seen thee, Tony Hill, yuh cheeky little bogger. Ah knows tha Dad. Tha wants some belt tha does,' a capper once shouted back.

Pigeon racing was an important pastime to many cappers. Both our next-door neighbours had pigeon lofts at the top of their gardens. Venturing into our back garden was a hazardous business. On more than one occasion I'd had to have pigeon shit washed out of my hair. And Mam was none too pleased to fetch in the washing only to discover her smalls had been blitzed by a squadron of speckled greys. Old Arthur to the left of us would, at times, have difficulty in getting his pigeons to go back in the loft. If one landed on a rooftop he'd stand there shaking a seed tin to try and entice it down.

'Come on. Come on, me beauty . . . come on, let's 'aye yuh ....come on, my beauty....COME ON, COME ON YUH FUCKIN' BASTARD....LET'S 'AYE YUH.' The pigeon continued to strut up and down the roof . . . Raight! that's it. Pigeon pie fuh tea.'

Arthur went into his house and returned with a pellet gun. His eyesight wasn't too good and his first shot put a hole in the Gregorys' (at no. 2) bathroom window. His fourth shot was a direct hit, the pigeon plummeted to the ground where our pet cat Fluff, who'd been watching intently, made her move, seizing the bird and running under a shed with it.

The main passion for the majority of the male population of Jacksdale, including my Dad, was football. Many of the miners, who worked together and drank together, played in the same team. And if the pit gave a sense of community then so did the football club.

In the post-war years attendances for local derbies against other village teams would put Wimbledon FC to shame. Even in the 1970s the noise generated by the supporters of Pye Hill Colliery Football Club (Jacksdale's pit was called Pye Hill), the all-conquering Mansfield Sunday League team, was such that match reports in the local press often gave praise to the crowd. Not many Sunday League teams could boast the same.

Liverpool had the Kop, Man United the Stretford End, and Forest the Trent End; but Pye Hill FC had the Palmo End, a muddy grass bank rising up behind one net, where me and my mates would mimic the chants and songs we'd heard on *Match of the Day*.

Unfortunately, although the average age of the Palmo End was only about twelve, there was a hooligan element that got us a bad reputation with visiting teams. Several goalkeepers complained to the referee that they'd been struck from behind by a mud ball just before conceding a goal.

Jacksdale. Football, beer, miners, pigeon racing, darts, dominoes and skittles. Not the sort of place Germaine Greer would want to set up residence in.

Local literary genius D.H. Lawrence (who was born and raised in the nearby town of Eastwood) neglected to mention Jacksdale in any of his stories, yet he mentioned all the other neighbouring pit villages. Rumour has it that he was going to write about Jacksdale, but one day, on one of his wanders out of Eastwood, he had the misfortune to call in at one of the pubs in Jacksdale, where he was knocked out for not supporting a local team. So he got the hump with the place. He'd certainly mentioned one of his adventures down there in a letter to his agent, though (at the time of writing *Sons and Lovers*): '*My sister and I were at a bit of a dance last night at Jacksdale – mining village four miles out. It was most howling good fun. My sister found me kissing one of her friends goodbye – such a ripping little girl – and we were kissing like nuts – enter my sister – great shocks all round and much indignation. But life is awfully fast down here.*'

All the men on my Dad's side of the family, as far back as anyone can remember, worked down the pit and played football. I have a photocopy of a document from Pinxton Colliery (the village where Dad was born and bred) dated 1840, which lists the children employed by the pit. On it is my Great, Great, Great-Grandad Hill.

'John Hill is 10 years old. Works on the bank. Goes to the Methodist Sunday School. Is in easy lessons. Cannot spell. Does not know what his clothes are made of, nor what flannel is,' reads the description of him.

So, right back to the early days of organized football, the men of the Hill family played and supported the game. It runs as deep as the mines in my blood. At family get-togethers I'd sit listening, spellbound, as the brown ale flowed and the stories got around to football.* Tales of how Grandad Hill (Les, nicknamed 'Toy' because of his diminutive size) in the early part of the century, was 'one of the first black footballers': he would go straight from working down the pit Saturday mornings to play for a local team in the afternoon, caked head to toe in coal dust. There were no baths at the pit head in those days. Grandad had four brothers: Tom, Joe, Louis and Herbert. All five formed the forward line for Pinxton Colliery FC, and on one occasion played against Albert Iremonger, the famous Notts County keeper. Grandad put five past him, so the story goes.

7

My Dad (Brian) had two brothers, Uncle Jack and Uncle Don. All three had been very good footballers, then Uncle Don married a Manchester lass and moved with her family to Blackpool in the 1950s. He was invited for a trial with Blackpool FC. This was when they had their great side, with legend Stanley Matthews in the team. Don was told to report to coach Alex Munroe's house. He went there at the time he was supposed to, but Mr Munroe never turned up, and Don never did get his trial.

Several years later Don became friends with ex-Blackpool players Jim Kelly and Bill Perry (the scorer of the winner in the 1953 FA Cup Final) and talked them out of retirement to play for the Sunday League team he coached.

Uncle Jack was a good player, but with one big drawback. He was a defender with seriously bowed legs, so he would be frequently nutmegged.

And then there was my Dad, an outside-left, who was such a good player that several big clubs had him watched. Manchester City showed interest, and Scunthorpe offered him a trial, which he didn't bother attending. Dad never talked about his footballing past much, but my uncles always said he should have been a professional.

One day when no one else was at home, I was looking through a drawer of family photographs, and discovered an old clipping from a local newspaper which read: 'Outstanding for Pinxton was B. Hill, who comes from a family of footballers. Only 18 years of age he has been invited for a trial with Leeds United.'

Dad had never said anything to me about this. And it was Uncle Don, years later, who told me what happened: sadly Dad had broken his arm in a mining accident a few days before the trial.

When I was a kid, Dad used to take me down to the local rec with a ball to try and teach me some of his footballing tricks. But for some reason his Stanley Matthews shimmey used to leave me rolling around the floor in hysterics.

The football recollections I would listen to most intently were those concerning Manchester United. There was a reverential tone in the voice of Dad and my uncles when they talked about the Busby Babes.

Uncle Don was called up to do National Service in 1952, joining the 55th training regiment at Tunfanau, North Wales. Their football team had been Welsh champions for seven years running. There was a reason for their success. R. S. N. Mclean, who ran the team, had connections at the War Office, enabling him to snap up the young professionals called up to do their National Service. Don played alongside Busby Babe Tommy Taylor, later to lose his life in the Munich air disaster. Also in the team were Keith Burkinshaw, George Showel (Wolves), John Newman (Birmingham), and John Wylie (Preston N.E.).

One day Don was called off the parade ground to join his team-mates to go and play against the Army Ordnance Corps, near Birmingham. Don played inside-right, and it was his job to mark the opposing team's left-half....the great Duncan Edwards. Don told of how the Manchester United legend scored the only goal of the game, lobbing the keeper from the halfway line.

All these stories intensified my passion for football, and in particular Manchester United. And I'm not going to make any apologies for living in Nottinghamshire and supporting Man United. Yeah, I can understand the scepticism people may feel about me, especially in the all-conquering Fergie years, when United became the dominant team and so many glory hunters attached themselves to the club. But the first season I can remember being a United fan, there was no bandwagon to jump on.

It was the 1973-74 season. Busby's great team had disbanded, George Best had gone AWOL, and United were heading for relegation. And in the penultimate match of the season at Old Trafford, there was the irony of ironies. United legend Denis Law, now playing for Manchester City, back-heeled into United's net to send them down. Thousands of United supporters invaded the pitch, causing the game to be abandoned. But the Football League ruled the result would stand.

It has been a trait of my character, right from an early age, to be different, an individual. And, believe it or not, when I was 8, back in 1973, being a Man United fan made me part of a rare species in Jacksdale. I was the only boy at infant school who supported them and the only boy in my class at junior school who supported them. I loved the attention it got me, being known as *the* Manchester United fan.

There was also no hereditary factor involved. Dad, for much of his young life, was too busy playing football on Saturday afternoons to go and support any specific team. When, in 1977, he started taking me to watch Nottingham Forest regularly, it was too late, I'd already sold my soul to the Red Devils of Manchester.

*Even when Mam told me I'd been close to The Beatles I wasn't as impressed. Well, actually I was just a three week old foetus inside Mam's womb, when her and Dad won a *Daily Mirror* competition to go to their Golden Ball at the Royal Albert Hall, and the Fab Four were in a private box the next-but-one to my

10

parent's. John Lennon bored with it all and wondering how many holes it would take to fill the Albert Hall.

The Flared Years

After the swinging sixties, the seventies were just . . . well, silly, really. No wonder that, as a kid in the ludicrous early 1970s, I thought life was one long comedy sketch, and those of us who were around at the time have all, years later, tried to destroy the photographic evidence of our hairstyles and the clothes we wore.

Long hair, the feather cut, delta-wing shirt collars, kipper ties, loon pants, twenty-one-inch bell-bottom flares with pockets on the side that went down to your knees, platform soles, silk football scarfs tied around wrists. These were the days of glam rock, the glitter bands, Slade, The Sweet, Wizard, Gary Glitter and Alvin Stardust (now we are talking silly). Then there were the pompous supergroups: The Eagles, Genesis; and the Take That's of the time: The Bay City Rollers, The Osmonds, The Cassidys. One day Mam had to console my older sister Elaine, who was sobbing uncontrollably. She and her school friends had travelled down to Heathrow Airport to see David Cassidy get off a plane from America. He hadn't turned up, thus ruining her life. Elaine's musical tastes became cooler, though, and I loved her T-Rex, Bowie and Roxy Music records.

I was at infant school, and for a time in 1973 became seriously ill. While off school sick with chicken pox, our pet cat Fluff scratched me as I played with her. The scratch caused an infection which developed into septicaemia, leaving me out for the season.

For the second time in my young life I was seriously ill (when 13 months old I'd had gastroenteritis, so bad that Mam and Dad couldn't even hold me, I was separated from them behind glass, in an isolation ward at Nottingham City Hospital, they thought they'd lose me. I made a come back). One of the chicken pox on my swollen head was the size of a 2p piece, most – all over my head and body - were 1p size (all would leave me scarred for life). The doctor – when he finally came out after Mam's pleading and sobs down the phone had convinced him I was seriously ill – had seen nothing like it before. Fearing I'd developed some sort of mutant version of the illness that was highly contagious and could wipe out mankind, he put me in quarantine, immediately. Even my brother and sister (when they came home from school) were turned away (they had to go stay at our grandparents). Dad asked if he should paint a black cross on our front door.

The Red Devil child, who looked like something from a Hammer Horror film, a freak. The word spread, an alien plague had come to Kitson Avenue. One boy dared to peer in through a gap in the curtains into the Goose Fair sideshow booth (which was our living room, where my bed had been brought down from upstairs), Nigel Lenton. He knocked on the window, and when I raised my delirious, moaning head that looked like it had been dipped in a toxic bath of a Marvel Comic villain, he screamed and ran in terror. Ha! At least I had revenge. He'd previously had me running in terror, to go hide behind the settee, when he'd come to our door (to call for my brother), dressed in a *Dr Who*, Dalek costume. Neither of us wanted to exterminate each other, though, Nigel was the only other United fan I knew.

In those days no one from my background could afford the luxury of more than one TV in the house, so being in the front room I at least could watch that during my illness. Children's books – borrowed from the library – were also at hand. The first book to really ever catch my attention and set my imagination on fire was Maurice Sendak's *Where the Wild Things Are*: the walls of the room melted away, I ran through woods into the land of monsters, played football with them. Or tried to, these weren't the friendly monsters like in the book. They kicked me, pulled my hair, bit me and chased me out of the woods then down a maze of back brick alleys. But the illness had put me in a state of delirium at times, hallucinating, so it could have been the Leeds United team of 'bite yer legs' Hunter, Bremner, Charlton, Giles and other malicious beasts on *Match of the Day*? By 1974 I was back to full fitness and out playing football all day again.

Football aside, the only other interest I had was what sweets 10p would buy me, and television. Catherine Bell, a girl in my class, had sent me a valentine's card and kissed me at her eighth birthday party, but that was just soppy stuff, I thought. And I was also a member of the Tufty Club; that was pretty important.

Kids' TV was great: there was *Captain Pugwash*, with its dodgy character names like Master Bates and Seaman Stains; *Mr Ben*, who liked to dress up and act out his fantasies; and every weekday morning during the school holidays they showed the same programmes year after year, things like *Stingray, Champion the Wonder Horse, The Banana Splits* incorporating *The Arabian Knights* ('size of an Elephant'), *Skippy the Bush Kangaroo* and *Tarzan*.

Saturday mornings was *TISWAS*, the kids' programme for adults, with Chris Tarrant, the bucketeers, the phantom

13

flan flinger, Spit the dog, and voluptuous Sally James, who, while wearing fishnet stockings, would pull on garters sent to her by sailors on one of Her Majesty's battleships, causing a sensation in my Y-fronts that I didn't quite understand.

Saturday nights were the best, with *Morecambe and Wise*, *Parkinson* and *Match of the Day*, hosted by this funny looking chap with a pointy, bearded chin, who talked about football in a way that I didn't understand. I would turn to Dad for an explanation, but even he had been reduced to silence and just sat there staring at the screen, bewildered look on his face.

The Family was a BBC fly-on-the-wall documentary series. For twelve weeks the cameras invaded the lives of the Wilkins family from Reading. This was supposed to show the everyday lives of an ordinary working-class family. Of all the flies on all the walls of working-class-family homes in England, they had to choose this one. What a dowdy, stupid lot they were. The flies on the walls of the Hill household were getting much more entertainment.

We lived in a semi on the 1950s council estate in Jacksdale. There was my sport-loving Dad (Brian). He'd left the pit in his late twenties and since then had had a variety of industrial jobs. A small man approaching his fortieth birthday, his thinning, slicked-back, Brylcreemed 1950s hairstyle was now mutating into more of your Bobby Charlton look. When mad he expressed his anger by slamming shut every door in the house.

Dad loved jazz music and the big bands, Ted Heath was his hero (the band leader, not the fat Tory). Dad also had a fine taste in comedy, introducing us to the splendours of Laurel and Hardy and the Goons, but for some unfathomable reason two of the worst jokes in history would nearly kill him with laughter. Every time he's drunk at family parties (even to this day) he will tell these jokes, which we have to participate in the telling of, as if we've never heard them before:

Dad: 'My dog's got no nose.'

Me: 'How does it smell?'

Dad: (now doubled over with tears of laughter streaming down his face) 'Terrible.'

Dad: 'I've got a dentist appointment tomorrow.'

Me: 'What time's that?'

Dad: (now on his knees, punching the floor, laughing uncontrollably, he is unable to give the answer.)

Me: 'What time's that?'

Dad: 'Toof . . . hurty.'

Mam (Dorothy), a towering 4ft 10', worked as a secretary for a firm that manufactured creosote, so would often come home smelling like a garden shed. Mam stayed neutral in family disputes, acting as the peacemaker. Although a quiet woman she had a loud, ebullient laugh. She wasn't interested in going out to the Miners' Welfare for a game of Bingo and to hear the village gossip, preferring to stay at home reading her Catherine Cookson novels while listening to Johnny Mathis or Nana Maskouri records, or knitting little woollen animals for the children of friends and relatives. Mam would get a bit attached to her woollen creations, though, often taking a collection of them to the bench at the top of the garden for a group photograph, before reluctantly giving them away.

Elaine was the eldest child, seven years my senior. Her pretty looks and slender frame masked a fiery temper, ignited by a fuse as short as the ones attached to sticks of dynamite in a Loony Tunes cartoon. She was intelligent, very good at art, and determined to leave Jacksdale and do something with her life.

My brother Brian (five years older than me) was the quiet, sensible one. He never really liked football, his heroes were Kung-Fu legend Bruce Lee and motorbike ace Barry Sheene rather than Kevin Keegan or Stuart Pearson.

May 1974, and Elaine's sixteenth birthday was drawing near. After much pleading and behaving as the model daughter, Mam and Dad reluctantly agreed to let her have a party to celebrate the event.

The evening of the party arrived. I was off out for the night with Mam and Dad to the Miners' Welfare. Brian was staying at home to act as DJ. As we walked down the hill into the centre of Jacksdale, a service bus pulled up about two hundred yards in front of us, and out of it emerged about thirty rowdy teenagers from the neighbouring village of Selston, carrying cans of Watneys Red Barrel and Party Sevens. They started up the hill in our direction.

'I hope this lot's not going to our Elaine's party,' said Mam, nervously.

'They'd better not be; she's only supposed to have invited ten close friends,' said Dad.

As the teenagers passed by, a youth dressed in white tartan-edged Bay City Roller flares, and obviously already pissed, stumbled into Dad.

'Zorry, mate . . . yuh gorra fag?' said the youth.

'No! I dunt smoke,' snapped Dad.

'D'ya know where Kitson Avenue is?' (The name of our street.)

Dad didn't answer. He just looked at Mam and frowned. Hours later, about 11.15 p.m., we headed home from the Welfare. As we walked down the road that led to

16

Kitson Avenue, the electrifying sound of T. Rex's 'Twentieth Century Boy' filled the night air.

'It's not still gooin on,' said Dad, his face reddening slightly.

Mam looked worried. I smiled in anticipation of what we were about to receive. As we turned the corner into our street, the youth with the Bay City Roller flares (now completely rat-arsed) fell into Dad.

'Zorry, mate . . . yuh gorra fag?' he slurred.

'I dunt bloody smoke!' shouted Dad, becoming increasingly embarrassed and angry.

The youth looked like he was going to say something back, but just tippled over sideways through somebody's hedge. We carried on down the street. 'Teenage Rampage' by The Sweet came blasting out of our house.

Across the road Mr Williams stood in the doorway of his house, wearing striped pyjama bottoms, a string vest and a flat cap. 'Aye thi oppun'd a naightclub, Brian?' he shouted to Dad.'

Old Arthur next door popped his head out of his bedroom window as we came to our front gate. 'Sort 'em airt, Brian. Ah's pigeons gunna sleep wi that racket gooin on?' he complained. Dad's face was now a deep red. Mam opened the front door. Sitting on the stairs was a youth, blood pouring from a gash on his forehead.

'Are you all right, duck?' asked Mam.

'No. I fell down the stairs and put me head through that,' he said, pointing to the smashed remains of Mam's china cabinet, which Dad, Brian and me had, earlier in the day, carried out of the front room and put in the porch at the bottom of the stairs to prevent it getting damaged. Dad, in the words of Barry Davies, went mad, and he'd every

17

right to go mad. In the front room the remaining partygoers, seeing the smoke coming out of Dad's ears, scurried for the nearest exit. Elaine ran and locked herself in the toilet.

Cigarette burns peppered the arms of the three-piece-suite; the carpet, strewn with Babycham bottles and cans of beer, squelched underfoot. Vomit overflowed from the plant pot holding Mam's rubber plant. Worst of all Dad's record collection lay scattered on the floor beneath the broken doors of the stereogram cabinet.

'What the bloody hell's gone off here? A riot?' stormed Dad.

Brian, who'd been in hiding, crawled from behind an armchair to the back of the settee in a vain attempt to sneak out of the room and escape to bed. But he'd been spotted.

'BRIAN!' bellowed Dad.

Brian stood up from behind the settee.

'Look at that stereo. You were supposed to be looking after it,' said Dad.

Brian shrugged his shoulders, then keeping his distance from Dad, sidestepped his way around the edge of the front room until he reached the door that led to the stairs. His gaze still fixed on Dad, he fumbled for the handle, opened the door and ran upstairs to bed.

The leftovers of the buffet, that Mam had lovingly prepared, decorated the walls and ceiling of the kitchen the aftermath of a food fight Hal Roach would have been proud of. Out in the back garden two youths lay brawling in the middle of Dad's prized rhododendrons.

Elaine was still locked in the toilet. Mam sat sobbing on a chair in the kitchen, her broken copy of Val Doonican's *Twenty Golden Greats* in one hand, the decapitated head of one of her knitted woollen animals in the other. I sat in a chair at the side of her, a smug smile on my face at the thought of being the favourite child for at least a week, and the benefits that could bring me.

But even I couldn't escape Dad's anger.

'Tony! Don't you even think about wanting a sixteenth birthday party.' (I was 8 and a half at the time.) Dad slammed shut every door in the house and went to bed.

A minute later there was a commotion upstairs, and footsteps could be heard running across the landing and down the stairs, as Dad chased the young couple he'd found shagging in his and Mam's bed, out of the house. My smugness soon disappeared when I went upstairs. Someone had taken a marker pen to my poster of Man United striker Lou Macari, and had drawn a penis coming out of the top of his head. They'd also scrawled:-

DICKHEAD

LIVERPOOL RULE

And when I got into bed I discovered a strange-looking party balloon, that I thought someone must have tried their hardest to blow up because of the amount of saliva it contained.

A month later the posters of Manchester United stars on my bedroom wall were joined by one of Johan Cruyff. In England's absence, I supported Holland in the 1974 World Cup. At the start of the 1974-75 season, I bought *Shoot!* football magazine which gave away a 'League ladder' on which you could follow your team's fortunes throughout the season. Each team's name was printed on a small separate piece of card, which you inserted into slits on the chart to show their position in the League. You could write down the scores in another section.

In August I placed Man United at the top of the Second Division table, and didn't have to move them for the rest of the season as they stormed their way to the Championship.

Jumpers for Goalposts, Isn't It

When I was in the first year at infant school, a teacher organized a game of five-a-side football in the playground. My team won 6-5, and I scored five of the goals. The other boys in my team lifted me on to their shoulders and carried me back into school. Suddenly, because I was good at football, I became popular. So, George Best may well have scored six goals for Man United away at Northampton in the FA Cup looking like he was suffering from a hangover, but scoring five goals in the school playground was good enough for me.

I think it's mainly due to my love of football that I had such a great childhood and so many friends. Life was so simple, pre-adolescence. All that mattered in life was Manchester United. In fact, I didn't realize there was anything wrong with the world, or that bad people existed, until I came across the dinner ladies at infant school. There was Hilda and Hilda, and they looked like, erm, Hilda Baker from the 1970s sitcom Nearest and Dearest.

They were trying to poison us. I was convinced they were. What other explanation could there be for every school meal tasting as if it had been doused with bleach? At lunchtime at school I couldn't wait to finish my dinner so I could get out in the playground for a game of football. I was a star player, my team needed me, and on one particular day we had an important match. A bag of cola-cubes was the prize for the winning team. Every pupil had finished their dinner and gone out to play - all except me. I sat prodding the mound of vegetables and mashed potatoes in front of me, and lifted the cardboard pastry lid off the pie to try to identify its contents. I didn't know what it was, I'd tasted one mouthful and spat it out under the table; and worst of all, the dessert was semolina pudding . . . oh Jesus . . . semolina pudding. (I'm writing this now with a bucket at the side of me.)

Hilda and Hilda insisted I eat every last morsel on my plate and lick my dessert bowl clean before I could go out to play. Hilda 1 stood over my shoulder. Hilda 2 guarded the door in case I made a dash for freedom.

'There's people starving in Africa, you know... they'd think they were in heaven if they were sat in your place,' Hilda 1 said, leaning over my shoulder.

My friends were banging on the windows beckoning for me to join them.

'Look at your friends enjoying themselves. Eat up, eat up, and then you can play,' said Hilda 2.

I bet Sammy McIlroy at United doesn't have this problem, I was thinking. I'd never heard Tommy Docherty say he'd dropped one of his players because they hadn't eaten their dinner.

To the cheers of my friends, I finally made it to the playground, with ten minutes of break remaining, but by then I felt too physically ill to play football, and had to sit and watch as my team crashed to a 6-11 defeat. The cola-cube trophy was lost.

I woke up screaming one night, after I'd had my reoccurring nightmare. I dreamt the two Hildas (laughing manically) were holding me by the ankles, upside down over an enormous vat of bubbling hot semolina. Mam came into my bedroom to see if I was all right, and I told her my sob story about school dinners.

A few days later she came up with a solution to my torment. A boy in my class lived just fifty yards from school, and went home for his dinner. Mam had arranged for me to go with him. I soon wished I'd kept my mouth shut. Firstly, it turned out that this boy's mother used to be a school dinner lady too - she cooked exactly the same unappetizing meals that were on offer at school - and, secondly, she would continually humiliate her son in front of me. One dinnertime she stormed into the kitchen and dangled a pair of the boy's underpants in front of his face.

'Look at this dirty article, you dirty, dirty boy. Shit stains all over 'em. What you reckon, Tony?' she said, turning to me. 'Nine years old and he still needs a potty.'

I looked agonizingly down at my chocolate custard covered chocolate sponge. My stomach gave a long groan.

Then there was antiquated teacher Miss Timms, with her fusty smelling Miss Marple clothes and horn-rimmed, thick lensed spectacles, giving her an evil owl gaze you couldn't escape from if you were her prey, which I was; her Victorian values and superstitions led her to brand me a 'devil's child.' Not just because my mate, John Leathers, and me did wax crayon paintings of people being fed to mincemeat machines, no, my more heinous crime was that I drew them – and wrote – with my left hand.

'That's raight miss, a red devil's child,' I beamed, thinking she was paying me a compliment, and to prove my point showed her the said devil on my Manchester United silk scarf.

Timms, momentarily, staggered back, then snatching the scarf from my hands she started tying it around my left

22

wrist. I was quite chuffed at this, at first, another teacher had told me off for wearing it like a Stretford Ender. Maybe she's not an old fuddy-duddy after all, I was thinking. Before Timms yanked my arm behind my back, using the scarf to secure my devil idle left hand to a chair, forcing me to write away my demons with my good Christian right-right hand. In response I started writing back-to-front, mirror writing, and I've sort of been that way ever since; a defiant, alternative, red devil.

Back in the playground I was in my element playing football with my mates, and when the bell rang to signal the end of break, I was already looking forward to when school was over and I could play football again.

Everywhere was our Wembley: school playgrounds, the rec, twenty-a-side, jumpers for goalposts, isn't it. In the street we'd use people's gates or hedges for the net. Friends' backyards or lawns would do for a pitch. Coming back from the chippy we'd often use a crumpled piece of paper or a tin can for a football, and a bus shelter or shop doorway as the goal.

Mam and Dad had bought me a Mitre leather casey for Christmas, and I was never to be seen without it, even when on errands, or on my way to school, I'd run through the street with the ball at my feet. It was like a pet to me. So when we were playing football on the rec one day and a lad booted my pet football over the crossbar and on to the road, where it was flattened under the wheels of a passing car, it left me devastated. I even placed the squashed remains in a plastic bin liner and threw it in the canal.

Although I was good at football, I had a major technical problem when selected for the school team in my second year at junior school. I felt uncomfortable in football boots.

23

There was a reason for this: the pair I had on my feet were a family heirloom. They had once belonged to Grandad. I wondered if he'd taken them with him when he was a soldier in the First World War, and worn them to play in the famous football match between the British and German soldiers during the ceasefire on Christmas Day. They looked more like rugby boots, were two sizes too big for me, weighed a ton, and had what seemed like six-foot-long laces which I had to wrap round and round the boot before I could tie a knot. The studs were bigger and harder than Sam Fox's nipples on a photo shoot on Blackpool seafront in January. When I put on these boots, I looked like Bambi wearing Doc Martens walking on corrugated iron.

I was also the smallest boy in the team, and had to wear a kit that was a standard size and miles too big for me. I'd have a shirt that came down to my knees, shorts that reached to my shins, and socks that I could pull up to my bollocks. So what's my honours in football? Well, I won a Cup winners' medal for two years running, the Cup in question being the annual village gala five-a-side knockout competition, even though only four teams entered.

I once won at Wembley...on a muddy field at the back of our council estate. Wembley's the game where you start with about fifty players, all playing against each other, and you have to score to get through to the next round. The last player on the pitch who hasn't scored gets eliminated at the end of each round. After playing for about three hours, I eventually got through to the Final, where I was up against Chris Knowles, the best player on the estate, who had a professional club interested in him. He was older than me and about two foot taller. I scraped a 2-1 victory, the highlight of my career.

24

I also won the World Cup, or a four inch plastic replica, for beating my friends on our street at Subbuteo in a knockout competition. I had to have all the football games and toys when I was a kid. I had Subbuteo with its little plastic figurines that you would accidentally kneel on, so after a few months you would have half your team out with broken legs. I also had Striker, with the little plastic footballers that would kick the football when you pressed their heads down.

And I had one of the earliest TV computer games. You got three games (all in black and white) - football, tennis and squash. The football game consisted of four rectangular shapes on each side that you could move up and down the screen. These represented the footballers; the nets were two open spaces at each side of the TV screen, and the football was a small square of light, which made a BLIP sound when you hit it.

The tennis game consisted of two rectangular shapes, one each end of the screen that you could move up and down; the tennis ball was a small square of light that made a BLIP sound when you hit it.

The squash game consisted of two rectangular shapes, that you could move up and down inside a box shape; the squash ball being a small square light that made a BLIP sound when you hit it.

If you had the deluxe version of the computer game you got a plastic gun that you fired at the small square of light that moved around the screen, and when you hit the square it made a BLIP sound.

I also had one of the early hand-held computer games (a football game). It resembled the first digital watches and calculators, with a red luminous display on a black background. The players were represented by movable little red dots. The player who had the ball shone brighter than the rest; the football itself was a flashing red dot. You couldn't see the display in daylight so you had to crawl under the table or under the bedsheets to play the game.

Back to my honours. I used to play football regularly with an England International, Championship and FA Cup winner. Her name was Jackie, and we used to play on the local rec as kids. No one even questioned that she wanted to play football with the lads; she was always one of the first to be picked when selecting teams and could run rings around most of us. And of all the lads dreaming of becoming a footballer and playing in the FA Cup Final, the only one of us to make it was a girl. Jackie later played for Doncaster Belles and England.

Wembley Dreamers

In 1975 I had my first visit to a football stadium. Jacksdale Junior School organized a trip to Wembley Stadium to watch a schoolboy international - England v the Netherlands. Wow! Wembley! I couldn't wait and felt sick with excitement for days before the trip.

The morning of the match, and I was throwing a tantrum with Mam. As usual, when I was going on a school trip, Mam wanted me to wear my Sunday best clothes - black, straight and sensible trousers, a blue shirt, blue v-neck sweater, black, thoroughly polished shoes, and a tie that had a poncey purple squiggly design on it. It was one of those children's ties that you didn't actually have to tie around your neck, because it had a piece of elastic on it that you simply pulled over your head. I hated wearing it. Other boys would grab hold of this tie, pulling it down as far as the elastic would stretch, before letting go for a painful slap under the chin.

I had come downstairs wearing my denim jacket, denim flared jeans, a t-shirt, trainers and a Manchester United silk scarf tied round my wrist.

'You're not going looking like one of them hooligans,' insisted Mam.

'It's what you dress like at a football match. All my mates will be wearing the same,' I said, and showed her a picture of supporters queuing outside a football ground from *Shoot!* magazine to prove my point. 'Tell her, Dad.'

'He's right, Dot*. It's not how we dressed in my day, but you don't want your best on at a football match.'

*Dad's nickname for Mam

Mam gave in and agreed to let me go as a mini-1970s Stretford Ender. She then handed me a Co-op carrier bag full of strawberry jam sandwiches (strawberry being my favourite jam because of its United red colour) and told me to behave myself, before waving me off.

I met with my friends outside the school, waiting for the coach to arrive. Mr Duly the PE teacher was in charge for the day. He was a mild-mannered man, who always had a smile on his face and never shouted at us. If you showed an interest in sport he'd give 100 per cent encouragement, but I'd still not forgiven him for dropping me from the school team halfway through the season, for a lad younger than me and who supported Liverpool.

Nigel Mason came walking around the corner. His appearance was greeted with howls of laughter. His family had allowed him to dress as a football supporter all right, but one from the 1930s. He wore a flat cap, and a large knitted blue-and-white striped scarf was wrapped twice round his neck (but still reached to his knees). An England rosette the size of a dinner plate was pinned to his jumper, and in his hand he clutched a rattle.

'Who are yuh? Who are yuh?' we chanted, mockingly.

'This lot's me grandad's. He told me he wore 'em to the 1966 World Cup Final,' Nigel said, proudly.

We were impressed. The mickey-taking stopped.

'One Nigel Mason - There's only one Nigel Mason.'

The coach arrived. We piled on and set off for Wembley. As a kid I always suffered from travel sickness. We had been on the bus for about an hour when my stomach began to feel dodgy, and when the boy in front of me took out his bad fart smelling egg sandwiches, I knew I couldn't keep the carrot stew down any longer. I started to run down the aisle of the bus to warn Mr Duly and the driver, but as I ran some boy stuck out a foot, sending me crashing to the floor.

'Penalty, Ref,' someone shouted, and laughter roared out as I lay there vomiting into Tubby Thompson's red-and-white bobble hat, which I'd pulled from his head as I fell.

An hour later I'd recovered enough to sing along with the football songs, as we travelled through the outskirts of north London.

'It's there!' a lad shouted.

A few miles ahead stood the twin towers of Wembley Stadium. To a football-mad kid seeing the twin towers of Wembley was as wondrous as seeing a pair of female breasts for the first time. And once inside, when I ran up the steps and looked out on to the pitch and surroundings, I thought it was fantastic. I didn't realize then what I know now, that it's a decrepit old shit hole.

'Maybe I'll play here one day,' I said to a friend.

The majority of the attendance that day was made up of thousands of schoolkids. Before the game we were supposed to participate in a sing-a-long with Ed 'Stewpot' Stewart, who sang a collection of songs that could only be described as Hell Island Discs: 'Tie a Yellow Ribbon Round the Old Oak Tree', 'Congratulations', 'Remember You're A Womble', 'The Wombling Song', etc. And there was no way Stewpot was going to get me to sing-a-long to 'Long-haired Lover from Liverpool' and 'You'll Never Walk Alone'. I did, though, with everyone else, sing the England chant continuously throughout the match. You know the one . . . somebody gives a blast on an air horn several times and then 'England!' The one from the 1966 World Cup, the one chanted to Noel Coward's character by the inmates of the prison in the film *The Italian Job*.

'Remember the names of the players, they're the stars of the future . . . the new Kevin Keegan could be out there,' Mr Duly had told us.

I still have the match programme from that day, and to my knowledge none of the schoolboy England team made it to top grade football: W. A. Gilbert, M. Rogers, S. Totty, W. Hurley and so on. Godfrey Ingram, the only black player in the team, was the one who really impressed, and we all agreed that he would be in the senior England team within ten years.

I've often wondered what happened to the players from that team and what they're doing today. Are they living unfulfilled lives, employed in jobs they hate, or even unemployed? All of them thinking of what could have been. What must it be like, to be considered one of the best eleven players in the country at the age of fifteen, be so close to your dreams, and then for everything to fall apart? You think you're going to play for a top side like Man United or Arsenal, and end up at Northampton, and maybe ten years on working in a factory doing a dead-end job. Have they happily got on with the rest of their lives, proud of what they achieved, or are they bitter with regret at not making it to the top?

When Dad used to come home from work in a bad mood, I would wonder if he ever reflected on what could have happened if he'd gone and had a successful trial for one of the professional clubs who were interested in him.

Football Mad

Shortly after the schoolboy international, I started to go with my best friend Paul Cope and his dad to watch Mansfield Town play. They're my local team, and I've watched them play all over the country over the years. I enjoy the contrast of watching and following Mansfield Town in the lower divisions, and also following Man United. There's nothing like going to Chester away (when in their old stadium) standing on open terracing, built on a grass hill, in the pouring rain, and sliding down the muddy bank at the back of the stand, fighting your way through nettles to have a piss up against a crumbling brick wall.

At Mansfield's Field Mill ground the men's toilets used to be in one corner, a piss trough surrounded by a brick wall, no roof. During one game, I can remember the match ball bouncing off a floodlight pylon and landing in the toilet. Thirty seconds later a man appeared, pulling up his flies with the ball under his arm. He then casually threw it to a player waiting to take a corner, to the applause and cheers of the crowd.

As a kid watching Mansfield I did my one and only pitch invasion, joining thousands (well, hundreds) of supporters on the pitch in celebration of Mansfield winning promotion to the old Second Division.

Around this time Dad took me to watch Notts County play Fulham. The reason for going to this game was that Bobby Moore and (more significantly for me) George Best were playing for Fulham. Best may have been heavier and slower than in his United glory days, but he was still my all-time footballing hero.

Before the game an old man with a walking stick emerged from the crowd. Unimpeded, he limped slowly across the pitch to near the centre-circle, where George Best and other players were warming up. Reaching Best, the old man removed his flat cap and shook the United legend's hand. Best patted him on the back; they exchanged smiles and chatted away. The old man turned and then slowly made his way back to the stands.

It annoys me when I'm in a pub and there's this man, beer belly resting on the bar, saying, 'George Best, what a waster.' Waster? He played for Manchester United, won two Championship medals, scored great goals, including one in Man United's European Cup Final triumph, was named European Footballer of the Year and shagged three Miss Worlds, where did it all go wrong? Yes the decline into alcoholism was heartbreaking in the end, and his days as a top footballer were over by the age of 27, but by then he'd achieved more in the game, in life, than the vast majority ever will, a legend forever, loved by United fans forever. And how many of us would wish to live just one of his years when at his 60's and early 70's peak? We have a strange mentality in this country. We like bringing down anyone who achieves any kind of success.

Something happened during the Notts County-Fulham game. We were sat in Notts County's old wooden stand, and during the match, about fifty yards from where we sat, a small fire started. I don't know if some rubbish had accidentally caught fire from a discarded cigarette, or if someone had started it deliberately, but stewards soon brought it under control.

I'd forgotten all about this incident, until years later. May 1985, in fact, when, in the old wooden stand at Bradford City's Valley Parade stadium, a pile of rubbish caught fire, and the small blaze quickly took hold, engulfing the entire stand, killing fifty-six spectators. What I'd seen at Notts County that day was not to be the last time I'd witness incidents at football stadiums that would one day lead to disaster and loss of life.

Most Saturday afternoons between August and May were given up to listening to BBC radio's *Sport on 2*. I'd wait anxiously for news of goals at United's games. It was best when Peter Jones would announce, 'The electric scoreboard in the corner saying welcome to Old Trafford tells you that today's second-half commentary is the match between Manchester United and Everton [or whoever].'

Tommy Docherty had built an exciting young team at United, which reflected his flamboyant personality. They played expressive, attacking football and had two wingers at a time when it was unfashionable to do so. Gordon Hill was on the left, with Steve Coppell on the right. These were my favourite players due to the fact, like my Dad before me, the wing was the position I played in.

United had acquitted themselves well, back in the First Division, putting up a strong challenge for the Championship and advancing in the FA Cup. It wasn't until the mid-1980s, when I'd left school, before I was able to attend United games regularly. Until then I had to follow every season and big match (Cup Finals apart) by the blind, nerve-racking excitement of radio. On many occasions this was almost unbearable; it's a wonder I'd not suffered a heart attack by the age of fourteen. United would have to be about 3-0 up before I could relax.

I'd become obsessed with United, and incredibly superstitious. Between three o'clock and a quarter to five on a Saturday afternoon, I banned everyone from coming into the kitchen while I listened to football on the radio. I'd got it into my head that other members of my family brought bad luck to United. I couldn't go and shut myself away in my bedroom for the duration of the radio commentaries. I tried listening there, and United lost three times!, including a 4-0 thrashing by Man City to go out of the League Cup.

The kitchen had proved the luckiest place to be. I'd spent most Saturday afternoons in there since the end of November, and United had gone eleven games without defeat.

So there I was, sat on a chair at the side of the fire. On the kitchen table was a rectangular-shaped transistor radio, which represented a net; a small piece of crumpled paper was a football, and my two fingers running across the table, a United player. I did the commentary. Flicking the piece of paper with my finger into the top corner of the transistor radio.

'Pearson scores . . . what a fantastic goal! . . . United storm into a 3-0 lead over Villa.'

33

Elaine then came walking into the kitchen. There was an announcement on the radio at the same time: 'We're going over to Villa Park for news of Aston Villa versus Manchester United.'

'Twenty minutes gone and Aston Villa have just taken the lead.'

'Elaine! United are losing and it's your fault,' I said, angrily to my sister, who just laughed at me, and left the room singing 'He's football crazy, football mad.'

Inevitably after that Elaine and Brian would keep coming into the kitchen on purpose, just to wind me up.

Sometimes I'd find myself biting my nails during the match commentary. I'd think to myself, Oh shit, biting my nails is bad luck, the other team's going to score now. For some insane reason I also thought turning the light on was also unlucky for United. So even in December and January I'd sit there listening to the radio in the dark, with just the orange glow from the fire until a quarter to five. Mam would stick her head around the door and turn the light on. 'Can I make tea now?'

'No, you can't. They've still got five minutes to play yet,' I would reply.

Cup Final 76: My Perfect Cousin

The FA Cup: the oldest, greatest, most magical football competition in the universe. Every football-mad kid in every country in the world has heard of it, and dreamt of playing in the Final at Wembley. And I was no different; one day I was going to score the goal that would win the Cup for United in a 4-3 victory over Liverpool. But to go and watch United in an FA Cup Final would be a dream come true. I'd settle for that.

So when United beat Wolves 3-2 to reach the semi-final and Wembley was in sight, I excitedly rushed to give Dad the news and asked him if he would take me to the Final if they got there. Dad sat me down and I listened sulkily as he tried to explain the complexities of the FA's ticket distribution and the token scheme.

'What about the royals and MPs? They're there every year, and I've never seen them in a football shirt,' I argued.

'That's different. They're VIPs.'

'VIP? What's that mean?'

'Very important people.'

'So we're not important, then?'

'Not important enough to get a Cup Final ticket from the FA. There'll be United supporters who've not missed a game all season, who the FA don't think important enough to be guaranteed a ticket.'

'That's not fair, is it?'

'No...it's the way of the world.'

And so what would become my eighteen-year quest for an FA Cup Final ticket had begun.

In the semi-final United were drawn against Derby County. My friend Robert Howard, who lived directly across the road from us, supported Derby. On the afternoon of the match, Rob, Derby scarf around his neck, stood behind his front-room window listening to the game on the radio. I was doing exactly the same in our house, United scarf tied around my wrist, both of us making certain hand gestures to each other.

United left-winger Gordon Hill (nicknamed Merlin the Magician by United fans) scored. 1-0 United. I jumped up and down, waving my scarf to Rob and making a 1-0 sign with my fingers. He stuck two lingers up at me.

Later, Gordon Hill scored again - 2-0 United. I danced around the front room, then held my scarf up against the window and waved to Rob. He waved his fist back at me. United won 2-0.

Afterwards, all smiles and full of myself, I went across to call for my Derby County friend, who answered my knock at the door. 'You'd better start running,' he said.

So United were in the Cup Final, thanks to two goals from my cousin, Gordon Hill. Well, for a few glorious weeks he was my cousin.

One day, we were sat at the kitchen table eating dinner, and Dad declared: 'Tony, you know the left-winger for Man United - Gordon Hill?'

'Yeah, he's my favourite player,' I replied.

'Well, I think we're related to him.'

The meatball I was just about to eat slipped off my fork and landed on the floor in front of our pet dog Jackie, who gratefully gobbled it up. I was speechless. I thought all my birthdays and Christmases had come at once.

How had my Dad come to this conclusion? Well, he had a cousin living in the same area of London that Gordon Hill came from. His name was Barry Hill - 'Very good footballer in his day,' Dad had said.

Dad was sure his son's name was Gordon, and that he would be the same age as the United star. It was logical - Hill is not a very common name, is it? And London's not a very big city. It was good enough for me. Dad said to keep it quiet for a while; he'd write to Barry Hill to have it confirmed.

I had visions of a sports car driving on to our council estate and pulling up in front of our house. Gordon Hill would get out of it, having come to see us for Sunday tea, to the envy of my friends and the rest of the street. Then, in my mind, I could see him handing me a Cup Final ticket.

Walking to junior school on Monday morning with my best friend Copey, I turned to him: 'Can you keep a secret?'

'Yeah,' said Copey.

'Well, it's not confirmed yet, but Man United's Gordon Hill... he's my cousin.'

By dinner time the whole school knew, and I had a minor celebrity status. Other kids came up asking me if I could get them Gordon Hill's autograph.

'No problem,' I'd say.

'Are you going to bring him to school to play football with us?' a group of boys were asking.

'I'll see what I can do,' I gloated.

A few weeks later a letter arrived from London. It was from Dad's cousin Barry Hill. It read, 'Sorry to disappoint you, but my son's not a famous football star. His name is Alan, and he works on the buses.'

The disappointment was bad enough, but having to live it down at school was worse. I'd walk into the classroom and sit down, then the sniggering would start from behind me.

'Aye up, look who's here,' a voice would start. 'Gordon Hill's his cousin, Jimmy Hill's his dad, and Benny Hill's his uncle.'

A few years later it was discovered someone in our street did have a famous relative. A girl called Samantha Walters moved into a house across the road with her family. Her mother had been married to actor Richard Beckinsale, who starred in the comedies *Rising Damp* and *Porridge*, among many others. He was Samantha's dad, but had split from her mum when she was still a baby. Her mother had never told her who her real dad was.

They'd not lived on our street long before gossip started and it was revealed to Samantha who her father was. She started writing to him, then one day, a big flash car drove on to our council estate, pulled up opposite us, and out stepped Richard Beckinsale, and went into the Walters' house for Sunday tea, to the envy of the rest of the street, me included.

Richard Beckinsale first made his name in the series *The Lovers*. There was a film version of this in 1973, which includes a brilliant, touching scene were he takes his girlfriend, played by Paula Wilcox, to Old Trafford. This is now one of my favourite film moments, filling me with nostalgia and longing, with fantastic footage of an Old Trafford that no longer exists; in regards to authenticity and atmosphere. And heartbreaking, Richard Beckinsale was only 31 when he died of a heart attack. Samantha had only known him for a short amount of time.

Samantha later changed her second name to Beckinsale and made a career for herself as an actress, appearing in the series *London's Burning*, and several other TV productions.

*

Cup Final afternoon. No football star for a cousin, no ticket. I settled down on the sofa in our front room, next to Dad and Jackie to watch the game on telly.

Mam, as usual on Cup Final day, had gone out shopping.

Refreshments were sorted; Dad with his bottles of nut brown ale, a pork pie and cheese and pickle sandwiches.

Me with a couple of bottles of cherryade pop and a bag full of sherbet fizz bombs, and Jackie with a bowl of water and three Boneos.

There'd been the disappointment of United not winning the championship - they'd finished third behind QPR and Liverpool - but the winning of the FA Cup looked a formality. United's opponents in the Final were Second Division Southampton.

'I'll bet Pearson scores a hat-trick today, and maybe me cousin will get one, aye Dad,' I said.

Dad went red with embarrassment.

'We'll see.'

The Southampton players jumped for joy as the ref blew for full time. Bobby Stokes had scored the only goal of the game in the last ten minutes to win them the Cup. The United players trudged up the Wembley steps to collect their losers' medals. I sat there in tears; Jackie was whining.

'They're not fit to lace Stanley Matthews' boots,' said Dad.

Tommy Doc told the United fans that they'd be back next year.

Punks and Hooligans

1977 and we are going mad
It's 1977 and we've seen too many ads
1977 and we're gonna show them all
That apathy's a drag
        'Plastic Bag' X Ray Spex

Elaine was showing me a fashion magazine and newspaper cuttings of a new fashion in London: punk. There were stories of punks fighting with rockers on the King's Road in London, and these photographs of amazing looking people with blue, orange, green and blond spiky hair, wearing ripped clothes, safety pins, chains and bondage gear. That doesn't seem bizarre now, but at a time when millions of people had long hair, wore twenty-two-inch bell-bottom trousers, and listened to pop music from groups like Showwaddywaddy, ELO and Abba, these punks looked like people from another planet, with an exciting new look, sound and attitude.

Elaine started wearing tight PVC trousers and mohair jumpers. She cut her hair short and started going to nightclubs in Nottingham. One day she cropped and gelled up my hair, I put on the drainpipe jeans she'd bought me, and we set off into the city to meet up with her punk boyfriend and hang around with the punks in Slab Square; they called me 'Baby Punk.'

People in Jacksdale wearing flares, laughed; they thought we were the one's who dressed funny. I think punk gave Elaine the identity she was looking for. It wouldn't be long before she would pack in her office job, leave home to go to art college, and then on to study fashion design at a polytechnic.

Punks soon became a regular sight in Jacksdale. In fact the centre of the village was overrun with spiky tops on Friday and Saturday nights. They travelled from all over the country to see punk groups like The UK Subs, The Ruts, early Adam and the Ants, The Members, Angelic Upstarts and others perform at the infamous Grey Topper club.

A mining village was a bizarre place for such a club. The building had started life as the Jacksdale Picture Palace, but had been turned into a nightclub and music venue in the 1960s. Many well-known music names played there, including Billy Fury, Gerry and the Pacemakers, Bill Haley, Ben E King, Jimmy Cliff, The Sweet and Bay City Rollers.

Groups that were little known or didn't even have record deals at the time, but would become world famous, appeared there: The Stranglers showed up in early 1976 (in Jet Black's ice cream van that they were using as a tour bus at the time), The Pretenders dodged spit, Simple Minds played to a handful of people in 79. And in the pop magazine *Smash Hits* in the early 1980s they asked Chris Cross from the group Ultravox to name ten gigs he never wanted to play again. At the top of the list was the Grey Topper, Jacksdale. 'There were more people in the chip shop across the road than at the gig,' he said.

In the punk years the Topper had a reputation for outbreaks of violence. Brawls would often spill out on to the street, and it wasn't long before local residents tried to have the place closed down. Bus drivers refused to stop in the village after 10 o'clock at night, and there was regularly a row of police cars and vans parked outside the club.

A local milkman stored crates of his empty bottles down the side of the Topper, which unfortunately turned out to be a convenient armoury for two rival gangs from nearby towns as they battled it out in the street after one gig. The Topper eventually closed after a mysterious fire. It re-opened again in the eighties as a club called Woody's, but today it's a lampshade factory.

The full incredible story of the Grey Topper is told in my book *The Palace and the Punks*.

I loved the sounds of punk and new wave, and began my record collection. My musical tastes didn't entertain my Dad's ears, though. I was in my bedroom listening to the track 'Holidays in the Sun' from the album *Never Mind the*

41

Bollocks, Here's the Sex Pistols: 'Now I got a reason....now I got a reason....now I got a reason, and I'm still waiting,' sang Johnny Rotten, when Dad stuck his head round the door.

'I got a reason as well, to turn the bloody thing off. What's the problem with this lot? What they trying to prove? It's just a racket. I can stick a Bing Crosby record on, go t'top of garden and still hear every word he sings. You can't do that with these bloody punk groups,' Dad lectured me.

Me and Dad still had a strong bond when it came to football. And when one day he asked me if I wanted to go to a match with him I jumped at the chance. Dad had to work Saturday mornings and couldn't drive, so I was disappointed when he told me he wouldn't be able to take me to Manchester to see United. I had to settle for Forest, who were a Second Division team at the time.

Dad had taken Brian to a Forest match before, but he never really liked football, and when he made it clear that standing in the rain, being jostled by drunken adults, watching a sport he shirked from playing, was not his choice of entertainment. Dad didn't bother him again, and hadn't been down to Forest for five years. Consequently, Dad was a bit out of touch with the seventies terrace culture, otherwise he would have been a little more selective about Forest's opponents when taking me to my first big match. He chose Forest versus Millwall. Clearly, he didn't know about the fearsome reputation of the south London club's supporters, with such notorious hooligans as 'Harry the Dog' amongst their ranks.

Me and Dad sat in the old East Stand at the City Ground, which was one of those stands with seating in the upper section and terracing below. The away fans occupied one half of the terracing in the stand, the Forest fans the other, with a small empty section separating the two.

I can't remember the score between Forest and Millwall, or any of the match. I spent the afternoon transfixed on the scenes on the terracing below us. I'd seen television news coverage of football violence, and I'd read about it in the newspapers, but here it was in blood-spattered 3D.

Half house bricks, bottles, stones, coins, full cans of beer were flying through the air, from one section of the terracing to the next. Millwall to Forest; Forest to Millwall. Half a brick smashed into the face of a Forest fan, blood poured from a gaping wound as he stumbled to the floor. The St John's Ambulance Brigade bravely pushed their way into the crowd to go to his aid. A bottle came down into the Millwall section, connecting with the head of a Millwall supporter; blood poured from another head wound.

The referee blew his whistle for half-time, and hostilities ended.

The same warring supporters stood there reading their match programmes, drinking Bovril and eating meat pies. Fifteen minutes went by, the players came out for the second half, the ref blew his whistle, a brick flew through the air from the Millwall supporters and landed in the Forest section. Ceasefire over. The barrage of missiles began again. The violence got more intense in the second half. Several supporters from each section broke through police lines and battled it out in no man's land. Several fans were led away on stretchers. From up in the seats above I watched with a mixture of fear and excitement.

I couldn't wait to brag to my friends that I'd seen real hooligans. Dad decided we should leave fifteen minutes before the end of the match.

'For Christ's sake don't tell yuh Mam what we've seen today. She won't let us go again,' he said.

But we did go again; Dad would take me regularly to Forest for the next three seasons.

Cup Final '77: Doc's Cup

On the Saturdays that Dad didn't take me to a Forest game, I was back in the kitchen listening to *Sport on 2* football coverage on the radio. Man United were off on an FA Cup run again, eventually beating Leeds in the semi-final to reach Wembley. Liverpool were the other finalists.

I entered a newspaper competition to win two Cup Final tickets. I wrote down the answers to the football trivia questions on a postcard and sent it off. I was sure I would win. Radio 1 DJ Jimmy Saville hosted a television programme called *Jim'll Fix'It*, where he made children's dreams come true. I wrote to him.

Dear Jim,

I'm a mad Man United fan. I need a Cup Final ticket.

Fix it for me, please.

Tony Hill.

Cup Final afternoon. No prize-winner's ticket in the newspaper competition. Jim hadn't fixed it for me either. I settled into an armchair in our front room to watch BBC TV's coverage of the game. We had watched the previous year's Cup Final on ITV, but United lost, so ITV was bad luck now. Dad and our pet dog Jackie sat on the settee. I'd sat I there a year ago, but United lost, so sitting on the settee watching United was added to my bad luck list.

Mam, as usual on Cup Final day, had gone out shopping.

Refreshments were sorted. Dad with his bottles of nut brown ale, a pork pie and cheese and pickle sandwiches. Me with a couple of bottles of cherryade pop and a bag full of wine gums, and Jackie with a bowl of water and three Boneos.

Manchester United versus Liverpool. 'The clash of the century,' wrote the newspapers. Liverpool had one of their greatest teams ever. They'd just won the Championship for the second successive year and had also reached the European Cup Final. They could achieve a unique Treble. It would be a tough game for United, but League positions have never meant anything when United play Liverpool.

Three o'clock, the match gets underway, my heart's pounding with nervous excitement. The first half was goalless, then in the fiftieth minute of the match, Stuart Pearson fires United in front.

'Yes. It's there!'

Dad and me are up out of our seats, Jackie barks. I run around the room, scarf held aloft, chanting, 'United. United.'

'Liverpool are at their most dangerous when behind,' comments Dad.

'Liverpool are at their most dangerous when behind,' comments the BBC's John Motson.

It's 1-1 moments later, Jimmy Case having equalized for Liverpool. I'm bursting to go to the toilet, but I can't go. Going to the toilet when United are playing is on my bad luck list. Liverpool would score.

It was lucky I didn't go, a few minutes later United were back in front. Lou Macari shoots, the ball bounces off Jimmy Greenhoff's chest and flies past Liverpool keeper Ray Clemence into the net. I didn't celebrate as much this time, as Liverpool had soon equalized after United's first.

'There's a long way to go yet,' said Dad, optimistic as ever.

Any football fan knows what it's like when your team only holds a slender lead; time drags on and on, your watch or the clock seems to stop. I looked at the clock on the front-room wall. Twenty to five, still five minutes of the match remaining. I paced up and down chewing my scarf, my heart pounding more than ever. I looked at the clock: twenty to five. Don't keep looking at the clock, it will make matters worse, I thought. I looked at the clock. Twenty to five. Suddenly the ref blew for full time. I looked at the clock. Twenty to five. It really had stopped. I raced out of the front room chanting, 'United. United!'

Swinging my scarf above my head I ran through the kitchen and out into the back garden, where I booted my football. It shot over the fence and thumped into the next-door neighbour's kitchen window. I ran back inside. United captain Martin Buchan was leading the players up the Wembley steps to collect the Cup. The Duchess of Kent handed him the trophy. He turned and raised it to the roars of the United fans. It was only from my armchair, but I'd seen United win the Cup. It was a great feeling. A nice bit of gloating to come at school on Monday.

Tommy Docherty placed the lid of the FA Cup on his head, as he joined the Wembley lap of honour with his United team. A few months later Tommy Docherty was sacked after it was revealed he was having an affair with the wife of the club's physiotherapist, Laurie Brown. The following season the Stretford End sang 'Knees Up Mother Brown.' David Sexton became United's new manager, and I had my first visit to Old Trafford.

Family Divisions

I'd told Mam I'd got stomach-ache so I could get the day off school. I was faking it, not just because I wanted to escape the tedium of a Tuesday at school (no PE, which meant no football) but also because if I was off sick I usually went up to Grandma and Grandad Lane's house in Selston, and that was always a treat.

They lived at the edge of Selston, in a big old end-terrace house situated at the top of a steep hill, from where you got a view over the fields to Underwood church (both pit villages are mentioned in D.H. Lawrence's brilliant - my favourite - short story *Odour of Chrysanthemums*. Grandad, Trixie dog and me walked along the path of the old railway line in the story). To the right were the headstocks of Pye Hill Pit; on the left derelict land where Selston colliery had once stood was being transformed into a golf course.

Grandma always bought me bizarre presents when she went into town. The last time I saw her she'd given me a book called *Wacky Facts: Useless Information You Just Can't Do Without*, which included gems like, 'If you removed the skin of every living person in Britain and sewed it together it would cover an area of 35 sq. miles' On one page there was a drawing of a footballer with the caption, 'SOLITARY VICE'. It continued: 'The Southern Transvaal Synod of the Dutch Reform Church has condemned organised sport and masturbation on Sundays.' I asked Grandma what masturbation was, and she told me it was an Olympic event.

47

Grandad was such an endearing character that I wanted to be in his company as often as possible. A semi-retired miner (now with the prestige job of bath superintendent at Pye Hill) he was like a cross between Eric Morecambe and Captain Mainwaring from *Dad's Army*. He'd actually been in the Home Guard during the Second World War. Mam told me that he and the other men used to practise manoeuvres with broom handles because they didn't have real rifles.

Grandad had a glass eye, having lost the real one when he battled cancer in his fifties. He kept a replica glass eye at the back of a drawer in order to play tricks on people. He would make a sucking sound and pretend to pull out his glass eye. Then revealing the fake one in one hand would begin to polish it on his trousers while covering what people thought was the empty socket with his other hand. Taking one step forward he'd always trip up and make out he'd dropped it on the fire.

'Me eye's on fire! Me eye's on fire!' he'd shout, jumping up and down.

The person Grandad was playing the trick on would then dash to his assistance by grabbing a poker and sifting through the burning lumps of coal to try to find the eye before it broke with heat. Grandad would then roar with laughter and the person would spin round to see that he still had his eye in place and he'd be holding up the fake one at the side of it.

'Eye, eye. What's all this, then?' he'd say.

When we were little kids Grandad would tell us daft stories. As he sat in his armchair by the fire in the darkened living room, his face lit up by the orange glow from the flames which cast a huge spooky flickering shadow on the wall behind him, we'd all gather round by his feet and then he'd begin.

'T'was a dark, dark night, and on a dark, dark lane was a dark, dark house, and in the dark, dark house was a dark, dark room, and in the dark, dark room was a dark, dark cupboard [Grandad would now lean forward and lower his voice almost to a whisper], and in the dark, dark cupboard was a dark, dark box and in the dark, dark box was a AAARRRGGGHHH [he'd shout, making us all jump] was a pig's ear.'

At other times I'd go with him on long walks across fields with his dog Trixie, when he'd point out landmarks and tell me the local history. Or I'd help him tend his huge garden. Grandad was, though, a Derby County fan, and none too pleased that I supported Man United and that Dad was now taking me to watch Forest. So this day when I'd told Mam I had stomach-ache and been given the day off school I walked into my grandparents' house wearing a woollen red-and-white striped hat, one which Mam had knitted for me and sewn on a 'United Forever' patch. As we sat supping our cups of tea Grandad frowned as he eyed my hat.

'Tha's still not supporting them, ah thee?'

'Yeah.'

'Ah thought tha'd of grown out of 'em by nah, and started supporting a good team like Derby.'

'No way.'

'An ar've 'eard that tha dad's tekin thee ta see Forest nah.'

'Yeah.'

'Ah never thought ah'd see day when a grandson of mine supported Man United and Forest,' he said, shaking his head disapprovingly.

'Ah dunt support Forest,' I protested.

'Yuh goo'n watch 'em - that's bad enough. If wey'd still got Cloughie wey'd be top team. It's a cryin shame he ad t'end up we them boggers. Grandad then attempted to save me from my sins. 'Tell tha dad that tha dunt want t'watch them wassocks any mooer an is'll tek thee to see a proper team at Baseball Ground. He then began to bribe me in the hope of stopping what he thought was my allegiance to the enemy. He went over to a drawer, took something out of a folded handkerchief, and shouted me over.

'Hold out tha hand, lad.' In it he placed a Second World War defence medal that he'd been awarded for serving in the Home Guard.

'What dust tha reckon ta that?'

'Brilliant!' I replied.

'Tek it, it's yours.'

'Thanks.'

'An 'ere thee are a bit extra pocket money,' he said handing me a 50p coin from his pocket.

'Thanks, Grandad.'

Grandad then looked me in the eye.

'Think worra ah said about goo'n ta Derby wi me instead of Forest.'

Dad, who had by now caught Forest fever and become an ardent supporter, didn't take too kindly to the actions of Grandad.

On Christmas Day morning I found two similar sized parcels for me under the Christmas tree. One from Dad, the other from Grandad Lane. I excitedly tore open Dad's present then, disappointed, chucked it to the floor. It was a Forest shirt. And yeah, Grandad had bought me a Derby County shirt.

With Grandad and Grandma Lane and other relatives due down our house on Boxing Day for a family get - together, I came up with a cunning plan. I wrapped up both football shirts. On the parcel containing the Derby shirt I attached a tag which read: 'To Brian from Harry (Grandad's name) - Happy Xmas.' And on the one containing the Forest shirt: 'To Harry from Brian. Happy Xmas'

On Boxing Day night when the beer had flowed and they were in good spirits, I got Elaine to hand each man one of the presents. Wearing my 1977 Cup Winners' Manchester United shirt I watched them from a seat in the corner trying not to smile. In synchronization they opened their presents then looked at each other indignantly. Not being able to contain my laughter any longer I burst into a fit of giggles, catching their attention.

'Yowl koppit,' said Grandad, shaking his fist at me.

'He's got a mind of his own, Harry,' smiled Dad.

'This'll mek a good dust cloth,' laughed Grandad, chucking the Forest shirt towards Dad.

'I reckon we're out of toilet paper, but this'll do just raight,' quipped Dad, crumpling up the Derby shirt.

Grandad began to sing:

'Roll a long Derby County, roll a long

Put the ball in the net where it belongs

With a bit of bloody luck

We'll win the FA Cup

Roll along Derby County, roll a long.'

Dad responded with 'Brian Clough's red-and-white army',

and I came in with 'Glory, glory, Man United.'

The Mighty Red Cauldron

Dad continued to take me to watch Nottingham Forest. They were now a First Division side and had started the 1977-78 season well, under the management of Brian Clough and Peter Taylor.

Forest had just beaten their arch East Midlands rivals Derby County 3-0. Dad and me were walking over Trent Bridge amongst the Forest fans making our way home. On the other side of the bridge thousands of Derby County supporters (bitter in defeat) were being escorted by the police back to Nottingham railway station. A Forest supporter walking just in front of us, suddenly took out a brick he had been holding on the inside of his coat, and hurled it into the Derby supporters. A policeman came up to the youth who had chucked the brick, pushing him firmly in the back.

'Get off this fucking bridge - you prat,' he ordered.

Several incensed Derby supporters broke from their police cordon and started clambering over the bonnets of cars stuck in a traffic jam on the bridge. Forest supporters met them halfway across the road. The rival fans punched and kicked each other, and as the police battled to regain control, Dad hurried me away from the scene.

On another occasion during that season two Aston Villa fans were grabbed by Forest supporters and pushed over the side of the bridge into the River Trent below.

A youth off our estate who supported Man United suddenly stopped supporting them one day and became a Forest fan. 'Manchester's too far to travel and it's too expensive to follow United,' he told me.

I thought about what he had said. I wondered if I should do the same. I'd still not seen United play, but I'd seen many Forest games.

Judgement day came in November. Forest v Man United. We had tickets for the game. By the morning of the match I already knew where my allegiance lay. There was only one team I wanted to win. Forest beat them 2-1. The disappointment I felt confirmed it for me. United would always be my team.

'Why don't you support a local team?' I've always had people asking me this question. I do; Mansfield Town. The people who usually ask me this question are Forest fans, and why do they support Forest and not Notts County or Mansfield? Could it be that Forest are the more glamorous option? So I threw the question back at them. 'Why don't you support Notts County?'

'Oh, I've always been a Forest fan.'

'You've got a season ticket, then?' I'll ask.

'No. Can't afford one.'

'Been to many games this season?'

'Well . . . er . . . I've not been this season.'

I do get a barracking from genuine Forest supporters, but it's so fucking annoying to be asked why I don't support a local team from people whose commitment to watching their team goes no further than their armchair or the local pub. More often than not I've seen more Forest games than they have, and it would have been an easier and cheaper option for me to support Forest. Many of my friends support them, Nottingham is within easy travelling distance from where I live, and between 1976 and 1981, when Dad used to take me to Forest regularly, they were a much more successful club than United, winning the Championship, two European Cups and two League Cups. Most of the lads in Jacksdale who at the time supported Liverpool or United or Leeds, conveniently became Forest fans. I could have easily done the same.

Of course, there are no United supporters who actually live in Manchester. I get that all the time, usually from people who have never been to Manchester.

'I've got a friend of a friend of a friend who's a Man City supporter and lives in Manchester. He says that all Mancunians are City supporters,' they'll say.

These people have never travelled on a tram or bus from the centre of Manchester, twenty minutes before kick-off on a Saturday afternoon with thousands of Mancunian United fans. They never saw the terrace houses at the back of City's Maine Road ground with United pennants and pictures hanging in the window. The United fanzine *United We Stand* once did a readers' poll. One of the questions they asked was, 'Where do you live?' Greater Manchester polled 50 per cent of replies.

I'll go to matches that don't involve United and I've no scruples about doing this. Above all I love football, and if a friend would ask if I wanted to go to a match with them, more often than not I would go regardless of who they supported, resulting in me witnessing some momentous occasions in the game over the years.

December 17th 1977 (the date is etched in my memory). Dad took a Saturday off work, to give me an early Christmas present, he was taking me to see United against Forest at Old Trafford. I hardly slept I was so excited. We caught the train to Manchester and once there, under grey skies, we made our way to the famous stadium, entering the away supporters' section. I wanted to stand in the Stretford End, but Dad wasn't having any of that.

Over 55,000 people packed into the mighty red cauldron of Old Trafford. The atmosphere before the game was incredible. I'd never heard a noise like it. There were United supporters standing on terracing in three different sections of the ground. A corner section to the left above the Forest fans, the Stretford End and the United Road paddock were singing and chanting different songs all at once. The thousands of travelling Forest fans responded with, 'Two-one . . . Two-one . . . Two-one.' United fans in all sections of the ground joined in unison, chanting a roof-raising, 'United! United! United!'

I was in heaven. But heaven turned to hell. Forest, now looking a Championship challenging team, won 4-0. But that night, lying in bed, the noise of the pre-match atmosphere was still ringing in my ears.

Forest did win the Championship that season. I was there to see it, but it didn't mean anything to me. I was happy for them and my friends who supported them. Dad even took me to see them play Liverpool in the League Cup Final at Wembley, and the replay at Old Trafford, Forest eventually winning 1-0.

Pre-Hillsborough 1

Forest, having won the Championship, qualified for the European Cup. Liverpool were the holders of the trophy. In round one the two English teams were drawn against each other, and Dad took me to the first leg at the City Ground. Everyone wanted to see this game.

We arrived at the ground early to queue to stand in the old East Stand. Liverpool fans were allocated in another section of the stand. We were among the first few hundred through the turnstiles, letting us get a standing place at the front of the terracing. Metal fencing had been erected at the City Ground, a standard feature at most big football clubs by the late seventies, due to the continuing violence and pitch invasions.

As kick-off approached I realized there was going to be a bigger crowd than average at the City Ground. They seemed to be letting in more people than usual on to the terracing.

By kick-off time the pressure of people behind was pushing me uncomfortably up against the metal fence in front. Peering through the fence, I grabbed on to the bars with each hand.

I didn't care about the match any more. I was anxiously wondering if the pressure on my body from people behind was going to get worse. And it did. When the match got underway, each time Forest attacked the crowd surged forward. It was even worse when they scored - twice. The air was pushed out of my lungs. A little boy at the side of me was crying.

At half-time I asked Dad if we could find a less crowded position, but even then the congestion was such that we couldn't move. For the first time I wasn't enjoying the experience of being at a football match.

At the end of the match we let the stand empty a bit before making our way out. Outside the back of the East Stand was a concrete channel about twenty yards wide, with a wall on the other side. Holding on to Dad's arm we pushed our way through the crowd. Further down the back of the same stand, Liverpool supporters were emerging.

Fighting broke out between the rival fans, and the congestion became as bad as inside the ground. People started pushing and shoving in all directions to escape the trouble. Losing grip on Dad's arm I stumbled and fell to the ground. There was jostling and shouting; people towered above me. In panic-stricken fear I shouted, 'Dad.'

'Give us space - there's a lad down there,' a voice shouted from above.

Dad's arm grabbed my shoulder and dragged me to my feet. We finally pushed our way through the throng of people to the breathing space on the banks of the River Trent. For a long time after that I suffered from claustrophobia, and had a fear of standing on the terraces, insisting on sitting down at games.

Over the years, as I grew older, I became hardened to standing in the congestion of the terraces, eventually always preferring to stand at matches.

Through experience I learnt the unwritten rules of the terraces - like don't stand behind crush barriers at big games, unless you want bruised ribs.

The Infiltrator

'What yuh on about, yuh don't want ta goo?' Dad fumed.

'I can't.'

'Why?'

'I'm a Man United fan.'

'I had ta pay a tenner over cost price fuh these,' he said, waving two Forest v Southampton League Cup Final tickets in front of my face (local coach driver Les Walker obtained all the Forest tickets from Brian Clough's butcher).

'Why dunt yuh support Forest, like everyone else?' he continued.

'United's my team.'

'Well, yuh gooin.'

I did want to go, really. I'd go to any football match if I had the chance. Only a lad at school, who was a year older than me and supported Forest, had heard I was going to the Final, and threatened me in the corridor at breaktime.

'I know all the Forest fans, so dunt tek owt to eat when yuh g'ta Wembley. Cos if I see yuh there you'll be getting plenty of knuckle sandwiches when I tell 'em yuh a United fan,' he warned.

And I was now a teenager, and thought it uncool to go to matches with my Dad. I was trying to be all grown up. I'd had a wank, I'd smoked a fag, which nearly killed me - this when I'd bunked off school one day and had the house to myself. No one in the family smoked, so I couldn't nick a fag off them. No problem, I thought, cigarettes are just made from dried leaves - I'll make my own. I pulled a leaf of Mam's cheese plant and stuck it under the grill for ten minutes, then crumbled the parched remains into the cigarette paper I'd made from an envelope. I put the thing to my lips, lit it, inhaled, and almost choked to death as the room began to spin. I rushed outside for some fresh air. Arthur, next door by his pigeon loft, looked flummoxed as I stood there swaying about and coughing up my guts with what looked like a blazing five-inch-long joint sticking out from between my fingers. I threw up for the next hour, and when Mam came home I looked so bad she gave me the rest of the week off.

'Brian, come and look at our Tony,' she shouted to Dad, who then came into the room.

'Don't you think he looks a greeny colour?'

I was a teeny-punk-bopper with a Sex Pistols t-shirt, a cheap one with the lettering done with glitter, which I bought when we were on holiday in Great Yarmouth. And I had an ever-expanding record collection. Me and Brian would play a cruel trick on Mam. Every Saturday when she went out shopping we'd give her a list of the singles we wanted her to get for us. She'd laugh at the names of the groups and song titles.

"Banana Splits" by The Dickies; Ian Dury and the Blockheads, "Hit Me With Your Rhythm Stick" - you're winding me up, aren't you? They're not real groups.'

So from then on we'd make up groups and songs and add them to the list for Mam to ask for in the record shop. And then wait for her coming home, Saturday teatime.

'Mam, did you get those singles we asked for?'

'Not all of them. I got the ones by Blondie, The Police and The Jam, but they'd never heard of "I Got An Itch" by The Spitting Shysters, or "Oi Pig, Up Yours" by Punky and Perky on pink vinyl.'

Me and Dad were travelling down to Wembley for the League Cup Final with the Forest fans who frequented the Social Club in Jacksdale. The coach departed at 9.30 a.m., but Dad insisted we be at the Social at 7a.m., because that was when the pub was opening its doors to allow regulars to get a little liquid refreshment before the long journey. I was wearing my snorkel parka, which I hated, but today it was an essential garment to avoid identification. All day I had my face safely hidden deep inside the fully zipped-up hood. In the Social someone knocked on top of my head.

'Ost tha in theer?' a capper said, peering into my hood. 'Dunt look s'glum, lad, wes'll win. Up tha redsa.' He then gave me 50p to buy a programme with.

There'd been heavy snow in the Midlands, with huge drifts blocking many side roads. To reach junction 27 of the M1 the coach would have to travel down one of these roads. Urged on by the already intoxicated Forest fans, the driver slammed his foot hard down on the accelerator and, to loud cheers of approval, smashed his vehicle through a drift barring the way. Every available space on the coach had been stashed with crates of beer. By the time we reached London, empty bottles were strewn all over the place.

There was a big contrast in the weather in the capital to that of the Midlands - blue skies, warm sunshine, spring flowers. And I was melting inside my parka. Under the influence of alcohol, the singing and chanting on the bus was so loud that Forest fans making their way through the streets surrounding Wembley towards the stadium would stop and applaud when they heard us pass by. Champion guzzler Abbo had his bare arse pressed up against the back window of the coach, mooning to any Southampton or London football supporters spotted.

'Abbo, show 'em yuh arse; Abbo, Abbo, show 'em yuh arse,' everyone chanted.

An Arsenal supporter walking down the street started making wanking gestures and kissing the badge on his Arsenal shirt while we were stuck in a traffic jam.

'Abbo, show 'im yuh arse; Abbo, show 'im yuh arse,' erupted the chant on the bus. Abbo showed him his arse.

In the street the Arsenal supporter pulled down his trousers and pants and mooned back. Then both rival fans raised their thumbs to each other in mutual respect.

Jacksdalians stumbled from the coach parked up at the stadium and headed for the nearest pub for a little more liquid refreshment. I was swept away by the atmosphere created by 100,000 people inside Wembley, and following the custom of the Argentinean supporters at the World Cup (which had taken place in their country eight months previously) a blizzard of tick-a-tape greeted the arrival of the players on the pitch, before what turned out to be a tremendous match. Forest won 3-2 having had two goals disallowed.

A happy lot of Forest Jacksdalians piled back on the coach after the game. The capper peered into the hood of my parka.

'Theer y'are, lad. What did ah tell thee: up tha redsa,' he said, and swung his rattle.

A coach collided with ours, smashing a window, as the driver had slowly tried to edge the vehicle out of the stadium car park. As much shattered glass as possible was gathered up and a Forest flag and sheet of polythene were taped over the broken window. We eventually reached the M1 and headed north for about sixty miles before it was unanimously agreed to leave the motorway to find a pub for a little more liquid refreshment. Twenty-stone Harry Roberts, up on a table leading the singing, got into a heated argument with a couple of Leicester City fans. Sending pint pots flying he dived from the table bringing down both men at once.

Several hours later we rejoined the M1. Now back in the Midlands, the weather had deteriorated, the flag and polythene were blown down from the window and snow swept into the bus, covering the people at the back, who having had a little too much liquid refreshment, slept on oblivious.

Two months later Forest became European Champions and one day the European Cup was on display at our school. I joined the queue, and when it was my turn I was allowed to hold the famous trophy.

Cup Final '79: Paper Lad

Jimmy Greenhoff stooped to head United's winner in the FA Cup semi-final replay over Liverpool, taking them to the Final for the third time in four years. At school, a friend of a friend's cousin's next-door neighbour worked at Derby County's Baseball Ground. He could get me a Cup Final ticket, I was told, but it would cost £30.

I did everything I could to raise the money. At home I helped Dad in the garden, washed the dishes, and went on errands to the shop to earn extra pocket money. I sold my Grifters push-bike for a tenner, resulting in a bollocking from Mam and Dad, who'd bought me the bike for Christmas. And I got myself a job as a paper lad.

The first day of my paper round didn't go too well.

'We've got a problem,' the owner of the newsagent's said to me.

'What's that?'

'We've run out of newspaper bags. Are you OK to carry the papers around without one?'

'No problem,' I replied, wanting to show I was eager for the job.

Halfway through my round everything was going fine. I placed the pile of newspapers on top of a small wall. Picking up a *Sun*, I folded it and walked down the front path of a house to push it through the letterbox. On my way back from the house, a gust of wind lifted the top newspaper in the pile into the air, separating the pages. I desperately ran around gathering up the scattered sheets of newspaper. There was a stronger gust of wind, the remaining newspapers in the pile lifted one after another into the air. All the pages separated and blew in different directions. They lay everywhere: in hedge-bottoms, on top of parked cars, in people's gardens, on rooftops. In a panic I ran to our house, a few hundred yards away. Dad was just about to go to work; Mam was clearing away the breakfast things. I burst through the door and blurted out what had happened.

'Bloody hell! I've got a bus to catch,' shouted Dad, never in the best of moods when off to work.

Mam and Dad strode up the street to help me collect the scattered newspapers. I traipsed behind them, head down, thinking, Please God, don't let anyone from school see this. I didn't think anything could get worse. It did. It was the day for the dustbin men to empty the bins on our estate. When we reached the scene of the disaster, the dustbin men were collecting the sheets of paper blowing around, screwing them up, and chucking them into the back of the lorry.

'No! No! Stop,' shouted Dad. 'They're today's newspapers. Me lad's still got to deliver them.'

One dustbin man handed my Dad a pile of crumpled paper from the back of the lorry; the other dustbin men, laughing, helped us gather up as many pages of the papers as possible. Back in our kitchen, we placed the pile of retrieved papers on the table. Dad stormed off to work. Mam, bless her, told me to get off to school. She told me she would put all the newspapers back together and deliver them before she had to go to work.

I think Mam must have put the newspapers back together a bit too hastily. There were complaints to the newsagent that day from numerous customers on my round. *Daily Mail* readers rang up to complain that they had opened the front page of their paper, only to be confronted by the bare breasts of a *Sun* page-three girl. Irate *Sun* readers rang up complaining that they had opened their newspaper, expecting to see a pair of tits, only to be confronted by photographs of Maggie Thatcher and Geoffrey Howe. (I could understand the *Sun* readers' frustration; they wanted tits, but instead they got a pair of arseholes.)

I'd actually kept one of the Page 3 girls for myself, Angela, 19, from Brighton, found hiding behind Mester Timms's coal bunker when the scattered newspapers were being collected in. I quickly glanced over my shoulder, then folded her up and shoved her into the pocket of my parker. I'd become fascinated by breasts and had been so, so close to victory; getting a glimpse of a real pair. I'd managed to cop a feel, actually I had no choice...

My Derby County supporting mate Rob was going out with a girl called Mandy, from the neighbouring pit village of Selston. One night he'd pissed me off by saying he couldn't play street football (the floodlights were back on, the council had fixed the lamppost light on our street), as he was off up to see his beloved.

'I've been promised more than fish fingers t'naight,' he said with a cheesy grin, then talked me into going up to Selston with him; she had a sister, Lorraine, who was looking for a boyfriend.

'Er, what do I do?' Said I, blushing.

'Owt yuh want, I've heard she's a right slag.'

The rendezvous point was wooden bush shelter that reeked of piss, but at least this had bench seating, and the roof wasn't too vandal damaged if it started raining. Ne'mind fish fingers, I thought I'd been stitched up like a kipper. Whereas Rob's Mandy was demure and pretty, her 'sister' was a foul-mouthed, beer swigging, fag inhaling, tomboy. I don't think it was love at first sight for her either (i.e. I wasn't in Rob's image: tall, handsome, athletic): 'Is this him? Bit of a weedy twat, cute though, he'll do I suppose,' she said with a smile that put the fear of Norman Hunter in me, then pulled me by my Man Utd scarf down into a darkened corner.

Whilst Rob wandered off arm-in-arm with Mandy, Lorraine, in quick succession, thrust beer, a fag (that I quickly spat out onto the floor not wanting to repeat my previous experience of smoking. For this I received a thump on the arm. 'Yuh twat.'), then her tongue into my mouth. I let it sit there for a few moments, not sure what to do, I gave it a little bite.

'Oi, you'll have me tongue off,' she laughed. 'But if you like biting.' She clasped her teeth onto my neck.

Fuck, I'm with a vampire, I thought, terror-stricken. I was impressed with her tits, though. Just then she ordered me to do something with my hands which were grasping the edge of the bench for dear life. Taking the lead she pulled one onto her left breast. I was enjoying this now and Lorraine was just pulling up her t-shirt, when a couple of lads showed up. One theatrically jumped forward into the shelter.

'Oi, what yuh fuckn' doin' wi my lass?'

Lorraine pushed me away. 'He's a dirty bastard Bill, had his hands all ower me.'

'Yuh lying slag,' I replied in my defence.

'He's a bloody Jacksdalien n'all, and arve seen him at back of bike shed nicking girlfriends,' was the other lad's evidence for the prosecution.

65

Bill yanked me up onto my feet by my United scarf. 'A Jacksdalien, United scum and a woman thief, who d'yuh think yuh bloody are?'

'A Jacksdalien, a United fan, but you can keep her,' I replied.

'Smack the cheeky bastard Bill,' put in Lorraine.

Bill gobbed on his Doc Martins boot. 'Is'll kick yuh arse cheeks all the way back to Jacksdale.'

'Yeah and you'll be dead, I know all the Topper punks, they're as vicious as Sid.'

'Topper punks, dunt gi mi Topper punks, I know Hell's Angels, and the Notts Outlaws, they'll kill em wi bike chains.

'Smack him Bill, if yuh love me.'

Bill cuffed the side of my ear, swung a fist, I ducked, it put another hole in the shelter.

Just then Rob returned from whatever he'd been up to with Mandy on the waste ground that used to be Selston Colliery. Rita ordered Lorraine home. 'Mam said stay away from Bill.' And the lads scuttled off knowing Rob was older and could handle himself.

Cup Final afternoon. The friend of a friend's cousin's next-door neighbour, who worked at the Baseball Ground, had sold his tickets to a group of foreign businessmen for £100 each.

No ticket. No push-bike. I settled into an armchair in our front room (my lucky 1977 Cup Winners' scarf tied around my neck). Dad and Jackie sat on the settee.

Mam, as usual on Cup Final day, had gone out shopping. Refreshments were sorted; Dad with his bottles of brown ale, a pork pie, and cheese and pickle sandwiches.

Me with a couple of cans of shandy, and several packs of salt 'n' vinegar crisps, and Jackie with a bowl of water and three Boneos.

Eighty-five miserable minutes of the game gone. Arsenal were leading United 2-0. I was slumped in my chair; my lucky 1977 Cup Winners' scarf discarded and lying on the floor.

Then Gordon McQueen pulled one back for United; a glimmer of hope, but surely they'd left it too late. I picked up my lucky scarf from the carpet; Sammy McIlroy collected the ball on the edge of Arsenal's area.

'McIlroy is through. McIlroy is through, and McIlroy has done it,' screamed John Motson, as the ball nestled into the back of Arsenal's net: 2-2.

I ran around the front room, scarf swinging above my head.

'I don't believe it,' said Dad.

The dog barked. Time was nearly up. United would win in extra time, I thought. Arsenal attacked. Graham Rix centred for Alan Sunderland, who slid the ball into United's net: 3-2 Arsenal.

'I do not believe it. I swear I do not believe it,' the commentator on the radio said. (I was listening to *Sport on 2* through an earphone plugged into my lucky transistor, while simultaneously watching TV.)

The final whistle blew. I slumped in my chair; the discarded lucky scarf lying on the floor. I thought I was getting a bit too old to be doing this now, but a tear or two trickled down my cheeks.

At school the United haters took the piss all day long and Lorraine kneed me in the bollocks in the corridor; I was finding being a teenager could be so unfair.

Baggy Trousers

The only lesson I ever really looked forward to at Matthew Holland Comprehensice School was PE, for the twice-a-week football game. Sometimes, though, I'd take my football boots along, looking forward to a game, only for the PE teacher to turn up looking a bit hungover and announce, 'No football today, lads. Cross-country. You know the route. Off you go.'

When we did play football, the games were straight out of the film *Kes*, with the teacher joining the game, showing us his skills, dribbling his way around as many thirteen-year-olds as possible, before smacking the ball as hard as he could into the net.

The worst PE teacher we had was a stand-in teacher from Nottingham called Mr Nightingale, quickly nicknamed Florence. Whenever one of the regular PE teachers was sick or on leave, Florence would come and take their place. He took us for PE once when I was in the first year, and one of the lads back-chatted him in the dressing room. Florence rushed over and laid into him with his fists. Later, he swore and shouted at us on the football pitch.

When he took us again we were in the fifth year, and the lad who had been hit was now as big as Florence, and asked him if he could remember the occasion. Florence, now friendly and polite replied, 'I did that? Sorry, lad, I was under a lot of stress at the time.'

The next day I saw him taking the first years for PE, and there he was, the Florence of old, shouting and swearing.

Over the thorn hedge at the bottom end of the school playing fields were several houses. One was a crumbling old house with an orchard, overgrown grass and bushes. An old man lived there. If a football went into that garden, unless someone went through the hole in the hedge and retrieved it a bit sharpish, it would be gone forever. The old man would appear from nowhere, walking stick waving, grab the football and disappear back into the house. There were rumours that he had a shed with so many footballs in it (some from the 1950's and 60s) that they went right up to the roof. Sometimes during a PE football game you would see this old man sat on a chair at the top of his garden watching us play. If a shot at goal went astray and the football was heading towards his garden, he'd be up out of his chair, walking stick aloft, yelling, 'If it comes over 'ere, I'll 'aye it!'

Once, Florence was taking us for PE, and someone shot wide, the ball landing in the old man's garden. Florence turned to the lad who'd had the shot.

'Go and retrieve the ball, lad.'

'I can't, sir. There's a madman lives there,' replied the lad.

Florence, booting the lad up the backside, retorted, 'Don't be stupid, boy. Go and get the ball.'

'Honestly, sir, he's a madman. He comes after you with a stick,' insisted the boy.

'Nonsense. You have only to ask him politely. I'll show you.'

Florence pushed his way through the hole in the hedge into the garden. He never made it as far as the football. The old man appeared from behind a tree, walking stick aloft, shouting, 'I'll 'aye yer! Yer bugger. I'll 'aye yer.'

'Now, now. Let's be sensible,' said Florence.

WHACK. The old man's stick smacked on to Florence's back. WHACK - another swipe, this time connecting to the side of Florence's legs, who then turned swiftly and started legging it back towards us. About five yards short, he took off, diving through the hedge, landing at our feet on the school playing field. He got to his feet, red-faced and breathing heavily. We all had to turn away, we were laughing so much. Florence tapped me on the shoulder, and said, 'Go to the PE stores, boy, and fetch a football.'

Most of the teachers at comprehensive school appeared to be insane or on the verge of a nervous breakdown. The music teacher was the barmiest of the lot. It was like he'd been there for ever. You'll talk to someone who was at the school forty years ago and they'll say he taught them. I once saw a school photograph from 1902 and I'm sure that Mr Bradshaw was standing at the back. Same old suit.

In his classroom, up above the blackboard, hung a plastercast copy of Beethoven's death mask. Mr Bradshaw's biggest obsession, however, was the Victorian operetta writers Gilbert and Sullivan, and he'd have his classes act out scenes from their work. We once had a music lesson when Mr Bradshaw turned up with a box full of plastic policemen's helmets and truncheons, (the sort you see being sold on Blackpool or Skegness seafront). He had us all put on these helmets, truncheon in hand, the tables and chairs cleared to one side of the room. We then had to walk around the room in comical policeman fashion, singing, 'A policeman's lot is not a happy one.'

'A happy one,' Mr Bradshaw would sing in a deep voice.

What made it worse was that the music room could be seen by all the other classes from across the playground, so you could expect to have urine extracted at breaktime.

Some teachers seemed to victimize certain pupils. For example, one teacher, Mr Hopkin, always appeared to have a go at one particular lad, just because he was overweight. One day the lad arrived late for Mr Hopkin's lesson.

'Good God, lad! I know you've got more weight to carry than anyone else, but it's no excuse for being five minutes late,' shouted Mr Hopkin.

'Sorry, sir,' the lad replied.

'Have you done your homework?

'I did, sir, but our dog ate it this morning.'

'Right, I see. Tell me something, boy. Do you know about Isaac Newton?'

'No, sir.'

Mr Hopkin walked over to a cupboard and took out four thick, dusty old volumes.

'Well, I'll tell you about Isaac Newton,' said Mr Hopkin, carrying the books over to where the lad sat. He then held the books about twelve inches above the lad's head. 'Isaac Newton discovered something called gravity. One day he chucked an apple into the air . . . and, guess what?'

'What, sir?'

Mr Hopkin dropped the books on the lad's head. 'Gravity pulled the apple back to earth. That's what, just like these books.'

I suppose some teachers had to have sadistic tendencies to be able to control certain classes. When I was halfway through the fifth year, a new physics teacher joined the school. I was in level 3 physics class. I didn't like physics. It was just one of the subjects you had to take if you chose engineering as one of your career options, which I had.

The new physics teacher, poor chap, had to take us, a load of couldn't-give-a-fuck fifth years who, despite there being Thatcher in power and millions unemployed, couldn't wait to leave school. He rambled on about Z=MP², zinc and copper, etc, without getting any attention from any of the pupils.

The classroom must have doubled as a biology room; there were two glass cases, one filled with baby locusts (or whatever you call young locusts) and one case containing several frogs. As the lesson deteriorated, one youth snook over to where the glass cases were situated, and removed the lid from each case. A mini swarm of locusts flew across the room; frogs hopped across the tables.

Someone at the back of the class had discovered a drawer full of bottle tops, which were soon whizzing across from one side of the room to the other. Two girls sat at the back smoking. There was a lock on the classroom door, and with a few minutes of the lesson remaining, the physics teacher strode over and locked the door.

'I'm the master here,' he roared.

Everyone became quiet and looked in his direction. Locusts flew over his head, a frog (locust in mouth) hopped across his desk.

'None of you have listened to a word that I have said for the last fifty minutes. So when the bell sounds, you're going to sit here through your break and listen to me,' said the teacher.

The bell sounded for break. Everyone rushed to the side of the classroom, clambered on to chairs, opened windows and jumped into the playground, followed by a dozen locusts and two frogs.

The headmaster was a bit of a bumbling forgetful old soul. Coming back from the chippy one dinner time, me and a mate found a purse containing £5. Well, it had contained

£10, but me and my mate decided to reward ourselves with a fiver. Then, seeing how we both had a detention coming up, we thought we would hand in the purse (with the rest of the money) to the headmaster to get in the good books. We knocked on the headmaster's door.

'Enter,' came the voice from inside.

'Sir. We found this purse at dinner time,' I said.

'Splendid, boys! Splendid. Honesty will get you a long way,' said the headmaster, rising from his chair.

'Who's your form teacher?'

'Mr Perry, sir,' answered my mate.

At school they had this system (I don't know what the use of it was) where if you did anything good, they gave you a merit (a pink piece of paper with 'merit' written across it). If you did something bad, you were given a D merit (a green piece of paper with 'D merit' written across it).

The headmaster looked at us nodding his head approvingly. 'Tell Mr Perry to . . . erm . . . to give you . . . to give you . . . erm one of those . . . erm . . . one of those pink things . . . to give you one . . . tell Mr Perry to give you a pink one . . . a merit.'

By now me and my mate were doubled up in laughter.

'Now, now, boys. Don't ruin your good deed,' said the headmaster.

Even the school nurse was allegedly an alcoholic. Before assembly one morning, not feeling too well, I was sick in the playground, and a teacher came over to me and enquired how I was.

'I've got an upset stomach, miss,' I replied.

'Go and see the nurse,' said the teacher.

I made my way over to the nurse's surgery. I knocked on the door. There was no answer, so I went inside and sat on a chair in the corner of the room to wait for her. About five minutes later the door opened, and in walked the nurse. Not noticing me, she gave a big sigh, and placed her bag on the table. She opened the bag and was just pulling out what appeared to be a bottle of whisky when I gave a cough. Dropping the bottle back into her bag, she spun round, giving me a cold stare.

'What the fuck . . .' she muttered. 'What are you doing here at this time, boy?'

'I've been sick - a teacher sent me.'

'Well, are you going to be sick again?'

'I don't think so.'

'Then take an aspirin and go away.'

The art teachers were nice enough, if a little pretentious and precious; at least they gave me praise for doing my own thing, to be free thinking, well to a certain extent. I did a CND protest poster: this showed the planet earth, but it also looked like one of those cartoon bombs with the fuse coming out of the top. Two arms reached up to this, one from the USA and one from the USSR, each had a lighted match in its hand. Mr Abbey liked this, but said I couldn't put it on the wall in case the headmaster thought he was cultivating leftie revolutionaries in his class.

My sister, Elaine, was studying for an Arts Degree at the time, she told me to do some modern art in class if I wanted a good mark as art teachers were suckers for this style. So when another art teacher, Mrs Wheatcroft, asked us to use our imagination and paint anything we liked for one lesson, I put my Picasso head on. I painted three connected 3D shapes, a trapezoidal prism in the middle and two parallelepiped ones on either side (OK I've had to look on the internet - and it took a bloody hour - to find out just what shapes I'd done back at school, let's just say a truncated pyramid with sloping rectangular shapes each side). Each had a square tunnel running through them. Into these entered - in orderly lines - red triangles on the left side, white circles in the middle and blue squares into the right one. They all emerged out of the middle tunnel and became jumbled up.

'Oh Tony, I really like that,' commented Mrs Wheatcroft, staring at my masterpiece in wonder. 'It really speaks to my soul, I see what you've done, the chaos theory, the rejection of regimented order, so profound. But that's just my interpretation, art is so subjective, so tell me what you're trying to say with it.'

'Well miss..'

'Wait.' Mrs Wheatcroft turned to the rest of the class. 'All gather round, Tony has painted a wonderful picture and is going to explain it to us all.'

They formed a circle around me.

'Well miss, lads n lasses, it's like this int'it. The red triangles represent United, the white circles the ball and the square blues is Citeh. Nah you can look at it two ways, they're the players coming out the tunnel and getting mixed up as the match gets underway or they're the supporters coming out at the end of the match and it's all kicking off, chaos, like.'

Sniggers came from the crowd. Mrs Wheatcroft had the look on her face like a goal had been given against her team which was clearly 5 yards offside. The Ref's whistle for full-time, the bell for break, saved her embarrassment. We were all filtering out when she called me back.

75

'Er Tony, I believe it's your turn to wash out the brushes.

I couldn't help myself in winding people up, not always intentionally. I don't know where it came from, what came first, the heedless – rather than headless – chicken, it was just in my nature to do my own thing and be cheeky; or the cracked, scrambled egg, caused by punk or growing up in a constantly piss-taking mining village?

I even snapped the patience of a mild-mannered science teacher, Mr Lockingly. One day he was on patrol in the Lower Unit (where our form room was this year). For some reason you weren't allowed to stay in there at break and dinner-time; but it was pissing it down this particular day. So me and a mate came up with a another cunning plan: make out we'd turned over a new leaf. We persuaded Mr Lockingly that we wanted to do some extra swotting up, could we use our break-time? He was delighted and obliged (ah, my innocent blue eyes). And all we did was laugh at those pupils getting wet in the playground, and every time Mr Lockingly passed by the open concertina doors, with his mug of tea, nodding approvingly as we pretended to scribble away, we'd rush over and make rude gestures behind his back. Only – on the third time – I tripped noisily over a chair and dived into the corridor with jacks already raised. In a rage he yanked me up by the scruff of the neck and threatened to throw me through a window. Then the look that came on the poor man's face as he came to his usual scientifically calmed senses, and he just showed us the door. He had me in later that day for a heart to heart chat.

'Your brother was never disruptive like you, a lovely lad, why can't you be like him?'

'Because I'm not him, I'm me, I wanna be me,' I replied obstinately.

What chance did I have of advancing academically in this environment? I'd gone backward. At Jacksdale junior school I'd won handwriting, spelling and art competitions (I was to stand on stage at morning assembly to show off my painting of a kingfisher). Now after five years at Matthew Holland Comp my handwriting was the anarchic scrawl of a madman and my art deemed subversive.

When it came to my careers interview it really was like the scene out of *Kes* when Billy sits there apathetically, with no idea what he wants to do; he just wants out of there, to be free. I just wanted to escape a school in meltdown and breakdown. Not realising I'd be out of the frying pan into a Thatcher world of petrol bomb fires and the break up of the only kind of society I knew. I did a Billy two fingered salute to them both.

The school leavers disco sums up our class of 82. Fights broke out, the result of large amounts of alcohol being sneaked in, girls screamed, dancers slipped on vomit. A teacher found evidence of rule breaking in the shape of several vodka bottles, and took to the tannoy to say they were pulling the plug. We responded by chanting 'Bastards, bastards, bastards.' A riot ensued, bricks went through classroom and car windows. The police turned up in numbers not seen since the punk nights at Jacksdale, Grey Topper. School discos were banned at Matthew Holland Comp for years afterwards, this was our legacy.

The following week a group of us were sat in an empty classroom, capping off from a lesson. We were counting down the days until we left now. No teacher dare confront us, not after the disco, they knew we were the generation that didn't care, beyond hope. A teenager called Spot, the most anarchic punk of us all, announced he was leaving that very moment, well he just stood up and said 'I'm outa here.' He walked through the doors and put his fist through the classroom window and walked away into the big bad wide world leaving a trail of blood.

A few weeks later I'd dramatically leave the bloody school in a bloody way too.

1980's

The Wilderness Years

When routine bites hard and ambitions are low
And resentment rides high but emotions won't grow
And we're changing our ways taking different roads
Then love will tear us apart again
    'Love Will Tear Us Apart' Joy Division

From early 1980 to the summer of 1982 my interest in football waned. I hardly went to a match and didn't play at all. Football wasn't the be-all and end-all any more. My life had been turned upside down. I was no longer a cheeky football-mad kid, but a sullen teenager. Adolescence had smacked me in the groin and exploded on my face.

My favourite person in the world was dying of cancer. Grandad Lane had been in and out of hospital for months, having several operations. I went around to see him when he came home, and the sight of him left me devastated. Grandad had become a withered old man; the cancer had not only eaten away at his body, but also destroyed his pride. I knew he didn't like me seeing him like that, but after that I never did. He died a week later.

Music, girls and getting drunk became major diversions from football. I saw the film *Quadrophenia*, started listening to the 'Two Tone' music of Madness, The Specials (who played at Jacksdale's own music venue the Grey Topper at the time 'Gangsters' was released), The Selector and The Beat, and became a mod. I was a failed mod; I'd always been a scruffy little fucker, and couldn't handle the wont of this fashion for looking smart all the time. I soon went back to my first love of punk.

One day my brother Brian, who never really liked football, walked into the house wearing a Leeds United shirt. His friends supported Leeds, so he decided he would too. It's ironic that at a time of my football dispassion, Brian should become a fan of the game. His interest didn't last long, though. With his friends, Brian went down to Nottingham one Saturday afternoon and unwisely wore his Leeds United shirt. He was punched and kicked to the ground by a gang of Notts County supporters in the Broadmarsh shopping centre. Brian had never really liked football; he hated it now.

I was at a loss when it came to going out with girls. Paula was thirteen and I was fifteen. Paula looked eighteen; I looked thirteen. She was taller than me, had a full figure, short-cropped brown hair and brown eyes. I'd seen her around at school, but I'd never spoken to her. I was in the fifth year and her friends kept coming up to me asking if I'd go out with her. She fancied me, they said. So a date was arranged.

We stood arms around each other in the corner of a bus shelter on the main road in Brinsley (the village where she lived; about a mile from Jacksdale). We'd been in the same stance for twenty minutes, in near total agonizing silence: what the fuck do I talk to her about? . . . she's a stranger . . . she's a girl . . . what the fuck do you talk to a girl about?. . . I only ever talk about football . . . you never know, she might like football. Then I spotted the football pitch across the road. I was away.

'I used to play on that pitch.'

'Did you?'

'Yeah. I played in the Brinsley under-13s team.'

'Oh.'

'We weren't that good, though. We played Clifton All Whites and they beat us 10-0. Best thing about it was they were called Clifton All Whites and all their players were black. They were brilliant.'

'Really.'

'Yeah. We did beat Priory Celtic, though, 3-1; and they were a good team, Forest star Tony Woodcock used to play for them'

'I hate football. It's all my dad talks about.'

'Oh.' (Music - that's it. Music - what groups does she like?)

'What groups do you like, Paula?'

'I've not got many records. I like Haircut 100. Nick Heyward's cute. Oh, and Bananarama. They're good.'

'You've not heard of Public Image Limited, then?'

'No.'

'Joy Division?'

'No.'

'Killing Joke?'

'No.'

'The Jam?'

'Yeah, I've heard of them.'

'They're brilliant, aren't they?'

'They're OK; not really my taste, though (OK. OK . . . she thinks The Jam are just OK . . .)

'Are you going to kiss me, then?' asked Paula. It wasn't conversation she was after; she just wanted a good snog, and for me to try and undo her bra strap. We lasted about a month.

In April 1982 I dramatically left school earlier than expected. During the Easter holidays I wheelied someone else's motorbike (I say motorbike to sound cool, yes it was a motorised bike but only a purple Yamaha 'Fizz' 50cc, not a Honda Gold Wing) through a hedge in the middle of

Jacksdale, breaking my wrist and cutting my face, leaving me unable to take my school exams (the school wouldn't let me take the exams at a later date. Eleven years of school wasted; but I'd enjoyed them, I realize now).

After crashing the motorbike, I lay on the pavement with my back resting up against a wall, waiting for an ambulance. A crowd had gathered around me. Blood ran from cuts on my face; the bone in my wrist, completely broken, stuck out at an awkward angle. I was in pain. Down the street walked Dad; someone had rung him up.

'I've got some more bad news for you,' said Dad.

Wiping blood from my eyes with my good hand I looked up at him.

'What?'

'Man United lost.'

I was out of school into the big shitty world of Thatcher's Britain, the Falkland's War was raging, I signed on the dole, donned punk clothes, listened to any music Radio 1's legendary DJ John Peel introduced me to; buying indie and punk records from Selectadisc record shop in Nottingham, and reggae and dub from a stall at the indoor market in Victoria Centre. Me and several mates would travel to rock concerts all over the North, sometimes crashing at student digs, at other times sleeping in railway stations after gigs; Theatre of Hate was my first gig, 50p to get in at Sheffield University.

Pil in Blackburn stands out: I went with Feff, one of the punks from the Jacksdale Grey Topper days, who spiked up his bright orange hair using loads of Harmony hairspray and a can of oxtail soup. He wore original 'Seditionaries' gear (an 'Only Anarchists Are Pretty' shirt, red cord bondage trousers) and a pair of grey beetle crushers. I had on a blue and orange parachute shirt, a battered old leather jacket (that at least six punks had owned before me) with the Birthday Party song title 'BIG JESUS TRASHCAN' painted on the back in big red letters, ripped jeans, black 'Seditionaries' boots and a Sid Vicious 'She's dead, I'm alive, I'm yours' handkerchief hanging from my studded belt. Both of us carried our rolled-up sleeping bags on our backs.

The train we were travelling up to Blackburn on had been delayed for forty minutes, which would give us little time to make the start of the concert. And as we passed through the sprawl of Manchester, heavy snow began to fall from the skies.

In a blizzard we trudged through the streets of Blackburn until we spotted the venue, King George's Hall. Snowballs in our hands we burst through the doors like Butch Vicious and the Sundance Punk, a layer of snow flattening our spikey tops. Just then Pil stormed into a version of 'Anarchy In The UK' (which Lydon was playing on this tour for the first time since the Pistols). We hurled the snowballs towards the stage then pogoed our way into the heaving mass of punks. I was sent spiralling straight back out again my head connecting with a speaker. As I lay there, dazed and confused, melting snow running down my face, there was a mystical moment. I looked up, stars spinning in front of my eyes, to see John Lydon looking down at me, holding a neon halo behind his head as he sang 'Religion.'

Me and Feff participated in the snowball of snowball fights involving about 100 punks after the gig, before retiring to the palatial surroundings of Blackburn station waiting room. There we unrolled our sleeping bags on the benches and had just got our heads down when a station guard came sneaking into the room, prodded us with a sweeping brush handle, then ran out again, shouting, 'Oi, Punks, you can't sleep here. On your way.'

A train was coming in heading south, which we boarded, leaving it at Crewe. There we went into the waiting room, unrolled our sleeping bags, got our heads down, were just dozing off when we were awakened by a message on the station tannoy: 'Wake up. Wake up, punks in the waiting room (there was then muffled laughter). This is not a hotel, so on your way.'

A train was coming in heading south, which we boarded and slept in the empty unlit carriage. Occasionally I'd wake up and look out of the window into the darkness before dawn, lightened by the fresh untrodden snow, a still, beautiful scene. We left at Derby to get a connection to our home-town station. As we waited, we watched the suits at rush hour, who looked like busy little ants as they swarmed along the platform and up over the bridge.

Back in Jacksdale I trudged up Wagstaff Lane homeward bound just as everyone else was going to work. Many looked at me, my punk clothes, bedraggled state with contempt or amusement. I thought 'fuck you, I've had an amazing time, that I'm going to remember forever, now I'm off to bed, you're off to some mind-numbing job in 'chicken town.' I think I was right, how many of them remember Dec 11th 1983?

*

It took the great World Cup of 1982 to re-ignite my passion for football. And the management of Ron Atkinson at United rekindled my desire to be a Stretford Ender. Gone was the steady tactical-awareness football preached by previous United Manager Dave Sexton. Under Atkinson United attacked with flair and imagination. He brought striker Frank Stapleton from Arsenal and the great Bryan Robson from West Brom, along with Remi Moses. Terrace favourite Norman Whiteside had broken into the team at the age of 16.

Soon I would be off on the train to Manchester, getting to Old Trafford early to queue to stand in the Stretford End. I wasn't able to afford to go to every home game. But at last I was beginning to feel more of a sense of belonging to the team I loved.

We All Stand, United

I simply say: 'off on the train to Manchester', but this was just one stage of my pilgrimage. First I'd lift my hangover hammered head off my pillow at 6.00 a.m., wanting to hammer the alarm clock for telling me that so noisily, briefly wanting to turn over and go back to sleep - and in those teenage days I could sleep for England, usually not getting up until dinnertime on Saturdays. Then I'd remember just why it was set for that unfamiliar hour and the first flames of excitement were kindled; fuelling me to jump out of bed, have a quick shower, a few slices of toast, mug of tea, a couple of Anadins. Back up stairs, plug headphones into my stereo for quick snatches of some essential sounds (despite the hangover, but it's disappearing quick, amazing how one does when you have something to look forward to in a day) to really get my blood pumping: Killing Joke tracks 'Tension' and 'Turn to Red', Sham 69's 'If the Kids are United,' and I'm ready, 1,2,3,4, ok let's go....

....just pause here, on my first trip to Old Trafford, Dad was up early as usual, going to work on a Saturday morning, and made a lovely gesture, handing me a £10 note. Now for you Southern football sophisticates, who can identify more with a sophisticated football fan autobiography, who were earning loadsa fackin money in the 80's (OK a generalisation that all Southerners were earning shit loads of money in the 80's, even plasterers, just like us working class living north of Watford Gap are not all Jeremy Kyle lowlife, Neanderthals, OK?), this may sound a pitiful amount. But this was a sizable bite out of Dad's wages at the time. It wasn't a calculated economic decision anyway, it was Dad recognising how much this day meant to me, his way of giving me a helping hand to start taking my own journeys in life; it meant a lot at the time, that's all...

I'd leave the house and first had to run the gauntlet: the fast paced walk down past the terraced houses of Palmerston Street. Most Forest and Derby yowfs would be in bed at that time, but a paper lad with an affiliation to those teams might be cheeky enough to throw a stone my way on seeing my United shirt or scarf with the shout: 'Brian Clough's red and white army.'

I feared 'Dagger,' the local 'tramp', still being in a drunken slumber on the bench or rec bank. He did actually have a council house, but befitting his stereotypical tramp image – a feather adorned grubby fedora hat, atop a weather-beaten face, red nose, long beard, long Bolshevik overcoat, holed baggy trousers held up with an old leather belt, a knife hanging from this, Chaplin boots – he often crashed out in the open; on coming home from the pub or a night out shooting rabbits. The latter the most scary scenario as he'd have his twelve-bore tucked under his arm. He'd definitely have his dagger and walking stick, and he'd still have a whisky hangover.

He was jovial most of the time: when we were little kids playing football in the street and Dagger was off down the pub we'd shout: 'How yuh going Jimmy?' This wasn't his name, but he called everyone else 'Jimmy.'

'Ah, all in fine fettle Jimmys,' he'd shout back with a big hearted laugh.

But if he'd had 'too much pop' in the pub, been in an argument or lost on the horses or failed to bag a rabbit, and we could hear him coming back up the road muttering and swearing to himself, then the street football match would be hastily abandoned until he'd passed by (me and my mate Webby once were being right little bastards, deliberately kicking the ball into his front garden, then knocking on his door to ask for it back, 'Aye Jimmys go get it,' until about the sixth time when he chased us away threatening to shoot us). So I certainly didn't want to be his early morning alarm call by kicking a tin can and waking him; if he was on his bench I'd tiptoe by.

Some Saturday mornings cappers gathered up their racing pigeons into wicker baskets. These they placed on old pram bases to transport them to the meeting point, at the rear of a local pub, in readiness for a lorry to collect them to be taken to the race starting point. If I'd encounter one - or worse, a gang of them - coming the opposite way, there'd be pavement rage. My attire wasn't much better than Dagger's and just as disagreeable: again the United scarf or shirt mixed with my punk image; ripped DIY bleach patterned jeans (or black jeans), studded belt (sometimes with a 'Anarchy in the UK' hanky hanging from it), either a black leather biker jacket or customised denim (blue or black)

89

jacket with patches, pin badges - bands, CND and United, a few safety pins, small chain, maybe one of my sister's old knitted mohairs on cold mornings, black Converse boots. If I'd tried to spike up my dark curly hair the night before, the curls would now be winning back out, giving my hair a medusa look.

First the cappers would force me off the pavement - if there was gang there was the danger of being hemmed in - before a short lecture delivered: 'Aye up, bloody Stig o that dump up rowd [Manchester], dirty boggering town. You'd be proper bloody dirty alreet, if yuh wer where tha should be, dahn pit yowf.'

A group of 'wesher women,' delivering the village news themselves, gossiping at the front gates: 'Look what cat dragged in.' I'd hear them mutter with elbow nudges and nods my way just before I reached them. Then just after I'd passed them by I could hear them start on all the gossip about our family.

Then the wait for the C5 service bus from Nottingham, full of real men off to work on Saturday mornings, who'd give their forthright opinions on the state of my club. They were wary of my punk clothes, however; the Topper punks and Jacksdale still had a reputation, I just might be one of the originals little brother. I hoped the bus would be full, then sit near the rear of the top deck and hope the conductor didn't have time to reach me for my fare before I got off, just before the town of Alfreton. From here there was another mile walk down to the train station.

There'd be a group of Pinxton (another tough mining village) Red Devils on the platform here at times. This could be a good thing or bad: if other team's away fans were travelling through here, a group of United fans could be looked on as provocative. I saw a few scuffles break out at times, nothing major, and I'd stay out of it. I didn't hang out with the Pinxton crew, they were older than me - 70's rockers - and I was independent, this part of the journey was personal. I'm not a hooligan or street fighter (except when I had to stick up for myself or with words), if you wanted to stay out of the way you usually could, those who wanted to take each other on would.

You had to be on your guard if you had to change trains at Sheffield, though. This could be a hooligan hub in the 80's; with many football supporters of several teams passing through or on the way to or from Sheffield. An indication that potential trouble was on the way was when a mini army of police and dogs would turn up on a platform just before an Inter City pulled in; packed with fans - of whichever club - chanting and banging on the windows. Then it was best to find the entrance to platform 9 3/4 for a while.

After arriving at Victoria Station, Manchester, I'd quickly wander around the city centre, before catching one of the orange double-decker buses that went by Old Trafford. This could be a lottery too: some buses went off straight down Chester Road, but others would go all around the dodgy back streets of Hulme; many a dodgy character or bitter blue could come aboard here. The bus routes around where I live could have a few bus nutters, but the ones in this area were in a different league. I once had to stand in an aisle of a packed bus when a crazy Irish man got on and stood in front of me and started shadow boxing, shouting: 'Would you fight Joe Frazier for a million pounds?'

Excitement would start to build within me when - just after a huge mural on the side of a building showing scenes of industrial Manchester and an image of Denis Law saluting after scoring a goal - my Mecca became visible in the distance, Manchester United Football Club; standing proud amongst dilapidated old Victorian warehouses of Trafford Park industrial estate and Salford Quay (from the windows of these - in days gone by - hard grafting workers must have peered out through the smog to Old Trafford, looking forward to the great escape on a special Saturday, with a sense of longing and excitement I can only imagine).

I'd jump off the bus on Chester Road. In later years I'd sometimes call in at The Trafford pub, where you'd find hundreds of friendly Irish Reds (although I think some of them would have thrown down the gauntlet to Joe Frazier for a million pounds, if it was on offer, by the looks of them), and generous too; many got me a pint in. They created a brilliant atmosphere, giving the first airing of the songs you'd later hear on the Stretford End. This was several years later, though, when I had a season ticket (LMTB) and more time before going in the stadium.

Lunch was fish and chips from Lou Macari's. Then I'd stroll up to the ground (if you were early enough - which I was for my first few games - you'd see a few players arrive) and wander around the souvenir shop (the only one in the country at the time). Then follow the curve of the stadium corners to queue outside the Stretford End terrace.

You'd stand here, sometimes in the pouring rain, for over an hour, continually checking your watch, still on the outside world, lost in your thoughts at times, dwelling on your problems back home (no ipod, no mobile, not even a Walkman, couldn't afford one, to kill time. Some would have small transistor radios, the ones with a single earphone plug). Until getting into banter or in-depth team analysis with other Reds and starting to leave it all behind. At last the gates would open at 1.30 p.m., still an hour and half to the sacred hour, 3.00 p.m. That walk down the Stretford End tunnel, heart pounding, out onto the terrace, pausing to take in the view of the Theatre of Dreams, quiet for now, sparsely populated. Still it's best to head for your spot, lean on a crush barrier, read the programme, chat to other Reds you recognise, listening to the sounds the pre-match DJ is spinning.

The excitement builds, turn to red. The terrace begins to fill. You roll up the programme, slip it out of the way in an inside pocket or tucked into your jeans, as the first songs sporadically break out, banter between the United fans at this point.

'Shit on the [Stretford End terrace] tunnel, shit on the tunnel tonight....We are the left side....We are the right side...K-Stand give us a song K-Stand K-Stand gives us a song.'

I'm smiling now, I'm happy, it's bubbling up, the outside world and all its trials has melted away; the Reds will do our battles on the pitch. Thoughts of defeat don't enter your head, we'll win, in style, and everything in your world will be seen through Lancashire rose red tinted spectacles.

The tension, the tension builds, the excitement, the excitement builds, turn to red.

Around 2.20 p.m. the Stretford End has become a joyous, edgy, and noisy mass of United humanity. Time for the classic old songs to be sung:

'Hello! Hello! We are the Busby boys...and if you are a City fan surrender or you'll die, we all follow United....Bertie Mee said to Matt Busby 'Have you heard of the North Bank, Highbury? 'No,' said Matt, 'you cockney twat, but I've heard of the STRETFORD ENDERS!!'....If ever they are playing in your town you must get to that football ground, take a lesson come and see football taught by Matt Busby....from the banks of the River Irwell to the shores of Sicily, we will fight, fight, fight for United till we win the Football League....Oh Manchester, (oh Manchester) is wonderful, (is wonderful) Oh Manchester is wonderful, it's full of tits, fanny, and United; Oh Manchester is wonderful.... We'll drink a drink a drink, To Denis the king, the king, the king [to the 'Lilly the Pink' tune].....Number 1 is Georgie Best, number 2 is Georgie Best, number 3 is Georgie Best, number 4 is Georgie Best' - so is 5,6,7,8,9,10 and definitely 11 – 'We all live in a Georgie Best world, a Georgie Best world, a Georgie Best world' [to the tune of 'Yellow Submarine'].

The DJ sounds and words drowned out. The away fans start pouring in.

The tension, the tension builds, the excitement, the excitement builds, turn to red.

One arm now pinned to my side, one free to punch the air, then a pointing finger on an arm pulled back over the back over the head, then flung forward like a catapult mechanism, in the direction of the away fans. The Stretford End's attention is fully on them now, they're trying their best to provoke us, to outwit us, out sing us, but this is Old Trafford, they don't stand a chance, not pre-match.

'Who are ya, who are ya, who are ya?'

'We'll beat 'em at home and we'll beat 'em away, we'll kill any bastards that get in our way, we are the pride of all Europe, the cock of the North, we hate the Scousers, and cockney's of course, AND LEEDS! We are United, without any doubt, we are the Manchester boys, la la la la la la la la la la la la la -

OOOOOOOOOOOOOOOOOOOOOOOOOOO.'

Followed by specialised songs for different clubs. Sometimes spontaneous, made-up-in-the-moment chants will break out, like a little flame, then catch on into a forest fire. And even if we do go one down the response from the crowd to urge a comeback will be even louder 'United United United,' we never die. If, Sir Matt Busby forbid, we go two nil down then Stretford Enders threaten to settle the score off the pitch: 'You're gonna get your fuckin' heads kicked in.'

For the real notorious Red Army this is a real threat. For people like me it's a fantasy. I feel like the little kid who loved United and played with toy knights, building up my army, watching classic films, those great swashbuckling battles - the classic scene in *Zulu* were both brave opposing forces are trying to ousting each other before battle begins.

The tension, the tension builds, the excitement, the excitement builds, turn to red.

'Glory glory Man United, glory glory Man United, glory glory Man United, as the reds go marching ON ON ON!' Is delivered with such passion and venom – and again the catapult arms - that the force sends masses of reds tumbling down the terraces, like the damn has burst, and all before the torrent will be swept away and destroyed. The thrill of being in the midst of this, like a mini theme park ride with the safety guards removed.

War songs now temporarily turn to cheers, heads swing to the players tunnel, as the first United stars are coming out for their warm ups. Each one's name is chanted. Many of the favourites has their own song, we demand a wave, they salute us, a cheer. Some are loved more than others, you can tell that by the red roar o meter, Robson and Whiteside are ones turning it up to 11 at this time. They've shown they understand what it means to pull on a United shirt - one a great signing, great captain, the other keeping up the Busby Babe tradition of young players coming through the ranks - they never surrender, they have style and guts, we love them for it. The boos and piss taking - again often spontaneous - of the opposing players, who stay as far away from the Stretford End as they can.

The players have all gone back in now. Not for long, the clock's ticking down the final minutes to 3.00 p.m. All the songs are now drifting one into another, then a loud roar as they come out to do battle-

The tension, the tension builds, the excitement, the excitement builds, turn to red.

'UNITED UNITED UNITED,' it's deafening, rising to a crescendo as the ref blows the whistle, again tumbling down the terraces as United attack 'attack ATTACK'....

...and WOW, if/when that net bulges, that 'GOAL!' goes in. How do you describe that feeling to someone who's never stood on one of the great ends of football at that moment? I'll try, imagine spontaneously combusting with supercharged life-force, the atomic big bang in your inner universe, like pogoing to the opening chords to 'Anarchy in the UK' at a Sex Pistols concert (which I would do one day, but you can insert any band you like), inhibitions lost, dancing with delirium, a hedonistic head charge, all compacted into a few minutes. Never mind all that orgasmic bollocks, all I know it was one great feeling that can't be recreated in modern day all-seater stadiums, or even on modern German style terracing. I'm forever glad I experienced it, wish I could have bottled it, I'd drink it back down every day, a United alcoholic, no need to be anonymous.

A 1-0 victory over our greatest rivals would suffice, but against lesser opposition we'd expect a 3 or 4 nil victory at least, accomplished in our traditional style. One final giant roar at the final whistle, flowing out onto the street in a red river of euphoria. Waiting for the bus back into town on those dark winter nights, looking back at Old Trafford, floodlights lighting it up, lighting up the sky, lighting up your soul, then onto the buzz bus. Possibly there was time to get some vinyl in at Piccadilly Records. Run to the station, hoping the *Manchester Evening News* late sports edition the *Pink Final* would make it into the station before your train (it usually did and it amazed me they could have the reports in and printed so fast), so you can read about the match highlights again on the journey home (often in those old style compartments with a corridor running down one side of the train).

If I was in luck I'd catch the C5 bus straight back to Jacksdale. If not there was one to Selston, I could get off at Jubilee (a one-street village of terraced houses high on a hill above Jacksdale) and walk down into the dale through the grounds of Pye Hill pit. I quite enjoyed this, my childhood excitement and imagination had been rekindled. The pit - down below - lit up, with its strange collection of buildings, old and fairly new: the Meccano lift winding wheel tower, dwarfed by a huge rectangular shaped coal storage and preparation tower, looking like some 60's modernist architecture; an angled enclosed chute coming out near its top that sloped down to the lower buildings, like a giant's slide (as a kid I dreamed of sliding down it). The whole complex looking like some sci-fi castle or *The Lord of the Rings* fortress.

If the pit canteen was open at the bottom of the hill I could get a bacon butty and cup of tea, before heading up the 'jitty' path onto our council estate, looking forward to giving Dad the match report. Then up to my bedroom, spinning some vinyl, splashing on some Old Spice (which really didn't complement my United punk image), and heading off down to Woody's club in Jacksdale. Walking on air, chest out, guaranteed to have a good laugh with my mates in this mood. If I pull a girl that's a real bonus, but the weekends already a winner if I don't.

A feeling that will last for days, until slowly being stripped away by midweek dole day despondency. Relieved by Alan Bleasdale's *Boys from the Blackstuff*, bringing me close to tears, then definitely laughing, hysterically. Bleasdale a new champion, he knew this shit, I knew it and those characters. Or escaping my outer bedroom blues with New Order's 'Blue Monday' and *Power, Corruption and Lies* album, then stepping into Siouxsie and the Banshees *A Kiss in a Dream House*. Looking in the *United Review* at the home fixtures, circling the next one I can make it to, counting down the days until I can go to a real Theatre of Dreams.*

*But oh god, OH GOD, if United didn't score and the opposition did and went on to win. Then - on leaving the stadium - the low rolling Manchester storm clouds sank onto my shoulders (and I couldn't stop - you'll never walk alone through a storm - from invading my head, even if we hadn't played and lost to Liverpool, fuck off out!), even on a sunny day. And all those sections of my journey had to be retraced and seemed an eternity: drained, falling asleep on the train, heavy legged on the walking sections, rain soaking you to your aching bones. Pye Hill pit looking like a dystopian interrogation unit from *1984* or Mordor. Snap at Dad, slump on a bar stool, shoulders slumped, sorrows drowned in alcohol, a hangover that would last a week.

Pre-Hillsborough 2

Feb 19th 1983:

United reached the fifth round of the FA Cup and were drawn away to Derby County. I was unable to obtain a ticket to stand with the United supporters. I did, though, get hold of a ticket to stand in the home section of the ground, Derby's Pop Side.

I was late into the ground, as a result of there being no organized queues outside the turnstiles, and wasn't surprised to be faced by a solid wall of supporters when I reached the rear of the terrace. It was OK to arrive late on to the terraces and stand at the back if you were six foot plus; more than likely you would still be able to see the pitch.

If, however, you were five foot eight or below, then you were going to have to push your way into the crowd to achieve a decent view. But I was used to this, it was standard practice of life on the terraces, and was something I'd become accustomed to in the Stretford End.

This time it was different; it had taken a whole lot of effort to push myself just twelve yards down into the crammed mass of supporters, using the sway of the crowd to get me a little further each time. More late arrivals were making the congestion almost unbearable; my feet had been lifted from the ground several times.

'There's no way everyone in here's got a ticket,' I said to a youth at the side of me.

'I know. I haven't; none of my mates have,' he replied.

'How'd you get in?'

'Easy. Just slip a fiver to the turnstile operator and you're in.'

As the game got underway there was a surge forward. I caught my ribs painfully on the corner of a crush barrier. I'd had enough. I turned and, with a struggle, pushed my way through the crowd to the space at the back of the stand. I stood there for a few minutes catching my breath.

In the corner of the terracing was a floodlight pylon. I went over to the pylon and climbed up as far as I could to get a decent view of the pitch, joining other supporters already perched on the bars of the pylon. Some supporters climbed right to the very top of the floodlight.

I lasted about twenty minutes up there. I didn't have a proper footing, and my hands were blue from the cold and gripping the pylon.

Eventually, with a hand up from another supporter, I clambered up on to a narrow ledge at the top of a wall at the back of the stand. I couldn't see one net, and missed Norman Whiteside's goal that was enough to win the match for United.

Cup Final '83:
Brown Ale Albion v Pils Lager United

Norman Whiteside was again the hero of the day in the semi-final of the FA Cup, volleying home the winner against Arsenal. Relegated Brighton would be United's opponent in the Final.

I didn't have enough tokens from United matches to qualify for a ticket. I was talking to a youth in the pub who played for a local Sunday League football team. He told me that each season this team received two FA Cup Final tickets, which were used as first prize in the raffle at the club's end-of-season presentation night.

So of course I went to the presentation night and spent £10 on half a book of raffle tickets. And should I fail to win first prize, then I'd got the nod from at least a dozen people who were willing to sell me a ticket if they won.

With the help of several lagers I'd sat patiently through the speeches, the presentation of trophies for player of the season, leading goalscorer, best goal, best free-kick, best penalty, best corner, best throw-in, best foul and best celebration after a goal. I'd joined in the football songs and now, after three hours, it was finally time to draw the raffle.

I won third prize - a box of assorted vegetables. I won second prize - a two-foot-high pink cuddly bunny rabbit. 'Now for tonightsa starrr prrize - a two a Cup a Final ticketssa - the winning number issa,' announced the compére, 'a six.'

Yes, I'd got that.

'A two.'

Yes.

'A four.'

No..Fuck, fuck, bollocks, fuck.

'Oh, that's me. What a turn up,' declared the compére.

Carrying the box of assorted vegetables in my hands, with the pink cuddly bunny rabbit tucked under my arm, I went over to the compére.

'I'll give you twenty pounds for one of the tickets and throw in the vegetables and the bunny rabbit,' I said.

'Not a chance, son.'

'Thirty quid.'

'No.'

'Forty.'

'I can't sell them. My grandson's Manchester United daft. I told him I'd take him to the Final if I could get hold of a couple of tickets.'

'Oh, I see, convenient you won the raffle, then.'

'Yes it is, isn't it,' he said, with a self-satisfied smile.

Cup Final afternoon. No first prize in the raffle. Ten pounds out of pocket. No ticket. I settled into an armchair in our front room. At the side of my chair sat a two-foot-high pink bunny rabbit, my 1977 lucky Cup Winners' scarf tied around it's neck. Dad and Jackie sat on the settee.

Mam, as usual on Cup Final day, had gone out shopping. Refreshments were sorted; Dad with his bottles of brown ale, a pork pie and cheese and pickle sandwiches. Me with several bottles of Holston Pils lager and the remains of last night's Chinese takeaway warmed up in the microwave. And Jackie with a bowl of water and three Boneos.

Brighton may have been relegated, but they were up for the occasion, taking the lead within the first fifteen minutes. I knocked back my first bottle of lager and started on my second. I noticed Dad watching me with interest.

'What?' I enquired.

'So you think you can drink with th' best of 'em, d'ya?' Dad replied.

He then emptied his pint of brown ale and began to pour another. Four minutes later he'd guzzled that. 'Lager's a woman's drink,' he commented.

At half-time the scores stood:

Brighton and Hove Albion 1 - Manchester United 0

Dad Brown Ale Albion 4 - Tony Pils Lager United 3

Ten minutes into the second half Frank Stapleton equalized for United and I pulled level with Dad. We didn't leave Jackie out, he was lapping up the brown ale-pils lager mix we'd poured into his bowl.

In the 74th minute of the match (with me and Dad still even) Ray Wilkins curled in a spectacular goal for United that would surely finish Brighton off. I gave the pink cuddly bunny rabbit a kiss and, in quick succession, finished off two more bottles of lager.

Brighton and Hove Albion 1 - Manchester United 2

Dad Brown Ale Albion 5 - Tony Pils Lager United 7

Dad was soon only one drink behind. I was bursting for a piss, but going to the toilet during a match was bad luck for United. I had no choice this time, though my bladder couldn't take any more. I made a dash for the bathroom.

'It's there. They've done it,' came Dad's shout from the front room, causing me to piss on the bathroom carpet. I ran back into the front room just as Dad slammed down his empty pint pot on the coffee table and the Brighton players hugged each other on the pitch.

'We've equalized,' said Dad, with a belch.

The ref blew for the end of normal time.

Brighton and Hove Albion 2 - Manchester United 2

Dad Brown Ale Albion 8 - Tony Pils Lager United 8

The match moved into extra-time. I was out of Holsten Pils, but Dad had two bottles of brown ale left.

'Here, have one of these. It'll put hairs on yuh chest, and we'll call it a draw,' said Dad.

Minutes later Mam came home. Dad, me and Jackie were completely guzzled. She gazed at the clutter of empty bottles filling the coffee table.

'How many you pair had? Look at yuh . . . yuh tanked up.'

'Well oiled, Mam; well oiled . . . and Jackie.'

'Yuh softer than grease, both of yuh.'

It was the end of the first period of extra-time. United and Brighton were still level at two apiece.

'Your tea's ready when you are,' shouted Mam.

Dad and me pin-balled our way into the kitchen; Jackie, who'd become a bit edgy after a few beers, decided to savage the pink bunny rabbit.

Dad had picked up this plate of shepherd's pie from the kitchen table and was on his way back to the front room.

'Brian!' Mam called to Dad, who turned around with a silly grin on his face. 'That plate's been in the oven. It's hot, isn't it?'

Dad looked down at his plate, pondered for a few seconds, and then his silly grin turned to a grimace.

'Aaaarrrgggrhhh.' Dad dropped the plate on the floor and rushed over to stick his fingers under the cold water tap. Mam laughed. I tripped over Jackie, who dropped the lacerated ear of the bunny rabbit from his jaws and tottered over and cocked his leg over a pile of neatly ironed washing.

With a minute left of the match, it looked as though the Cup Final was heading for a replay, then Brighton player Gordon Smith received the ball unmarked in United's penalty area.

'He must score,' shouted Dad.

I closed my eyes, but he didn't score. Gary Bailey saved it, and five days later Dad, me and Jackie stayed sober to watch United beat Brighton 4-0 in the replay to win the Cup.

Scargill's Barmy Army

'Isn't it about time yuh thought what yuh going t'do?' said Dad, referring to me getting some kind of job.

It was a Tuesday dinner time and we were both sat at the kitchen table. Dad, off work sick after a fork-lift truck had run over and broken his foot, was eating his dinner. I, having only just got up, was having my breakfast. Many a weekday I stayed in bed until noon so as to shorten a long day with nowhere to go and nothing to do. In the eighteen months since leaving school I'd been unable to get a job and, now disillusioned, I'd given up. But I wasn't alone in my humdrum existence. This was the eighties: three and a half million unemployed, frustrated youths rioted in the cities.

It was the decade of Thatcherism; the greedy, uncaring selfish society being created by Margaret Thatcher, the so-called 'Iron Lady', who revelled in the sick flag waving patriotism of the Falklands War. Whether the war was just or not – the sinking of the Belgrano was certainly dubious – it wasn't the time for celebrating like a victory for the England football team. Hundreds of men - from both countries - had died; many British men horrifically burned and injured, physically and mentally scarred for life (PTSD - it has been claimed that more veterans have committed suicide since the Falklands War ended than the number of servicemen killed in the conflict).

When Thatcher used the words 'rejoice' it was because the Falklands gamble had - via some perverse WW2 nostalgia sweeping a country desperate for something to show that the land of hope and Empire glory still existed - elevated her status to that of a winning warlord, and guaranteed the floundering Tories an election victory. Then Thatcher would have free reign to go to war with her real foes, 'the enemy within' - the unions, miners, the industrial working-class Labour strongholds. She spat on her iron fist ready to smash the lot of them.

My Grandma Lane, who later would wear a BOLLOCKS TO THE POLL TAX t-shirt and refuse to pay hers, had the best comment for Thatcher. 'It's about time Denis shagged some sense into her,' she said.

Brian (out of the house at the Job Centre) was also now unemployed. He had been an apprentice printer until being laid off.

'I thought of gettin a job at pit,' I replied to Dad's question.

'Yuh dunt want to work at pit, there's no future in it any more. Pye Hill'll not be open fuh much longer, and if Tories get their way, all pits will be closed. Yuh better gettin yuh sen a trade,' said Dad.

A few months later: I'm with a couple of mates in the entrance corridor of Jacksdale Miners Welfare; playing on the arcade games in there, well pretending to, so as not to be thrown out into the street by one of t'committee – on guard in his glass fronted sentry box, just inside the doors. Only those with membership cards get past this point, especially on this day; the most important gathering of miners in pit donkey's years is taking place in the large function room.

Another committee guard has already blocked us from trying to sneak in there. But when serious looking miners come out the doors – to go to the toilet or to pass on updates to their spouses in t'other room (even Bingo can be interrupted for news this night, and that's unheard of) – we can see him. Up there on stage, jabbing his finger with conviction, delivering his sermon to mount his biggest challenge: to save the coal industry from destruction, and bring down Thatcher. We only catch glimpses of him, but he comes across as impressive, defiant, an aura around him, Arthur Scargill is in full-on strike building mode.

'We're all out on strike Monday,' said one miner, emerging from the function room, but there was a wry smile on his face. Others seemed to genuinely support the word of Scargill. But I know these men, I have black dust blood, they put no one on a pedestal. Get too big for your boots and they'll bring you down with a cutting remark or right hook. They're honest and straight talking, no one will bullshit them, no bastard will grind them down, bullies are not tolerated or feared and soon put in their place. Scargill may have won many Notts miners over to his cause that night, and if only he'd have given them the right to have a voice and vote through a national ballot he may have had their backing.

I admired Scargill and what he was trying to do. However, he didn't lay all his union cards on the table to the Notts miners, he kept some up his sleeve or under his comb-over, betrayed their trust, by not trusting in them, acted as a dictator in trying to force them out on strike. The Yorkshire and Scottish miners - given the go ahead by the NUM executive committee – started a national strike without a ballot. Notts miners chose to stay at work, as was their democratic right.

Months later: Me and a mate were walking through the centre of Jacksdale one afternoon. Two policemen with southern accents, walking in the opposite direction, stopped us.

'Have you seen any of those nasty Yorkshiremen hanging about?' one of the policemen asked us.

'No,' we replied.

'Well, if you do, let us know,' said the policeman.

Both men then walked away laughing. Apparently they were so happy because they were getting paid so much overtime, just for walking around a village all day.

One day a group of us doleys were playing a game of football against the police on duty at the entrance to Pye Hill. A couple of the policemen's tit-head helmets came in for good use as goalposts. With the match deadlocked 4-4, the ball was booted in my direction at a perfect height for me to connect with what I hoped would be the winning goal, when a tranny van screeched around the corner scattering us all and running over the helmets. It sped fifty yards towards the pit with the shout of 'Scabs, scabs' coming through the tannoy on top of the vehicle.

The van then span round, drove back towards us at high speed, out of the entrance and headed towards Jacksdale. The policemen hastily put their crushed helmets on their heads, ran to a police van and the chase began.

Weeks later: From the windows and garden of our house (at the edge of Jacksdale) I'm looking towards the mining village of Underwood, up on the hill in the distance. In the direction of the sounds of sirens and – carried on the changing winds – the shouts, chants and songs of a large group of men. It's like a football stadium on a Saturday afternoon, but you can't hear the City Ground from here.

Then they appear on the horizon, on the brow of the hill, flags flying, banners raised. I grabbed Grandad's binoculars. 'They're coming!' I shouted, my voice almost tremulous as they began to march down into the valley, hundreds of them. The general was sending in one of his crack battalions to try and take the rebel fortress of Pye Hill, the new Northern civil war had begun. We could clearly see and hear them as they passed down Barrows Hill Lane, not far from our house.

'Arthur Scargill's Barmy Army – Arthur Scargill's Barmy Army,' they chanted.

We're used to battles in this village, they'll never defeat Jacksdale. In the event a pit pitched battle is avoided: the police are here in force and ready for them, the opposing sides are kept apart, and Scargill's barmy army marches on to the next pit village on the war map.

In my heart - then and even more so now - I found it sad that the miners of Nottinghamshire and Yorkshire weren't united by Scargill. His heart was in the right place – we now know that his warnings of a secret Tory hit-list of over 70 pit closures to be true – but his ego overruled it, a hubris hangover we'd all suffer from.

Scargill would have been wise to win over the hearts and minds of the Notts miners by talking to them through genuine Labour MP's in the area who shared his views, like ours, Frank Haynes, who also warned: 'The government is gunning for you. I appeal to the whole trade union movement, stand together like the miners did in 1972. We can bring Thatcher down if we go about it the right way.'

*

The hangover of the doomed miners' strike was making me feel nauseous just a few years later. When a butterfly flaps its wings: when Thatcher, a Death's Head Moth, sweeps hers, making sweeping changers for economical means to an end; the end of thriving communities, of community spirit, the end of manufacturing and heavy industry, in a country that gave birth to the industrial revolution and built an Empire on the power it generated. The end of jobs for life, the end of union powers; So the Eton rifles could take pot shots at us and we'd have no defence. The cap on working-class wages. A land of milk and honey for the privileged elite and the money dealers and shakers, whilst grub, as nourishing as gruel by modern standards, from budget supermarkets and food-banks is on the table for millions living on the breadline. Don't ask for more.

A fiscal study or economic analysis put together in the ivory towers of Canary Wharf telling of the economic benefits of Thatcherism doesn't show those on benefits struggling to economise. Try putting a soul in an unemployment statistic and follow them home from the dole queue and take a look at the conditions they're living in. What's the human benefit of an administration that created banking power but sees the number of children living in poverty double from 1.7 million in 1979 to 3.3 million in 1990; the children of ship builders in a country of once mighty sea power that no longer builds ships; the children of miners, black gold still beneath their feet, but no longer the wish to extract it - the miners deemed more trouble than its worth, their quality of existence of little worth, the 'enemy within.' Let's import the coal, keep foreign miners in work, put food on their table; we don't have to deal with their wage demands, they're no threat to our party's power.

No wonder the Tories are now in favour of fracking as they've experience of fracturing mining communities and society and in the process unleashing a poison gas of social problems: drugs became the new currency along the underground seams of desperation and hopelessness in the coalfields. Hope you understand I can't go into much detail here, as the young woman in question was the onetime girlfriend of someone I know, the mother of their child. She became a victim of the modern plague that became prevalent in the advent of the destruction of the mining communities, she died of a heroin overdose; in a squalid drug den. A flat just a few streets from D.H. Lawrence's birthplace museum in Eastwood, Nottinghamshire (If D.H. Lawrence was around in modern times he'd have plenty of material to write about, a pit disaster of a different kind).

A girl I took out a few times fell in with a drug crowd. When I tried to intervene I was threatened, from half opened windows of passing cars with tinted windows. It was futile on my part anyway, her mind so drug warped she didn't give a fuck, even setting me up to try and have my flat robbed. One of her female friends, and her boyfriend, once lovely young people, became heroin addicts; robbing a woman of her handbag at knifepoint, desperate for the money to feed their habit, and going to prison. Before getting sent down I saw the girl heading down the street towards my home. She'd been welcome once, but now I had to hastily lock the doors and rush up stairs. She was desperate, banged on the door, shouted through the letterbox. I hid in the wardrobe like one of the living dead was trying to get in, welcome to the villages of the Tory damned.

I'd seen the buckled foundations of all this on that one Thursday, just a few years after the miners' strike and at the savage height of Thatcherism. Returning from signing on the dole in Alfreton, stepping off the bus in Jubilee to do that walk down into Jacksdale through the grounds of Pye Hill pit. You can see for miles up there; the smoke billowing up into the sky from Ratcliffe-on-Soar power station - 20 miles away - on some days. This probably fuelled with

111

imported coal, definitely not Jacksdale's any more: the buildings of Pye Hill pit, down to my left, now derelict; the downward sloping chute between two of them making it look like a sleeping dinosaur. It's fenced in, but there's no chance of it escaping, it's been shot with a deadly tranquilliser dart from the Eton rifles, powerful enough to ensure it never awakens again.

In the same grounds: the broken tubular rubble of the closed pipe works, and that of a brick works next to this. On one corner the abandoned haunted house of a manager of one of the firms; curtains blowing in the wind, graffiti on the walls, scattered remnants of a forgotten life. So many burnt out stolen cars lay strewn about that it resembles a war zone; Stanley Kubrick could have shot *Full Metal Jacket* here.

In the distance the ruins of the massive forge works at Ironville, where once upon a time they forged the steel for St Pancras Station (before it headed on industrial rail to Butterly to be pieced together). All this industry once provided employment for thousands of men in the local area.

At the bottom of the hill the huge windows of the pit canteen (that had the bath house attached), boarded up. It's the once well kept gardens – around the canteen – that breaks my heart more anything, as my Grandad (the one who'd died of cancer a few years previous) used to lovingly tend the garden; mow the lawn, plant flower beds, polish the 'Welcome to Pye Hill Colliery' sign, when he'd retired as a miner. Now I see it full of weeds, overgrown, flowers rotting dead.

Out of the Red and into the Black

Football may have been in a shambolic hooligan-infested state in the eighties, but it was still the game of the people: by the people, for the people and affordable to the people. Clubs accommodated for teenagers and people on low income by having cheap areas of terracing (£2.20 to stand in the Stretford End). This was in the days when Manchester United were first and foremost a football club and not just the brand name of a multi-million-pound merchandising industry. Now champagne corks are just as likely to pop in the boardroom in celebration of a rise in the share price or the announcement of pre-tax profits, as of the winning of a match or a trophy.

United reached the quarter-finals of the European Cup Winners Cup. There they would face the mighty Barcelona, who had Diego Maradona in their side.

Prospects didn't look too good for United after the first leg, Barcelona winning 2-0 in their Nou Camp Stadium. Back in Manchester 58,000 fans packed into Old Trafford and turned up the volume. It was once said the atmosphere in Old Trafford was akin to the sound of a jet taking off, this night it was turned up to Apollo 11: the ground shook, red hot lava flowed from the stands, hotter than Barcelona's Las Ramblas at midday, hotter than Buenos Aires. Maradona couldn't stand the heat, the onslaught of the Red Army, off and on the pitch, led by Robbo the Lionheart, it was his finest hour and a half. Robson totally dominated the midfield and scored two goals; Frank Stapleton got the other. United won 3-2 on aggregate. Thousands of United fans invaded the pitch, carrying Robson shoulder-high off the pitch in triumph.

Usually, if I attended a midweek game, I'd have to leave five minutes before the end of the match to enable me to make it back to Manchester Victoria railway station and the last train back to Nottinghamshire. But the Barcelona game had been such a glorious occasion (the first big United cup-tie I'd seen) that I stayed well after the final whistle to join in the celebrations, leaving me with no chance of making it to the station in time. The next train I could catch wouldn't be until five o'clock in the morning.

So with plenty of time on my hands, I decided to walk it from Old Trafford to the city centre. I'd wandered aimlessly for twenty minutes and was passing through the sprawling concrete crescents of the Hulme district of Manchester. I was naive about the realities of inner-city life; I had no knowledge of the crime-infested ghetto I was in. The same area where, years later, my sister's boyfriend lived and would be twice mugged at knifepoint. I slowly ambled my way through Hulme without a care in the world, reading the *United Review* match programme and reliving in my mind the highlights of the great game I'd seen. The speeding car that narrowly missed me when I'd stepped out in front of it startled me out of my blissful state, and a few seconds later I had to jump back on the pavement to avoid the police vehicle in hot pursuit. Then I replayed the moment when Frank Stapleton struck the winning goal, and went happily on my way. And when the girl on the corner wearing an incredibly short mini-skirt said to me, 'Yer lookin to score?' I just assumed she'd spotted my United shirt and mistakenly thought she'd asked, 'What was the score?'

'Three nil to United; Robbo got two.' I replied, cheerfully, as I passed her by.

114

I arrived safely at Victoria Station and crashed down on a bench for the night. I finally stepped off the service bus at about 7.00 am at the bottom of Palmerston Street in my village. The weather was grey and wet. Across the road, waiting to catch a bus to work, was Dad, hunched shoulders, coat zipped up against the rain. Gracious as ever in not standing inside the bus shelter to give space to the women in the queue. The thoughts of work etched on his face, until he saw me and his face lit up like the Old Trafford floodlights. 'Well done son, brilliant,' he shouted, like it was me that had won the match for United. Guess he was right in a way, the United fans certainly played their part, as good as a twelfth man, as it should be but is not now always the case.

United, without Robson, were knocked out by Juventus in the semi-final.

*

I contemplated going to college, but couldn't decide what occupation I wanted to enter into. I looked the part of a student. I'd by now drifted from punk into more of your *NME* reading, indie goth; into groups like Bauhaus, The Cure, Cocteau Twins, The Cult, Siouxsie and the Banshees, The Sisters of Mercy, The Jesus and Mary Chain and Echo and the Bunnymen.

I'd dyed my hair black, wore a black upside-down cross earring, either a black denim or leather jacket, black t-shirts, black sweaters, black jeans and black footwear (if only United's black away shirt had been around at the time). I was going to paint my bedroom black to create the right ambience when listening to my records. Only I was having to share my bedroom with Brian whilst Elaine (back from polytechnic) was living at home for a few months.

So I could only paint my half of the bedroom black, and, to achieve the desired goth effect, I had to lie on my bed turned on my right side with my left eye closed to block out the Led Zeppelin, Sam Fox and Rocky posters covering the magnolia-coloured walls of Brian's half.

I had mild rock-star ambitions and bought a cheap second-hand acoustic guitar, but all I ever managed to learn how to play was the intro to 'Warhead' by the UK Subs. My old punk mate Feff was now drummer with Sheffield indie group Ipso Facto, who were fronted by a charismatic singer who, on stage, bare chested and clad in black leather trousers, looked like Jim Morrison. The group had a big following in the city and had favourable record and gig reviews in the music press. With the prospect of the group becoming big, and maybe overseas tours to come, I decided to try to latch myself on to them with thoughts of getting myself a job as a roadie. When Feff invited me to watch Ipso Facto rehearse in a big old warehouse in Sheffield (Pulp rehearsed in the next room and Cabaret Voltaire in the same building) I saw this as my opportunity to get my foot in the door and meet the rest of the group.

The session deteriorated into a slanging match, however. Full cans of beer began to fly across the room. Fearing a head injury, I left and didn't go again. The group split several months later.

Not having much cash – and living 13 miles from the nearest city (Nottingham and Derby were about that equal distance away) – I was lucky in regards to my social life: the old and notorious Jacksdale punk club, the Grey Topper, had closed after a mysterious fire just before I left school.

But just as I was about to turn 18 another club opened in the refurbished building - Woody's 2 Mega Video Dance Bar no less. It was, again, pretty cool for a mining village, even ahead of its time with a line of TV screens showing music videos; if you could see them through the gloom. They pumped out so much dry ice smoke into the place that it was like someone had left the doors open and a 1970's peasouper had crept in. There were certainly ghosts from that decade swirling around the club: Simple Minds, Adam and the Ants, The Stranglers, Ultravox and The Pretenders; now multi-million records selling super groups, now re-appearing in Jacksdale via expensive videos on *MTV*. Just a few years previous they'd been little-known bands dodging pint pots and punk spit on this very spot, now a dance floor.

Me and my very small band - a mere handful of alternative types - weren't getting a much better reception when we were the only ones on there; trying to be all mysterious whilst doing our Goth and minimal shoegazing moves to the likes of Siouxsie and the Banshees and The Cure. Not exactly love cats out there, plenty of catcalls and the odd Holsten Pils bottle thrown our way (Robert Smith could have been a boy that cried and acquired his black-eyed scary panda look, years before he settled on that image, if he'd have faced the Topper punks. And he very nearly did, if you take a look at the *Boys Don't Cry* tour poster you'll see the Grey Topper on there as one of gig dates. They didn't show in the end, guess the club and village's reputation had reached their ears?)

Sometimes, though, if I'd come straight back from Manchester and a match, I'd be wearing a United shirt...and still receive the same kind of hostility (usually from outsiders as I was fine with most Jacksdaliens). One night a local Leeds fan (from Selston) was in there and threatened to rip it off my back and set fire to it. I managed to escape from him in the fog and in doing so bumped into a girl called Karen, knocking a drink out of her hand. I apologised and said I'd get her a new one in. Not only was she happy about this but also informed me it was her birthday and insisted on a snog as a present. I could grant that, I started to move forward, my lips puckered and ready...the machine at our side gave a blast of dry ice smoke akin to an air display vapour trail bursting out of a Red Arrow. When it began to momentarily disperse I found myself face to face with the glare eyes and sneer of the Leeds supporter.

For the rest of the night I was trying to avoid him and find Karen again. I'd achieved the former but had all but given up on the latter when it came time to leave Woody's for the night. There she was, looking lost and lonely stood at the bus stop across the road. I sauntered over and sweet talked her into the bus shelter (another girl, another bus shelter).

'Oi, this corner's taken,' came the shout from a lad called Webby, a randy bastard, sock up to the nuts with a girl he'd picked up in the club.

The bus to Selston came round the corner. 'You can come back to mine,' suggested Karen. 'My brother will out clubbing and mam and dad will be staying at the Welly [Miner's Welfare Club] for a lock in for a few hours yet.'

Karen was right, her house was in darkness as we walked through the front gate, at last I was to graduate from bus shelters to a house with a girl. She turned the key in the lock; we couldn't wait to get our lips and hands on each other, stumbled from the porch into the living room. When there was a sudden blinding light and a cacophony of noise and a burst of 'Happy Birthday.' All her friends and family had arranged to get back before Karen to finish off the night with a surprise party.

I was United red faced with embarrassment, but her parents and friends cheered and laughed at seeing us together. All except one, her brother, red faced with anger, my Leeds United foe from Woody's club.

He couldn't have a go at me there and then, biding his time to collar me in the kitchen.

'A Jacksdalien, United scum and fuckin' touch me sister and I'll fuckin' kill yuh, who the fuck d'yuh think yuh are?'

That's when the penny dropped, he was the same lad from a few years previous who'd caught me with his girlfriend in Selston.

'A Jacksdalien, a United fan and going to impregnate your sister with a Red Devil,' I replied, swaying about drunkenly, wagging my pointed finger in front of his face.

His penny dreadful dropped too, he kneed me in the bollocks, causing me to vomit on his Leeds shirt. Party goers flooded into the kitchen on hearing the commotion and the (obligatory) table cloth covered, food filled, decorating table, go over as we grappled.

I was shown the door and told not to darken it again. But I did pass through it again, in the dark, for secret rendezvous' with Karen when the coast was clear – i.e. I'd seen her brother come into Woody's and her parents were at the 'Welly.' Not for long, however, it had been just a brief fling of teenage sexual discovery, on my part anyway. Karen wanted romance, but the only 'Flowers of Romance' from me was PiL's and 'This is Not a Love Song.' She wasn't impressed with either.

There were plenty more girls faces that emerged out of the fog of Woody's dance floor: casual carousels of teenage kicks, amid swirling lights, whirling rhythms, twists and shouts, stars orbiting after a right hook to the chin, experienced via a spinning drunken head, a giddy blur, barely able to be recalled the following day, never mind through the dry ice fog of time...

....Writing this has actually regurgitated a memory to mind: after a night on Holsten Pils and rum and black chasers in Woody's, going to a house party on one of the terraced streets in Jacksdale. A woman, she was 24, a real woman to a teenage me then, with long flowing mousy coloured hair, a sultry stare from heavily mascaraed eyes, grabbing me by the hands and spinning me round the living room. Me having to hastily push myself away from her, to run to the kitchen, head in the sink vomiting purple and black sick, all over my black fingerless gloves. Dead or Alive's 'You Spin Me Round (like a record),' on in the background. Feeling fuckin' more dead, crawling up stairs looking for a bedroom to crash in. Finding the woman had moved on, into a bed with a real man. Crawling home, throwing up more black and purple sick at the side of my bed (on the cream coloured carpet, an ear-bashing from Mam on the way) stepping into it with bare feet in the morning, head pounding, head spinning, right round baby, like a fuckin' broken record.

None of the Madonna, Bananarama or Boy George clad girls on the dance-floor of Woody's 2 Mega Video Dance Bar made my heart dance, though. They weren't 'cool' enough or pale enough in comparison to the alabaster faced, black eyeliner eyed, black clad, rock chic, and indie enigmatic beauties in Rock City, Nottingham. How I desired to find a girlfriend there.

One night me and a few mates were going to see the all-girl indie band We've Got a Fuzzbox and We're Going To Use It at Rock City (the Nightingales and dead pan comedian Ted Chippington were on the same bill). There were bound to be loads of sexy indie and punkette girls in for this one we agreed. Fuzzbox's recently released debut EP was so sexy, so rebellious – 'Do I Want To?,' 'Rules and Regulations,' 'XX-Sex.' The only pictures of the band I'd seen were small ones on the back of the record sleeve. I couldn't wait to see and hear what they looked and sounded like live on stage.

Before the gig we called in at my Aladdin's cave: Selectadisc Records. Flicking through some vinyl was a beautiful indie girl with long hair streaked with pink and blue. I sort of casually positioned myself at the side of her and picked up the Fuzzbox EP as way of a conversation starter.

'You heard the Fuzzbox? They're cool as, they're playing Rock City tonight, you going?'

She smiled politely but there was a look in her eye that said: 'Yes I'm going but not with you.' It wasn't until Fuzzbox took to the stage that I immediately noticed the flowing hair with pink and blue stripes and I realised that I'd been trying to chat up the lead singer.

Although I'd take a girlfriend to Rock City, I didn't actually get off with a woman in there until in my 30's! Guess I was the one who wasn't 'cool' enough?

Rock City meant as much to me in regards to music as the Stretford End did to football; the same kind of energised buzz. The great dark rock cavern, with its sticky floor and an aroma of sweat mixed with cannabis and spilt beer. I've seen so many great gigs there and one of the best was around this time. When I heard The Jesus and Mary Chain's debut single 'Upside Down' on John Peel, followed up with a session that included 'You Trip Me Up,' 'Taste the Floor,' and the great 'Never Understand' (I still have this session on one of my John Peel C90 tapes) I knew, immediately, this was the band for my generation's alienation, the one I'd been waiting for.

A few days after hearing 'Upside Down' I called in at Piccadilly Records in Manchester city centre to buy it, after (I only made the mistake of buying a vinyl record and then standing on the Stretford End once) United's game against Ipswich in December 84. Then I snapped up a ticket for their first gig at Rock City in early 85. This gig was several months before their 80's indie era defining album *Psychocandy* was released, so there was only a few hundred - at most - in Rock City. They played for just 25 minutes. William Reid with his back to the audience for most of the gig. Primal Scream's (they supported them, if not at this gig, then the next one - with Pink Industry too) Bobby Gillespie banging away on a bass drum, and Jim Reid slumped apathetically over the mike. Yet stunning us with a brilliant set of songs drenched in feedback, no encore, no goodbyes, gone, perfection!

As with some United classic matches, as with several women, there are a few gigs missed at Rock City that I'll forever regret. In the autumn of 91 I saw Nirvana were to play Rock City and asked my mates if they were up for going. For one reason or another we all couldn't make it, 'We'll catch them next time,' I remember saying. This was a few weeks before the release of 'Smell's Like Teen Spirit,'

and after that blew up the music scene and fired Kurt
Cobain to planet rock star – where he never really wanted to
be and couldn't handle it – we'd never get the chance to see
them live again.

Of all the wise words and phrases - from older people
to me - that fell on deaf ears as a yowf, only two sayings
now have any substance with hindsight: 'If I knew then
what I know now' and 'seize the day' (yes I know you're
suppose to say the last one in Latin, but I went to bloody
comprehensive in the Notts coalfields in the 70's! 'Carpe
Diem' would be misinterpreted as 'Did you hook many
carp?')

Come Saturdays the black gear was off, the red shirt of
United was on, and I'd be off on the train to Manchester.

Rain and Tourists

I've been waiting for her for so long
Open the sky and let her come down
Here comes the rain, here comes the rain
I love the rain
Here she comes again
      'Rain' The Cult

Rain poured down from grey Manchester skies as I queued
outside the Stretford End before United's game against
Everton. There were still forty minutes to go before the
turnstiles would open, and I was already drenched. I
munched on a dodgy burger, from a nearby refreshment
van, rainwater from my soaked hair ran down the back of
my neck.

Two coaches turned into the road that led up to the
Stretford End. Fifty yards away they pulled up at the side of
the road. The coach doors opened and out piled hordes of

Japanese tourists, smiles on their faces, cameras hanging from around their necks.

With great excitement they walked up to the Stretford End, to the drenched queue. The tourists geared their cameras into action and started taking photographs of everything in sight: floodlight pylons, burger vans, police on horseback, the grey Manchester skies. They pointed to the lines of Stretford Enders, then turned to each other and chattered away in Japanese. Then, with smiles on their faces, they focused their cameras on us and started snapping away.

I turned around to look up at the stand, expecting to see a sign written in Japanese, that I thought would read 'Please Do Not Feed the Supporters'. I had an image entering my head: thousands of miles away, on the other side of the world, in a suburb of Tokyo, this Japanese couple were hosting a holiday-snaps party for friends and neighbours, showing each other photographs of exotic places of the world they've visited. And there, on a photograph, would be me, soaked to the skin, queuing with the Stretford Enders in the Manchester rain.

The turnstiles finally opened. I paid my money and took my place on the terrace, under the shelter of the stand. During the game I noticed three Japanese tourists standing nearby, who were more preoccupied with the reactions of the crowd than events on the pitch.

'The referee's a wanker!' chanted the Stretford End, none too pleased with one of the match official's decisions. The Japanese tourists all looked at each other, chatted away in Japanese, started laughing and nodding their heads, then turned to face the pitch and chanted, 'Ref-er-ree-a- ranker! Ref-er-ree-a-ranker!'

A Manc youth hoisted himself above the crowd, with the aid of a crush barrier, and shaking his clenched fist bellowed:

'Southall, yer fat fuckin shite,' to the Everton keeper.

The Japanese tourists stood in a line and punched their fists in the air, shouting, 'Southa, fat fuk sha.'

Ten minutes later a flowing United attack won us a corner, causing the crowd to surge forward. The tourists were unprepared for this red-and-white human tidal wave and were sent crashing down the terrace steps. In a bewildered state they were helped to their feet by several amused Stretford Enders.

The Japanese dusted themselves down, inspected the damage to their Nikons and hastily headed out of the stadium, shaking their heads and saying, 'You crazy people.'

Ron Atkinson had assembled a fine United team, and they were beginning to play some great football. Midfield dynamo Gordon Strachan had arrived from Aberdeen; Danish international Jesper Olsen dazzled on the wing, and a young Mark Hughes came into the side.

There was Robson, Whiteside, and McGrath, a great trio on the pitch and on the piss, and although United were slipping behind in the Championship race, they had again reached the semi-final of the F A Cup, where they would face Liverpool.

In the first match Liverpool twice came from behind to grab a 2-2 draw. In the replay at Maine Road, Paul McGrath headed into his own net to give Liverpool a 1-0 lead. It took Captain Marvel to pull United back, scoring what must be one of United's greatest goals. Collecting the ball just inside his own half, Robbo played a one-two with Frank Stapleton before surging forward to fire home a thirty-yard shot into the top corner.

Mark Hughes scored the winner and United were back at Wembley.

Cup Final '85: Elvis and Norman Whiteside

I could have been there, should have been there. I'd not missed many games during the '84-85 season. It's never guaranteed at United, but the number of tokens I would have had must surely have given me a good chance of qualifying for a Cup Final ticket. By April, though, I didn't have all the tokens from all the games that I'd attended because a few months earlier Mam, doing a bit of spring cleaning, had chucked a dozen of my United Review match programmes (tokens enclosed) away. And I'm not going to go into the argument that ensued, which nearly resulted in me leaving home.

The night before the Final. My mood of despondency wasn't eased any by the conversation I was having with the landlady of a local pub.

'Oh, I could have got you a Cup Final ticket,' she told me.

'You could! How! How?'

'I've a lifelong friend from Nottingham, who's a referee. He always gets hold of a number of tickets. He'd have let me have one for definite.'

'That's just typical.'

'If only you'd have let me know sooner,' she said.

That was it. I decided to go out and get fucking wasted.

Six o'clock on the Saturday morning, and the milkman, who found me asleep on our front lawn, woke me to see if I was OK.

Cup Final afternoon, seriously hungover, not on speaking terms with Mam, no ticket. I settled into an armchair in our front room, lucky 1977 Cup Winners' scarf tied around my neck.

Dad and our new dog Benny Hill (Jackie had died) sat on the settee, Elvis the budgie watched from the bars of his cage.

Mam, as usual on Cup Final day (and definitely for this one), had gone out shopping.

Elvis used to be called Joey and have suicidal tendencies, throwing himself off his top perch, landing with a thud on the base of his cage. One day we had the radio on in the front room. Joey was motionless on his perch, and Elvis Presley came on the radio singing 'Jailhouse Rock'. Joey suddenly burst into life and started running up and down his perch, bopping his head, chirping along to the radio. 'Jailhouse Rock' finished playing and Joey became motionless again. We wondered about the possibility of Joey being Elvis Presley reincarnated. From then on we called him Elvis, and would sing him or play Elvis records to cheer him up.

Refreshments were sorted; Dad with his bottles of brown ale, a pork pie and cheese and pickle sandwiches. Me with a pint of water and a bottle of paracetamol tablets. Benny Hill with a bowl of water and three Boneos, and Elvis with a pot full of Trill.

Everton were United's opponents in the Final. They were Champions, and a few days earlier had won the European Cup Winners' Cup. Ten minutes before half-time, with the match deadlocked at 0-0, the telephone rang. Dad looked across at me. 'That'll not be for me. I bet it's one of your mates.'

I reluctantly went and answered the phone, which was at the bottom of the stairs, from where you couldn't see the television screen.

'Hello.'

'Hello, Tony. It's Rebecca,' the female voice replied. Rebecca? Who the fuck was...then it all came back to me: the girl in the nightclub, the pretty art student I'd had the courage to chat up after six pints of lager and three Jack Daniel's.

'Hello, Rebecca. You all right?'

'Yeah.'

'Get it in there, my son!' Dad shouted.

I left the phone and looked around the door. It was only a goalkick.

'Tony, Tony - you still there?'

'Er, yeah. Sorry, Rebecca.'

'Who was that shouting? One of your mates?'

'No. That's my dad. He's watching the Cup Final.'

'Well, are we still on for Echo and the Bunnymen?'

Echo and the Bunnymen? . . . Oh shit, I'd told her that I'd got two tickets for an Echo and the Bunnymen concert and that there was a chance we could get backstage passes because I knew one of the roadies.

'Er, yeah, I'll take you to see Echo and the Bunnymen.'

'Load a crap!' Dad shouted at the telly.

'You don't sound so sure,' said Rebecca.

'Sorry, Rebecca. I've got a bit of hangover, that's all.'

'What you doing tonight?' she asked.

'Go on, Hughesy. Go on,' Dad roared, causing me to drop the phone and dash into the front room. Another false alarm. I went back to the phone and discovered that either Rebecca had hung up or I'd cut her off. Shit! I didn't have her number and couldn't remember where she said she lived. She's got to ring back, I was thinking. (Not straight away, but at half-time.)

The ref blew his whistle to start the second half. Rebecca hadn't rung.

Everton break dangerously into United's half. Kevin Moran brings down Peter Reid, the referee wanting to make a name for himself (I won't name him) decides to send off Moran, making him the first player to be sent off in an FA Cup Final.

Maybe the ref did United a favour. With ten men United looked the stronger side, determined not to be beaten by the ref's injustice.

There's a knock at the front door. Dad looks across at me.

'That'll not be for me. I bet it's one of your mates.'

I reluctantly go and see who's at the door. I open it and there stand two men - one black, one white, both with cropped hair, white shirts, black trousers and black shoes. The white guy takes one step forward preventing me from immediately closing the door and sticks out his hand for me to shake.

'Heyyy. Believe in Gahd, son,' he says.

They're American Mormons. Fuck, I don't need this. Fucking religious fanatics to get rid of, and I start flicking my upside-down cross earring to try to bring their attention to it.

'No, I don't believe in Mister Beardman,' I reply.

'Do you know who your saviour is, son,' says the black guy.

'Yeah, I've just been watching him on the telly. He's a Red Devil called Robbo.'

129

'Jesus, yuh useless,' shouted Dad at some inept piece of football on the television.

Then they notice the upside-down cross earring and I start quoting lines from Public Image Limited's song 'Religion', about 'Praying to the holy ghost when you suck your host'. The Mormons both took a step back as if they'd beheld Beelzebub himself.

'May Gahd save your soul, son,' said the white guy, and then they were gone.

Ninety minutes up and still no score; the Cup Final moved into extra-time. There was another knock at the front door. I looked across to Dad.

'That'll not be for me. You answer it this time,' I said.

Dad reluctantly went to the door. 'Oh, aye up, come in,' I heard Dad say.

What's he doing? I thought. It's a rule that we never invite anyone in when were watching the Cup Final. Dad walked back into the front room followed by a tanned Andrea and Alan and their two-and-a-half-year-old cherub of a son Adam, who signalled his arrival by tipping over Benny Hill's dog basket, kicking the contents (squeaky toys, an old slipper, half-chewed chewie sticks and one of my old football socks) around the room and squeaking as many squeakies as he could get into his hands in one go.

Alan, in his early thirties, was one of Dad's workmates. He, Andrea, and Adam had recently returned from a holiday in Lloret de Mar. Alan wore sandals, white socks, cream-coloured knee-length shorts and a 'Champions' sport vest, stretched tight over his beer gut. Andrea wore sandals, cream-coloured knee-length shorts and a short-sleeved floral shirt. Both wore his 'n' hers Reacta light Rapide sunglasses. They'd brought a pile of holiday snaps for Dad to look at.

'Wups! Owd that gerrin there?' said Alan, holding up a photograph in front of Dad's reddening face. 'There's no white bits on Andrea, eh, Brian,' he said.

'Ooh, Alan. What's he like, Brian?' said Andrea, and then she and Alan gave a synchronized manic laugh.

'Yuh norra Manchester United fan, are yuh?' Alan said to me, noticing my scarf.

'Yeah, I-'

'I bet y'don't know where Manchester is,' he interrupted.

'Yeah I do. I go to-'

'Yuh should support a local team.'

Don't get drawn, Tony, just leave it. Adam had climbed up on the arm of the settee and started jabbing his fingers into Elvis's cage, who chirped out a warning (something like, 'Don't step on my blue suede claws, kid.')

Adam didn't heed Elvis's warning and received a nasty peck on his finger. There were tears. Andrea cuddled him. 'What's the nasty bird done to baby?' she said, and then pulled out a squeaky toy hammer from her handbag for Adam to play with. He jumped down from his mam's lap and ran over and climbed up on the arm of my chair. Each hangover intensifying squeaky blow to my head was met by howls of laughter from Andrea and Alan. I gave a fake smile, and lifted Adam down on to the carpet.

Meanwhile, with the Cup Final looking like it was going to a replay, Mark Hughes collected the ball in midfield, turned and picked out Norman Whiteside on the right wing. The cowboy in the white hat gunned down the cowboy in the black hat. We were now watching the

Western on BBC 2. Adam had changed channels. I jumped out of my chair and ran over and flicked back over to BBC 1. Whiteside had advanced to the edge of Everton's penalty area. Adam's stretched-out finger was inches away from the BBC 2 button. The cushion caught him at the side of the head, knocking him sideways down on to the carpet. Whiteside curled the ball round Everton keeper Neville Southall and into the bottom corner of the net.

'Pick that fucker out, you scouse bastards!!!' I roared, jumping from my chair. Benny Hill barked. Elvis bopped his head and chirped.

'Well, I never did. Come on, Alan. Come on, Adam; we're leaving,' said a gob-smacked Andrea. Dad looked at them, gave a half smile, and shrugged his shoulders. Minutes later the ref blew the final whistle. Whiteside had done it again; his goal was enough to win the Cup for United.

A few months after the Cup Final I discovered I could have gotten into Wembley without a ticket to see United's triumph over Everton. A couple of United supporters I was talking to told me they had travelled down to Wembley on the day of the Final without tickets. Apparently they, with many other United supporters, had slipped a five-pound note to turnstile operators, who then let them into the stadium.

Everything seemed to be coming up roses in Ron Atkinson's garden. United started the following season with ten consecutive wins, and at one stage were ten points clear at the top of the League. In the Stretford End we dared to talk about United winning the Championship for the first time since 1967.

It was not to be. Injuries piled up, most importantly to Bryan Robson. At that time United always appeared to adopt an inferiority complex when Robson was out - it was as if the other players felt they couldn't win without him. Mark Hughes was being lined up for a transfer to Barcelona, and because of all the newspaper speculation about the transfer, his form suffered.

United finished the season in fourth place, the following season after a poor series of performances, Ron Atkinson was sacked.

United had played some swashbuckling football under Atkinson and won two FA Cups, but the Championship remained elusive.

Pre-Hillsborough 3

Not at a United match one Saturday, I travelled down to Nottingham with a couple of friends for a dinner-time drinking session. Forest were playing Champions Everton that day, the game wasn't all ticket, and my mate Jeff (a Forest fan) suggested we go the match.

Having spent two hours visiting about half a dozen pubs in the city centre, we were bevvied by the time we started to stagger our way to the City Ground, and didn't arrive until 3.35 p.m., by which time the turnstile doors were locked.

At the back of the West Bridgford End at the City Ground there was a big iron-barred gate. In our drunken state we decided we could scale this to gain entry into the stadium.

The lowest foothold on the gate was about five foot high, so me and my other friend Paul cradled our hands together for Jeff to step into them and be given a lift up.

With Jeff safely over the gate and Paul clambering off my shoulders to reach the foothold, I came to my senses. Who was going to give me a lift up? 'Oi. What about me,' I shouted.

Laughter roared out from above (the West Bridgford end at Forest was, at the time, open terracing - from the back of a the terracing you could look down on to the street below). I looked up to see hundreds of laughing faces looking down at me.

At that moment a steward appeared from under the terracing and observed what we were up to.

'What the fuck d'ya think you're doing?' he shouted.

Jeff ran off into the crowd. Paul jumped back down and stood beside me.

'We just want to see the game. Our car broke down; that's why we were late,' I explained to the steward.

'OK, OK. It'll cost you a fiver each,' he replied.

Me and Paul both gave the steward a liver. He then produced a set of keys, unlocked the gate and let us into the stadium.

Bag of Wind

When I was a kid I discovered that Paul Cope (Copey), a boy the same age as me who lived a few hundred yards up the street from us, had the same ailment as myself: acute Football Mania. We've been friends ever since. He was the one who grassed me up to the rest of the school when I told him in confidence that I thought Gordon Hill was my cousin. It was with Copey and his dad that I began to attend football games regularly, watching Mansfield Town in the mid-1970s. Unfortunately his first team is Forest, and not

Man United, otherwise we would have had a season ticket together for years.

In the 1980s, when neither of us had any non-football commitments, we often went to matches together. Sometimes he'd come with me to Old Trafford and at other times I'd go to the City Ground with him. We were both addicted to the buzz generated by vociferous partisan crowds. That was what made attending a big football game so special: the passionate atmosphere; the spontaneous way the Stretford End or United Road Paddock, would break into songs and chants, as one collective body, reacting to a bad refereeing decision or the taunts from away supporters.

Copey, me and another school friend Chico followed Mansfield Town (the Stags) all over the country. One Tuesday we joined up with half a dozen youths from the nearby town of Kirkby-in-Ashfield to go and watch Mansfield away at Preston North End. A van had been hired to transport us there.

The weather forecast was for hurricane-force winds. We were halfway across Derbyshire when it was announced on the radio that the match had been postponed due to structural damage at Preston's Deepdale Stadium, caused by the increasingly strong winds. Chico parked the van at the side of the road. 'What are we going to do now? We've got the van for twenty-four hours, if we want,' he said.

'What other matches are being played today?' someone said.

'Glasgow Rangers are playing at home. Fancy a trip to Scotland?' I said, looking at the day's fixtures in the newspaper.

'No way. It's too far; the game would be over by the time we got there,' said Copey.

'Well, there's Everton against Middlesbrough in the FA Cup fourth round, second replay,' I suggested.

'Yeah, why not? We're already heading that way,' said Chico.

We took a vote on it. Everyone was in agreement. Off to Liverpool.

The wind became stronger, buffeting the side of the van. Up on a bridge over the motorway an articulated lorry had been blown over. Further on, another lorry lay on its side. In Liverpool, after stopping to ask directions, we spotted the floodlights of Goodison Park. We parked the van in a car park about half a mile from the ground. As we piled out of the van, a little scouse kid came running up to us.

'A pound off each of yus, to look after the van.'

'Piss off yer cheeky little bastard,' someone replied.

'Yer all gimme a pound, and yer van will still have wheels when yer get back,' said the kid.

We got the message. We reluctantly gave him a pound each.

The wind was now so strong that the trees in Stanley Park, towering above us, looked like they could come crashing down at any moment. I dodged a flat cap flying through the air. Walking against the wind was near impossible. Outside the stadium we all gathered in a group.

'Well, are we going to put on our North East accents and stand with the Middlesbrough supporters, or put on our scouse accents and stand with Everton supporters?' one of us asked.

A policeman on a horse rode up.

'What's you fucking lot hanging around for? Get in the stadium,' he shouted.

We headed for the nearest turnstile and entered the stadium, standing with Everton supporters behind one net. Litter swirled around the pitch, and every time there was a dead ball situation the ball would roll away, pushed by the wind. Graeme Sharp scored for Everton. I pretended to be happy and clapped my hands. The Everton supporter at the side of me insisted on giving me a hug. I think the match finished 2-0 to Everton.

Back in the car park after the game, we saw a van with all its windows smashed. Had someone not paid the scouse kid protection money, we wondered. Our van was intact. Snow joined gale-force winds as we drove back over the Derbyshire hills. The van swerved from one side of the road to the other; in the back we fell over each other, banging our heads on the side of the van. Through a hole in a stone wall, down a steep bank, a bread van lay on its side. There was no driver.

The winds finally eased and the snow stopped falling as we made it off the Derbyshire hills into Nottinghamshire, and home.

'What lengths you nutters will go to just see a game of football. You travelled through that wind to see twenty two men kicking a bag of wind about,' said Kath, the landlady of the Corner Pin Pub, the following day.

There's some games, football fanatic or not, that you just wish you hadn't bothered with.

Me, Copey and Chico, decided to go and watch Mansfield Town playing away at Wigan one Saturday. Not the most glamorous of fixtures, but it was a game of football. We got lost in the fog driving there. Arriving at Wigan with only fifteen minutes to go to kick-off, we spotted the floodlights and headed in their direction. You've guessed it. They were the floodlights of Wigan Rugby League Club. We made it to the football ground at 3.10 p.m., only to discover the gates locked. One elderly steward came strolling up.

'A bit late, aren't we?' said the steward.

'We got lost in the fog and then ended up at the rugby ground,' I explained.

The steward laughed, shaking his head from side to side. 'I've heard that so many times,' he said.

I knew what to do next. Out came the trusty fiver. In fact, we each placed a five-pound note in the palm of the steward's hand. He pulled out a set of keys, unlocked the gate, and let us in. 'Oh, and by the way,' said the steward, as we walked towards the stand. 'You're losing 1-0.'

Ninety minutes gone and not another shot on goal, the ref blew the whistle for full time - 1-0 to Wigan. We got lost again in the dense fog driving home, going thirty miles in the wrong direction.

A few months later, though, I was at Wembley for Mansfield Town's greatest ever day of glory, part of an astonishing attendance of around 70,000, to see them come back to win a thrilling penalty shoot out against Bristol City (who had ex Man United striker Joe 'Jaws' Jordan in their team), to lift the Freight Rover Trophy, no less. They even won a team bus as a prize. I say team bus, it was actually a mini bus, the other half of the squad would half to make their own way to matches. At least they painted it in The Stags colours and put the club badge on there. Better than bloody Northern soulless Wigan, anyroad. If you'd have told me that one day they'd be playing in a plush new stadium, in the Premier League, beating a multi-million pound, champions, Man City, in the final in the FA Cup

Final, I'd have said your were a barm cake, off your head, delusional.

You'll Never Get A Job, Sign On, Sign On

January 1987. The first week after Christmas. I was standing in a queue in the dole office, waiting to sign on. This was the 1980s, when dole offices were grim-looking places, unlike today, after thousands of pounds have been spent on refurbishment, turning them into Employment Services, combining the dole office and jobcentre and having special coloured zones where you sign on: the yellow zone, the green zone, the blue zone . . . the fucking Twilight Zone more like.

Anyway, I was standing in this queue waiting to sign on, wondering if I was going to be grilled and patronized by an employee of the DHSS trying to force me to join some government scheme or Job Club or fucking Mickey Mouse club; anything to get the unemployment figures down with a general election coming up.

There was a youth standing further down the queue with a ghetto blaster. He was (we all were) listening to The Smiths singing, 'I was looking for a job and now I've found a job, and heaven knows I'm miserable NOW.'

An unemployed man sat down at the desk in front of me. He looked in his sixties, must have been near retirement age, and was getting an ear bashing from the dole office's chief interrogator. A middle-aged battleaxe called Ms Cotteril, who gave you the impression that she'd once been a school mistress in the way she talked to every unemployed person as if she was scolding a naughty child. It was impossible to reason with her. And her deadpan, hound dog, Walter Matthau in drag resemblance did nothing to enliven her demeanour.

'I'm NOT happy with your efforts to find work, Mister Henderson. I think we'll have to place you on a Restart Course or Job Club or a Community Programme. What do you say, Mister Henderson?'

The man made no reaction and stayed silent. 'Oh! no comment. Then, I think we'll have to think about suspending your benefit, Mister Henderson.'

'I'm deaf, tha knows. I've not heard a bloody word you've said for the last ten minutes,' replied Mr Henderson, scratching his head. He was then allowed to sign for his unemployment benefit.

It was my turn to sign on. I sat down to face Ms Cotteril.

'Have you done any work in the last two weeks, Mister Hill?'

'Yeah. I got some work with this fat bloke with a white beard, dressed in a red suit delivering parcels.'

'And was that just temporary work or could it lead to a full-time job?'

'It's seasonal work. I just helped him for one night.'

'And what did he pay you?'

'Nothing. We got the odd mince pie and glass of port, and he allowed me to ride his sleigh, which was nice.'

When the penny finally dropped, Ms Cotteril narrowed her eyes and stared directly into my face for about fifteen seconds. She then opened a draw in the desk and began flicking through some cards.

'Ah! Here we are, Mister Hill. Here's a job that I think you're suited for. It's a factory job mixing chemicals. One pound an hour.'

I somehow managed to get myself out of that one. I was doing a bit of work here and there, but I didn't declare it. I only earned a little extra to help me get by. A lot of unemployed people work on the side and they're not all the greedy cheating spongers the Tories labelled them as. For many of them, working on the side is a necessity, there was no minimum wage at the time and the money being offered for the majority of jobs advertised in a jobcentre was – and is – scandalous. Only a few years ago, the Tories stuck up huge posters in the streets and put advertisements in the newspapers, offering cash incentives for people to 'grass on a dole cheat'. How a load of sleazy, hypocritical, cash-for-questions-receiving, expenses exploiting bigots can call anyone else a cheat is beyond me.

I've heard of many a dodgy scam to make money. The most original and bizarre ideas came from Mad Malc, and were surely influenced by certain illegal substances. He was in his early thirties, stood a gangling 6ft 2in high, and wore his long matted hair tied back in a ponytail. He often wore a Pink Floyd 'The Wall' t-shirt, and had Led Zeppelin and Black Sabbath tattooed on his arms. Malc was constantly on whizz and when you spoke to him his dilated pupils would keep darting in all directions. He lived in a council semi on the main road through the village. I was walking by his house one day and saw him sat on his front lawn, painting a sign.

'What yuh doin, Malc?' I enquired.

'Fuckin' sussed it, man. I'm gunna mek a fuckin' mint, right.'

He lifted the sign to show me. In bright green letters it read:

MAD MALC'S
BACK GARDEN ZOO
£1 entry fee
Food 'n' stuff, if you want it.

'Listen, man, this is a fuckin' main road, right. All these fuckin' people in cars passin' by. If they've got kiddies with 'em and they see this sign for a fuckin' zoo - yeah, man - they're gunna want to stop and check it out, right?'

'Yeah, they would,' I encouraged him. 'What animals you got, though, I can only see rabbits?'

'That's it, man just fuckin' rabbits. But it dunt fuckin' matter, right, 'cos listen, listen, right, yeah. I can disguise the fuckin' rabbits as other animals, yeah?'

'Like what?' I said.

'You see the tin bath over there man, yeah. Do you know what that is, man?'

'Er . . . a tin bath?'

'No, man. That's the fuckin' seal tank, yeah. just fill it with water, yeah, get a fuckin' rabbit, yeah, dye its fur black, yeah, stick a fuckin' swimming cap over its ears and a fuckin' aqualung on its back, an it's a fuckin' seal, yeah, man.'

'Amazing.'

'Yeah, yeah. Yuh fuckin' seein' it now, man. And this fuckin' old dustbin lid, right: paint the fucker brown, yeah, strap it to a rabbit's back, yeah, put a fuckin' brown stocking over its fuckin' head, and there's yuh fuckin' giant turtle right, eh, man.'

On another occasion, when the crop-circle phenomenon was receiving a lot of press, Mad Malc thought he would be on to a winner if he went into a field and created his own 'extra-terrestrial markings' to substantiate the story he planned to sell to the newspapers of his abduction by aliens.

Only he came up with this idea in January, when a six-inch-deep layer of snow covered the ground. He told me of his plans in a local pub.

'The fuckin' snow, that's it, man. Winter, right; snow, yeah. Don't yuh see it, man . . . FUCKIN ' SNOW CIRCLES! There's the fuckin' novelty, man, yeah. That's the fuckin' sellin' point, right?'

'Snow circles! Your going to do some snow circles?' I asked, not quite sure I'd heard him correctly.

'Yeah, man. How come these fuckin' aliens only ever visit in the summer, yeah? Why the fuck don't they land their fuckin' spaceships in the fuckin' fields in the winter, eh, man?'

'You've got a point there.'

'Yuh seein it, man, yeah. That's the difference with my story, man. Fuck the local press, yeah. Yuh fuckin' nationals are gunna be knocking on me fuckin' door.'

Later that night Mad Malc attached two flat pieces of wood to the soles of his boots with insulating tape to disguise his footprints, and went into a nearby field. He hammered a stake into the ground, tied one end of a thirty-foot-long rope around his waist, and the other to the stake. He spent the entire night trudging through the snow to create three huge circles. In the morning, exhausted and out of whizz, he went home and slept till noon, by which time a blizzard had ruined his night's work.

Mad Malc regularly did the car-boot sales, but he didn't own a car. So he would fill a shopping trolley with a collection of dodgy items he planned to sell, and transport

143

them to the location of the car-boot sale by towing it on his push-bike.

One of the things he sold was a football 'authentically autographed' by the 1980 Forest European Cup winning team. Later, it turned out he had an unlimited supply of 'authentically autographed' footballs.

I also tried a few money-making schemes. I designed and sold football t-shirts. One season, with the prospect of Forest reaching Wembley three times - in the League Cup, Simod Cup, and FA Cup, I came up with a design. I drew a cartoon of a Forest fan stood in front of Wembley Stadium with a smile on his face, having climbed a ladder, crossed out the name Wembley and painted Nottingham Forest FC in its place. Above the cartoon I wrote FOREST WEMBLEY TAKEOVER. I had this printed on the t-shirts and sold them in a shop near the City Ground.

Later, I did a Stretford Ender t-shirt, but I was a bit late with that idea. By the time I had some t-shirts printed it was near the end of the season, when the stand was due to be demolished.

Eventually I was forced into slave labour: a Tory misgovernment 'training scheme.' Apparently it took a year to learn how to use a shovel; chained to your fellow detainee. This on a vast site where they were building exhibition centres, engine sheds and connecting paths for a railway heritage centre.

The Tories had a problem on their hands, us, millions of unemployed caused by their butchering of the industrial north. What to do with them? If only we could hide the blasted oiks down in the empty pit tunnels like we'd wish, let's force them into labour camps instead; call it a 'training scheme' so they're no longer unemployment statistics tarnishing our image in the opinion polls. Only we weren't playing ball, and chain, the hundreds interned, who didn't want to be there, didn't deserve to be there, given no option but to be there, deserved better (this wasn't a YTS, all ages were sent on here, including now unemployed miners), but had the threat of benefit sanctions if we didn't show up in the morning. Well ask a miner to pick up that shovel under the pretence of it being 're-training,' for nothing at the end of the week again, and they'll wrap it around your shins; but this was the general attitude off all sent on there. Welcome to Tory employment utopia.

As soon as they'd done the roll call in the morning many of us would disappear into the hidden corners and hidey-holes of the sprawling site (the main offices were at another old station up the line); full of wooded areas and embankments, winding paths and rows of dilapidated old railway carriages.

I was part of a small gang that discovered that the bolted doors of an old engine shed could be prised open at the bottom, enough to squeeze inside. In there was a big old red steam engine (it could have been used to transport German POW's to nearby Swanwick Hayes - just across the fields - during WW2, where, ironically, the only German soldier escapee fled from, as featured in the film *The One That Got Away*). We'd climb aboard, have a laugh, play three card brag, get stoned on the footplate there and back again, looking out for the fat bastard controller.

To signal I was part of the rebellion I dug out a few old tattered and torn old t-shirts to wear to 'work' – the Sex Pistols 'God Save the Queen' and 'Anarchy in the UK.' The only time I considered picking up a shovel for nowt was when I became part of an escape committee who'd drawn

145

up plans to tunnel under the barb-wired fence. Luckily, though, I didn't have to break sweat to break out, as I'd found a great escape by getting a real job, or thought I had.

That last morning at the *Carry On At Your Conservative Convenience Camp*. The chargehand, a nasty, jumped up, little shit (betraying his own kind just because he's been given a prefect badge and is important for the first time in his life, or thinks he is), coming up to me to throw a shovel at my feet. Said he knew I'd been skiving, but today I was going to graft or he'd grass me up to the JobCentre. I stood up, spat on the said shovel, told him to stick it up his arse, informed him I had a job and walked off down the railway line, in June sunshine, homewards and turntable vinyl bound, cheers ringing in my ears.

The 'real job' didn't exactly turn out to be the dream transfer: a wood furniture manufacturer. First I learnt the nuts and bolts of the job i.e. counting screws into bags all day long. The couple of fairly elderly (to me at that age) women I did this job with could switch off from the tedious task, and gossip away whilst putting the exact amount of screws in the bags at 5x the speed of me. Whilst I was numb with boredom 'fifty bloody one, fifty bloody two, fifty bloody three....'

I was promoted however, to the production line that had fearsome *Modern Times* machines: throwing out wooden drawer fronts that you had to quickly catch and stack, catch and stack, 5x20 high, onto pallets, Clingfilm wrap, all day long. Only I failed at this too. It was akin to a tennis ball training machine - firing out rectangular wooden shapes instead, at full speed, non-stop, at a novice. I sat on the floor, wood piling up around me like I was Guy Fawkes building his own bonfire, fearing decapitation as another missile flew over my head or hit me in the guts.

Deemed to be slow in body and intellect, the line manager put me to use stacking the larger, and heavier, wardrobe doors. These came out at a steady pace; if you had any fingers left to stack them. The 'experienced' wood machinist sawing these had three fingers missing, yet was instructing me to remove the off cuts left before the saw descended again each time.

This task done the doors had to be stacked again 5x20 high. This took two people to do, only the chap I was supposed to achieve this with was Norman Wisdom's long lost brother: he was about 55, 5ft 1, flat cap and braces. He omplained he had a 'dicky ticker' that nearly gave out as the stack reached above chest height. Resulting in loud groans, his bow legged knees buckling, causing several of the laminated doors to slide off and crash onto the factory floor; chipped they would have to be skipped.

A bollocking on the way from the gaffers you'd expect? But not a cross word came our way. It later transpired that the management – and several trusted employees – were corrupt, after being arrested by the police: they'd been removing the partly damaged pieces of furniture from the skip, patching them up and selling them on – kitchen units, wardrobes and other various pieces of furniture - for personal gain (apparently they knew the firm was heading for closure in the difficult climate for manufacturing and were making as much money as possible before losing their jobs).

Corrupt and a health and safety nightmare. Me and another young lad - who'd just started - were handed a huge spanner by one of the digit deficit wood machinists and told to change the massive 15 inch diameter circular cutting blades, whilst he went for a fag (in a wood factory!) Neither of us had any idea - or had been given any instruction on - how to carry out this order. We did manage to remove the 'blunt' one from the machine (which was still sharp and we had no gloves), the lad nearly dropping it on his trainer covered feet. Whilst I gingerly held the new one, ready to try and fit it in. When another worker casually strolled up and hit the big red off button and said, jocularly: 'Yuh daft twats, machine wer still alive, yuh could have lost an arm and probably have bled to death huh huh.'

Not surprisingly the place went into administration, I'd been there for about seven months. At least I still had all my fingers intact and earned enough for trips to United, beer and vinyl.

Music my saviour during the working week days of drudgery and despair: a memory personal Hi-Fi in my head. Drowning out the machines, not exactly producing The Kitchens of Distinction – the 'Prize.' The wage packet at the end of the week, 'How Soon is Now,' until then 'Destroy the Heart,' home to The House of Love and real sounds on the turntable or pop a compilation, 'C30 C60, C90 Go' or the NME C86 into the tape deck. Into bed, lights out with the Peel Show on the headphones, a friend in the darkness, playing strange lullabies. Sometimes the 'Spies in the Wires' drifting out, spies in the wires drifting in as the frequency slips on MW; Soviet voices, and classical music, strange bleeps. Fun spinning through the dial to hear more weirdness out on the late night airwaves, but always back to Peel.

Music my soundtrack, setting the scene as the slow motion days finally clock off on Friday. Away from Talking

Heads 'Road to Nowhere,' to Kate Bush 'Running Up That Hill,' on the 'Rise' with PiL, ready to stand with The Fall to 'Hit the North.' Away from the factory to *the* Factory favourites, New Order and 'True Faith' – United United United. The train in the outer suburbs of Manchester 'Strangeways Here We Come' passing the tower of the prison, into Victoria Station – The Wedding Present's *George Best* album, onto his Theatre of Dreams, 10,000 Maniacs *In My Tribe*, to stand with 10,000 Manc Maniacs, my tribe, M/A/R/R/S 'Pump Up the Volume,' United United United!

The Weather Prophets were right, it rains, but I 'Almost Prayed' with them when Alex Ferguson's first major signing, former Celtic striker Brian McCair announces his arrival, and potential as a new hero, with a stunning scissor kick volley against Chelsea. Strachan and Whiteside add the 2nd and 3rd goals for a 3-0 win. The cuts and blisters on my hands forgotten, the walk to work in the rain forgotten, I'm 'Happy When It Rains' on Saturday afternoons like this.

Maybe United are ready to reign again: other signings Steve Bruce and Forest veteran Viv Anderson are looking solid in defence; Robson is back to his best and injury free. United only lose five games all season, finishing 2nd to the still mighty Liverpool. We're after their crown now, signalled by the comeback at Anfield: 1-3 down to 3-3 with Strachan equalising in front of the Kop and cheekily giving them a two-fingered 'kiss this' sign. Fergie arguing with Dalglish, 'Big Mouth Strikes Again,' 'Frankly, Mr Shankly' I'm going to knock Liverpool off their fucking perch.

Pre-Hillsborough 4

Wed Oct 26th 1988:

Copey rang me up. Forest were playing Liverpool at the City Ground. It wasn't all ticket. He asked me if I wanted to go, it was midweek, and I had nothing planned, so I agreed to go with him.

There were huge queues outside the ground. Walking around the stadium we noticed that it was pay at the turnstiles for Liverpool fans as well. The Liverpool queues didn't appear to be as long. There were only fifteen minutes to kick-off, so we decided this queue would be our best option if we wanted to get in for the kick-off. The away fans at Forest were allocated terracing in the corner of the West Bridgford end.

Inside the stadium we stood at the back of the terracing. There was no choice - the whole fenced-in pen was jammed with Liverpool supporters. There was no way forward, and visibility of the pitch was poor. There was also a floodlight pylon on the terracing, obstructing the view. To the left of where the Liverpool supporters stood were two large empty areas of terracing, divided by a metal fence. To the left of these areas Forest supporters filled the rest of the space. Behind us in the top left-hand corner, an argument was going on between Liverpool fans, police and stewards. There was a Liverpool man with two little kids.

'I've paid good money to get in here, I can hardly see the pitch, and my two kids can't see anything. There's another empty section of terracing there, so why don't you open this gate and let us through?' the Liverpool fan said to a steward.

'This gate's staying closed. Just take your kids and make your way to the front,' said the steward.

'Haven't you got eyes, man? Can't you see there's too many people in here? How am I supposed to make my way through that lot?'

'They'll let you through when they see you've got kids.'

'Let me through? It's that packed they couldn't let me through if they wanted to, and there's still more people coming in,' argued the Liverpool fan.

The congestion became worse, more Liverpool supporters joined the argument, some youths forcibly pulled and pushed the gate.

'This fucking gate opens only when I say it opens,' insisted a police sergeant.

Ten minutes after the match started, the gate was opened, letting supporters on to empty terracing and relieving the congestion.

I've often wondered how many of the Liverpool supporters I saw and stood with that night were caught up in a far worse crush on the Leppings Lane terracing at Hillsborough, six months later. Did I look at faces that would appear in the newspapers, people who only had six months left to live?

Sweet and Tender Hooligan

He was a sweet and tender hooligan
Hooligan
He said that he would never never do it again
Of course he won't
Not until next time
            'Sweet And Tender Hooligan' The Smiths

'Stand and fight,' shouted the burly Mansfield Town supporter at me, his fists clenched, ready for action. I swept passed him, on my way to matching a 100-metres Olympic qualifying time. I was on the run from a frenzied mob of Chesterfield Town fans that we had riled about the score at the end of a prestigious Third Division derby. As books about hooligans sell so well, I wish I could go on to describe my role in the ensuing, legendary battle between Mansfield and Chesterfield, writing something like: 'I dun 'im with a bottle.' But being 5 feet 8 inches and 9 and a half stone (at the time) I always seemed to be on the sidelines when trouble kicked off.

Spurs were playing Notts County in Littlewoods Cup (League Cup) at County's Meadow Lane ground. Paul Gascoigne was in the Spurs team. Me and Copey wanted to see him play, so we went along.

Before the match, we sat drinking in a pub near Nottingham railway station. There was a group of Spurs fans in there, who looked like they'd had a beer or two. The landlord of the pub asked them to finish their drinks and leave. One of the Spurs fans walked up to the bar.

'What would you do if we smashed this joint up?' he said.

'Well, there's a police station only next door,' replied the landlord.

The Spurs fan threw his pint glass, smashing it against the back of the bar. 'It don't matter, we'll smash it up if we want to. Four pints of lager.'

The landlord served him, then the Spurs fan rejoined his mates. Gazza didn't disappoint, taking the piss out of the opposition by dribbling past players in his own penalty area. If only he'd have learnt that he didn't have to fly in with reckless tackles or use his elbows - his skill was enough to humiliate opposing players.

November 5th 1988:

Sat in K stand at Old Trafford during a United game against Aston Villa. Two Villa supporters sitting in the stand were getting on the nerves of the United supporters. At half-time a United supporter walked up to one of the Villa supporters and punched him in the face, leaving him out cold, sprawled across the seats. A policeman came rushing up and started giving the Villa supporter little slaps in the face to bring him round. The Villa supporter regained consciousness. The policeman asked him how he was, and then arrested him.

Alex Ferguson was now in his third season in charge of United, and was continuing his steady rebuilding process. Not just of the first team, but also laying the foundations for the future by developing the youth teams as well. Yet, despite his rallying call to 'knock Liverpool off their perch,' and being a constant thorn in the side of our greatest rivals in matches against them, the previous season's 2nd place in the League had proved a false dawn; Arsenal now looked more likely to snatch Liverpool's crown than United. There'd be no overnight success for Ferguson, and some of the football United played was far from exhilarating, causing rumblings of discontent among the United faithful who had now not seen their team win the Championship for over twenty years.

Ferguson had showed his shrewdness in the transfer market, buying striker Brian McClair from Celtic (in his first season McClair had become the first United player since George Best to score over twenty League goals). Mark 'Sparky' Hughes was bought back from Barcelona, a young Lee Sharpe was dazzling on the wing. But some of Fergie's signings were just baffling. I'd watched an inept Bristol City winger called Ralph Milne struggle all afternoon to get by Mansfield Town's full-back in a mid-table Third Division clash. A few months later he was in the Manchester United first team, and expected to produce the goods against the élite of the top division. The transfer listing of four Stretford End favourites - Whiteside, McGrath, Moses and Strachan (plus the loss of Gary Bailey, who retired due to injury) - dented United's confidence, and our belief, more than anything.

March 1989: United were mid-table and out of the League Cup, but had reached the quarter-final of the FA Cup, only to be beaten by 1-0 by Forest at Old Trafford. Brian McClair appeared to have equalized for United, but Dad's namesake Brian Hill decided the ball hadn't crossed the line.

Forest were drawn against Liverpool in the semi-final. The tie was to be held at Sheffield Wednesday's Hillsborough Stadium. My mate Paul Cope came around to see me. He could get hold of six tickets for the game, did I want to go? he asked. The FA Cup semi-finals were always an exhibition of English football at its very best. The games often being more exciting than the Final itself. And the atmosphere was guaranteed to be electric, with the teams just a match away from Wembley.

'Yeah, I'll go,' I told him.

Hillsborough

Friday April 14th 1989:
Friday afternoon and I was sat at home excitedly looking forward to the next day, the sort of day I loved. Saturday

out with the lads, drinking a few beers, going to a big football match. This time, an FA Cup semi-final.

I took two football books - which I had bought earlier that year - down off a shelf. I opened up Simon Inglis's *The Football Grounds of Great Britain* to read the section on Sheffield Wednesday's Hillsborough Stadium, where the following day's semi-final was to be held: 'Hillsborough is a stadium with all the grand connotations the term implies...To the left is the West Stand [Leppings Lane], with 4465 seats in an upper tier, and open terraces in front. Next to the other two stands it looks ordinary, but the view it provides is excellent, as are its facilities....a visit to Hillsborough on a crisp autumn afternoon remains one of the quintessential joys of English sport.'

I put the book down, and picked up *Back Page Football* by Stephen F. Kelly, a book about newspaper coverage of football from 1900 to 1988. I was up to 1970, and Brazil's victory in the World Cup Final. I turned the page, 1971, and there was a photocopy of a newspaper headline printed on the page: SOCCER DISASTER...66 die in big match panic.'

The headline was from the Ibrox Stadium disaster. I read about how there had been a crush on stairway 13 near the end of a match between Glasgow Rangers and Celtic. Hundreds of fans fell down the steps, leaving sixty-six people suffocated or trampled to death. It was 'the worst soccer disaster.'

Saturday April 15th 1989:
Saturday morning, a car horn pips outside the house – my mates picking me up for the drive to Sheffield. There were five of us in the car: Paul, Mark and Byrnie - Forest supporters, and Dave, a Liverpool fan, and me. I'd jumped

at the chance when Paul said he had a spare ticket. I was addicted to the buzz, excitement and atmosphere that was generated at a big football match, but, of course - being a Manchester United supporter, a Stretford Ender - I was also hoping to see my hated rivals, the all-conquering Liverpool turned over.

The Forest lads were full of confidence that this year they would beat Liverpool and reach the FA Cup Final. I'd been with them to the same fixture at the same ground (with both sets of supporters allocated the same sections of the stadium) the year before and that had been a great occasion, even though Liverpool won 2-1 I had to admit they were brilliant, as had the whole day out.

The sun was shining from a clear blue sky; it was a warm, beautiful spring day. With the car parked up in Sheffield city centre we headed for the nearest pub.

Paul, who had all our match tickets in his wallet, started handing them out to each of us.

'You'd better save mine, I'll only lose it,' I told him.

About two o'clock we left the pub to catch a bus to the stadium. Walking to the bus stop, Byrnie, Dave and me decided it was too early to go to the ground - we wanted another drink. Paul and Mark caught the bus to Hillsborough. We bought our drinks and sat down at a table. Then I remembered Paul had my ticket in his wallet. There was nothing I could do now he'd gone to the stadium - I'd have to hope to meet him there.

I struck up a conversation with a Liverpool fan in the pub and mentioned what had happened with my ticket...

'I haven't got a ticket either,' he replied.

'Are you still going to the ground?' I asked.

'Yeah.'

'Do you think you'll get in?'

'Yeah, no problem, I have done before.'

There was no reason for him believing he wouldn't get in without a ticket. A £5 note slipped to the write person could get you into any football ground. And at Hillsborough that day there would be no police cordon in the streets near the ground stopping anyone without tickets reaching the turnstiles (as there had been the year before). There would be no effective stewarding at Hillsborough; crowd control would be left in the hands of incompetent police. The FA's running of the game was a joke, they'd mismanaged the game for years. Crumbling old English football stadiums were a joke, even at the bigger so called glamorous clubs, chairmen and directors didn't want to fork out for improving facilities and making loyal supporters more comfortable when a new centre-forward could be bought.

So, OK, some football supporters hadn't been angels over the years, but I'm not going to have a go at fellow supporters - too many other people have done that, people who had never stood on a football terrace.

I'm not Lord Justice Taylor or a *Sun* newspaper reporter or Brian Clough; I'm just an average football fan who'd stood on many terraces. And the events I was about to witness that day, I'd unwittingly seen coming for years.

'I've just remembered from last year, the bus drops us off at the Liverpool end of the ground,' said Byrnie.

The bus down to the stadium turned onto Leppings Lane and the Liverpool end of the ground were we'd have to get off. From the top deck I looked down at the masses of Liverpool supporters converging behind the stand.

'Fucking hell! Look at the crowds,' I remarked.

157

We left the bus and made our way around the back of the Liverpool supporters, then walked down the road behind the main stand. We had tickets for Hillsborough's Spion Kop, a massive stand that allowed for 22,000 standing.

I did have ticket, but as we stood at the back of the Spion Kop, it was obvious my friend had entered the stadium with it.

The scenes behind the Forest end of the stadium were a big contrast to Leppings Lane. It was 2.50 p.m. now and the queues of Forest fans weren't even very long. The stand was so big that supporters were moving easily into the stadium.

I stood next to a turnstile talking to a policeman, I explained my ticket situation and he suggested I get a message to my mate on the stadium tannoy.

Following his advice I went back down the main stand and into the ticket office. They told me a pre-match DJ was behind a blue gate further down the stand and if I knocked on that he would open it up so I could give him my message.

The noise from inside the stadium told me the match must have got underway. I knocked on the blue gate. Nothing? I tried again.

'Oi what are you trying to do?' Shouted a police officer as he came striding up to me.

Again I told him about my ticket and that I was told to knock on this gate.

'Do you think they're going to open this just for you?' He firmly told me.

'What do I do now then?'

'That's your problem. Now move on,' he ordered.

A huge roar went up from inside the stadium. Had someone scored I wondered? [a Peter Beardsley shot had hit the crossbar] No the roar subsided to quickly. Back behind the Spion Kop just a few hundred Forest fans without tickets were hanging about. I saw the policeman I'd been talking to earlier and went over talking to him again. Then he received a message on his radio and ran off around the back of the stand, all the other police in the area did the same.

All the stewards seemed to have gone. I was stood right next to a turnstile, two Forest fans - without tickets - rushed up, pulling fivers out of their pockets, they thrust them into the hand of the turnstile operator and shouted 'Let us through.'

I followed them, I had a fiver ready as well, but the turnstile was still rotating so I followed the youth in front of me through and got in without paying. At that moment all the turnstile doors automatically slammed shut. I was the last one in.

I was sure I was going to get arrested, so ran fast as I could up the steps leading to the terracing, expecting any moment to be grabbed by the arm by a policeman or steward. Reaching the terracing I disappeared deep into the middle of the crowd. Then I noticed there were no players on the pitch. At the other end of the ground several hundred Liverpool supporters were congregating on the pitch, more were climbing over the barriers.

'What's happening?' I asked the man at the side of me.

'Some sort of pitch invasion,' he replied.

Sections of Forest fans - believing this to be the case - were chanting, 'You scouse bastards.'

I don't recall how long had passed before a man was carried by Liverpool supporters into the Forest half of the

159

pitch and placed on the ground, and one of the men who had been carrying him started to give him the kiss of life and heart massage. He tried repeatedly for five minutes to relieve the stricken man, but there was no movement.

'He's dead,' said someone nearby me in the stand.

The Forest fans were now silent. Everyone was becoming aware that something had gone seriously wrong. Access to emergency vehicles at Hillsborough was in the bottom right-hand corner, in front of the Forest supporters on the Spion Kop. It seemed to take a long time for the first ambulance to arrive; by then Liverpool supporters had already begun tearing down advertising boards to use as makeshift stretchers.

From the confused masses of supporters on the pitch in front of the Leppings Lane stand, emerged Liverpool supporters carrying the injured, dying and dead. They had to carry them the full length of the pitch to the corner down below us, where rows of ambulances were beginning to converge. Each time the Liverpool supporters carried a body across the pitch, the Forest supporters applauded them. What else could they do? They'd come to watch a football match, but were now witnessing a disaster unfold.

Soon there was a row of bodies, their faces covered with coats, lying on the pitch in front of us.

'I've seen enough of this,' I told the guy standing at my side.

I left the stand and walked slowly down the steps I'd raced up earlier. I waited at the bottom of these for my mates to emerge from the stadium. Someone passed by with a transistor radio: 'Nine people are now confirmed dead,' announced BBC radio's Peter Jones, who should have been into the second half commentary of a football match.

My mates emerged from the stadium. We began to walk back to the city centre. As we did, ambulances, police cars and police on motorbikes passed by at high speed, their sirens sounding.

The sun was shining. I saw a red balloon drifting up into the clear blue sky.

Halfway from Hillsborough to the city centre, we heard on a radio that at least twenty-seven people were feared dead. By the time we reached the city centre the number had risen to over fifty.

It just didn't sink in to any of us what we had just seen. That night I sat at home and turned on the television for *Match of the Day*. They showed pictures of the scenes in the Leppings Lane stand; there were interviews with Liverpool supporters who had been in the crush and had seen people die in front of them. Women and children had died along with the men.

Tears rolled down my cheeks. For the first time since my Grandad died of cancer I cried.

Ninety-six people died at Hillsborough.

*

Me, Paul and Mark had already bought tickets for the Simod Cup Final a few weeks after Hillsborough. Forest were playing Everton at Wembley Stadium. Before the game we sat on a wall outside a house in Wembley. There was a skip on the drive of the house piled with rubbish. I noticed some old newspapers amongst the rubbish, a two-week old *Daily Mirror*. On the front cover was a close-up colour picture of the dead and dying at Hillsborough, their faces pressed up against the barrier that was preventing their escape from the crush. Never to be yesterday's news. As much as the authorities and police wanted to bury the truth of what happened that day. *The Sun's* sickening, perverse version of 'the truth' deserved to be in the rubbish bin of history, in Liverpool the filthy rag will be forever.

I felt cold and guilty at being here at Wembley to watch a football match just a few weeks after the disaster. Even though the match turned out to be exciting, I couldn't get the haunting images on the front of the newspaper out of my head. I looked around Wembley Stadium and thought about the people who'd died, people like me; people who loved football and had just gone to Hillsborough to see their team get here to Wembley, for the Cup Final, a game of football.

*

Five years after the disaster I went back to Hillsborough for the first time since the semi-final, to watch Man United play Sheffield Wednesday in the semi-final, second leg of the Coca Cola Cup.

The tickets we were given were for seats in the lower section of Leppings Lane stand. I felt uneasy at the prospect of sitting on the terraces where so many people had died. In my opinion the whole stand should have been demolished in respect to those who died. But that would cost money - and money is more important than sentiment to most people in this world.

As we reached the stand, I couldn't believe my eyes. The perimeter wall outside the stand (where the crush of Liverpool supporters had built up before the disaster) was still in place. The blue gate (the opening of which had led to the disaster) was still in place. Inside, the tunnel under the stand (which funnelled the supporters to the central section) was still in place. The whole stand was like some huge black museum piece. If it hadn't been for the Taylor Report (recommending stadiums should be all-seater) I'm sure the directors of Sheffield Wednesday would have re-opened the Leppings Lane terrace as a standing area.

MaDchester United

December 16th 1989:

The train I'm on is on the slow arcing crawl round to Manchester Victoria Station, through a desolate landscape of derelict houses and factories; the rotting skeletons of the industrial revolution. The skies are slate grey, the tower of Strangeways Prison is visible in the distance. But I love what would be a dystopian scene to others, it sings to my soul, the landscape of my favourite soundscapes; Joy Division and The Smiths. Yet I'm minutes away from stepping off the train into a colourful cultural revolution coursing through the streets and realising things will never be the same again.

The train pulled into Victoria. I've only about £15 in my pocket. This, however, is enough for a fry-up at the greasy spoon café in the Arndale bus station or chips from Lou McCari's outside Old Trafford, maybe a record or two from Vinyl Exchange, the bus fare to the ground and most importantly entrance into the Stretford End; it was only about £2.80 to stand on the terraces.

I have a walk around the city centre before heading off down to Old Trafford and immediately I can feel the buzz, see the colour and hear the sounds of MaDchester: a Guy Called Gerald, 808 State, Inspiral Carpets, Happy Mondays and the Stone Roses are drifting out from the nearly every shop and pub ('Pacific State,' 'The MaDchester Rave on EP,' and 'Fools Gold'/'What the World is Waiting For' had all

163

just been released). An alternative country bumpkin still in my straight jeans, black Converse boots and old leather jacket I feel old and passed it - at the age of 24! - as I take in the colourful baggy fashion of the youths down in the streets.

Then I decide to call in to see my sister, Elaine; she's a fashion student graduate, recently moved to Manchester and working in Afflecks Palace. It's my first visit there and I feel like I've walked into a psychedelic Aladdin's cave: a former department store that had become an alternative emporium, with bohemian boutiques (one of *the* places to buy MaDchester gear), records, posters, piercing booths, hairdressers, bric-a-brac and accessories, a huge stuffed Yeti looking on. The place is as cool as fuck, as are all the people in there (it wasn't unusual for people who frequented Aflecks to be in the pop charts a few months later). Suddenly I've an inferiority complex developing. But I love it all and wish I were part of the revolution of ecstasy.

I catch the orange double-decker bus down to Old Trafford, this goes straight through the concrete crescents of Hulme. My sister's boyfriend lives there: Edward Barton, an eccentric music maverick who'd appeared on *The Tube* singing 'I've got no chickens but I've 5 five wooden chairs,' wrote the Inspiral Carpets b-side 'Two Cows,' the Top 40 single 'It's a Fine Day' (twice entering the charts, the original was sung by Jane, then Opus 3 released a new dance version) and directed the first James 'Sit Down' video (my sister would go for dinner with him to Tim Booth's flat at the location of the original Factory offices at 86 Palantine Road).

He had a room in his Hulme flat full of drift wood where he'd sit on a wooden throne. When my sister visits

Edward in Hulme she has to run for her life from the wild packs of dogs that roam the estate. Wild alternative gatherings take place by bonfires in the middle of the green (it's like the make-believe urban counter-culture areas of after hours Glastonbury but real) and Edward is twice mugged at knife-point. A no go area for the police, they've given up on it.

Edward did me a great MaDchester compilation cassette (which I still treasure) with tracks from A Guy Called Gerald (who he also worked with), De La Soul, Electribe 101, the Todd Terry Project, Jungle Brothers, S'Express, Phuture, Man Parrish, 808 State, Stakker Humanoid, 101 ('As Long As I Got You'), and one of his own tracks, the brilliant 'All of My Life' produced by A Guy Called Gerald.

Soon I'm in my element, an electrically charged, vociferous element, swaying in the mass United youth (then the average age was about 24 – now it would be about 44 I'd guess) on the terraces of the Stretford End; one love, one United entity. The heart of Old Trafford, as much an essential pulse and noise to the United experience as the MaDchester revolution - coursing through the city centre streets earlier - was to the culture of the city. The terrace supporters seem to have a collective consciousness in the way they respond to chants from the opposing fans or fuck up by one of their players. The atmosphere is not orchestrated or rehearsed, it's spontaneous and immediate, often funny, sometimes threatening. Several areas of the Old Trafford terraces are all singing different songs at once, then as United attacks they all join into one thunderous chant of United United United! Deafening, the hairs on the back of my neck stand up, this is real atmosphere.

But the writing's on the wall – and in the match programme – for the terraces. In the wake of the Hillsborough tragedy, earlier that year, plans are already drawn up to make Old Trafford all-seater and flatten the Stretford End; and as a consequence flatten the real atmosphere forever. I was at Hillsborough, saw the scenes outside of Leppings Lane at 3.00 pm and dying bodies on the pitch; this I'll never forgot. Yet terraces weren't the sole cause - incompetent policing of the match and other factors all played their part.

Some of the chants of the Stretford End are against their own manger 'Fergie, Fergie, Fergie, out, out, OUT,' sporadically breaks out. In his programme notes Alex Ferguson talks about going through a difficult spell, the reaction of the fans at him leaving Mark Hughes on the bench as 'the worst experience of that nature of my career...I hope that in the light of the day the United fans will have to realise that it was not intended as a snub of the player, but something which had to be done in the pursuit of the excellence we all want to see at Old Trafford....I am sure fans would not want me to sit back and just hope things would come right. It was time for action.'

Ferguson has been there for three years now, won nothing and some of the football has been dire. The performance of his team this day adds fuel to the fire: their opponents Tottenham outclass United. None more so than a young lad in midfield, outclassing the mighty Bryan Robson, his name is Paul Gascoigne. At his impish best, maybe to be as good in the future as *the* Best, George. Two years later the dark side - that seems to be the side effect of so many genius's - will see him implode in front of millions on Cup Final day and never fulfil the potential; to be one of the greatest footballer's of all time. I'm convinced that was possible on the evidence of what I see on display this afternoon. Gazza slips the ball to another England star, Gary Lineker, who scores - what he will consider the best goal of his career - curling the ball into the top corner from outside the box; it's the only goal of the game.

United are in the bottom half of the table, the knives are out for Fergie again. That Christmas the fanzine *Red Issue* will have a cartoon showing Santa giving out presents to the United players, when he comes to Fergie there are no presents left, only the sack. Fittingly, when I made it back into the town centre, heading for the train home, I saw that the massive inflated Santa Claus (in his United colours of red, white and black), on the tower of the Town Hall, has been shot; hanging there looking sad and deflated. United kids look up at him feeling the same.

This day, however (despite United's woeful performance), match and feeling, in the city centre and at United, has stayed with me. The 80's only had weeks to go before the dawning of a new era, much of what I witnessed that day has now gone. Yes glory days were to come for Ferguson, United and me - some of the most memorable days of my life just over the horizon - but are all things better at United and in Manchester than on that day in 89, in terms of atmosphere, culture and music?

1990's

Cup Final '90: Fools Gold

I was actually working, doing a mundane job in a warehouse. At least I'd got enough cash together to learn how to drive and get a car on the road. I bought a clapped-out Ford Escort - red, of course.

My sister Elaine now lived in the Didsbury area of Manchester, just a ten-minute drive from Old Trafford. Therefore United and Manchester had become much more accessible to me. The problem was I had to work shifts and every other Saturday morning, resulting in me missing a number of United's games, which again cost me dear at the end of the season.

I would often stay at Elaine's flat in Didsbury for the weekend, which gave me a chance to check out the Manchester nightlife. I went to The Hacienda, which had become so much 'the place to be' that it was as difficult to get into as the Stretford End. After queuing for an hour I went inside and the sight before me left me stunned. There were hundreds of wild-eyed, drugged-out teenagers dancing like they'd watched too many Gerry Anderson programmes, and nearly all wearing flares. I was so embarrassed about the photographs of me wearing flares as a kid in the 1970s that I'd put them all in a sealed cardboard box and placed it in the darkest corner of the attic. And here were loads of kids who thought 70s gear was trendy.

Then someone offered me an E and everything suddenly made sense: a sensory, heightened sense of euphoria, part of the Bez Borg Collective, a blurry joyous swirl of 'Voodoo Ray' zapped faces, a hypnotic beat, bodies moving to it en mass.

This was a brief flirtation with the scene, though. My clothes remained decidedly unbaggy: scruffy, straight jeans, black Converse boots, and my leather jacket stayed in place. As ever I couldn't be arsed to change (goes in circles that look - The Strokes would make it popular again and round and around) and anyway another band more suited to my image and musical tastes had caught my ear on John Peel, Nirvana. It was ok to take a drug that released your inner Jesus and love everyone and everything in your otherwise mundane milieu (apparently hooliganism dropped following the E 'Summer of Love.') But I liked music (and lit/media) that made me angry, energised and reactionary against an authoritarian Tory state. A regime that called working-class people, who spoke up and fought for their rights, 'the enemy within,' and sent troops in against them, disguised as police (who could be brutal enough). Not only against trade unions and striking miners, but also against peaceful hippy convoys.

I loved the music of the MaDchester scene, have a very eclectic taste in music (again thanks to John Peel's influence, and my Dad, brother and sister I'd say), enjoy sounds that take me to another place: like ambient, folk, psychedelia and the ethereal, beautiful, escapism of the Cocteau Twins is some of my favourite ever music. But noisy guitars will always strike a chord with me in more ways than 3 (the Stone Roses are essentially a great guitar band, I mean John Squire, few better). From The Beatles and the Stones, the Who, Led Zeppelin, The Stooges, but mostly the Sex Pistols, classic punk, post-punk and those alternative and indie guitar bands. They're the one's to release the rebellious spirit in me; nothing energises me more (except maybe anger stemming from an injustice). If music is my drug, then howling guitar tracks are LSD, speed, ecstasy and heroin rolled into one super drug.

One of my favourite bands of the time was actually an underground indie guitar band called Loop - like Spacemen 3 but darker, edgier and better: black-magic-spellbinding looping guitar riffs that harnessed dark matter as fuel and headed for and through a black hole into another dimension in space, a *2001:A Space Odyssey* far out trip into Jupiter (they were big Kubric fans and sampled his classic space film on the album *Heaven's End* – 'my mind is going,'). Lead 'soundhead' singer Robert Hampson is a United fan (so is Mani, Ian Brown, Richard Ashcroft, Thom Yorke, United have the coolest of fans don't ya know?).

These were the sounds I would listen to before a United game to fire me up, or before going out for the night, to fill me with life and energy. Seeing these bands live was the only events that could give me the same buzz as being on the Stretford End on match days. Being a professional footballer or rock star were the only entities that we could aspire to become to escape our humdrum existences. In the back streets of Manchester two brothers called Gallagher were breaking into that dream to put together the framework for the classic album of our times; the one that told us we could get there, definitely, maybe?

My bedroom - Spacemen 3 - revolution, dreams and sounds still didn't impress Dad though. I was listening to the Loop's *Fade Out* album, heading into a 'Black Sun' ready to take on the world, when Dad stuck his head around the door.

'Oh, it's your music is it, I thought someone was drilling.'

*

The '89-90 season had started so well for United: property tycoon Michael Knighton had supposedly bought the club from chairman Martin Edwards. He told supporters that he would pour money in for ground development and new players.

On the opening day of the season United played reigning Champions Arsenal. Before the game started Knighton ran on to the pitch in a United kit, juggled a ball a few times with his feet, before shooting it into the net in front of a cheering Stretford End. He blew kisses to the crowd and left the pitch.

United beat Arsenal 4-1, with Neil Webb (United's new signing) scoring on his debut. Alex Ferguson later bought Paul Ince and Gary Pallister. Things looked promising.

Things looked different by January. Knighton's promises were bullshit. He had backers that pulled out, the club stayed with Edwards (I bet he's glad about that now). Neil Webb ruptured his Achilles' tendon playing for England (and would never be the same player again) and United were in the bottom half of the League.

In the FA Cup third round, United were drawn away to Forest. It was rumoured that if United lost, Alex Ferguson's job would be on the line. United scraped a 1-0 victory, Mark Robins getting the vital goal, and the rest is history; United have never looked back.

They reached the Final of the FA Cup in 1990. I'd missed so many midweek games that I was well short of having enough tokens to qualify for a ticket. I tried the touts around Old Trafford but couldn't talk them down to a price I could afford. I went and stayed at Elaine's in Manchester the week before the Cup Final in a last-ditch effort to get hold of a ticket. Nothing turned up, though.

On the Friday night I sat drinking in the basement bar (the dimly lit basement bar) of the Barleycorn pub in Didsbury. I was feeling sorry for myself and thinking I would never see United in a Cup Final. Jokingly I asked one of the bar staff if he knew anyone with a spare Cup Final ticket. He gave me a negative response. But two streetwise-looking Manc youths overheard and shouted me over.

'Yer looking for a Cup Final ticket?' one of them asked.

'Yeah. Why?'

'This could be yer lucky day; we've one left.'

My eyes lit up. 'You have!?'

'Yeah, we were gonna flog it tomorra at Wembley.'

'What you asking for it?' I said, eagerly.

'What yer got?'

'I've got fifty pound on me.'

Both youths sat shaking their heads from side to side.

'We're looking for more than that. It's a thirty-pound seat.

We'd get at least a hundred at Wembley.'

'It's all I've got.'

The two youths had a whispered conversation with each other.

'Fuck it, mate. Yer can have it for fifty. We wanna get pissed tonight, anyway,' one youth spoke up.

My wallet was straight out and I started counting out the money. 'Not in the open, under the table,' one of them instructed me and then pulled out the ticket from his jacket pocket.

175

I couldn't wait to get my hands on it and quickly handed over my cash without inspecting the ticket. The deal struck, both youths stood up.

'What yer drinking. I'll get yer one,' said the youth I'd given my money to.

'Cheers. A pint of lager,' I replied, and they walked off towards the bar. I was looking down at the ticket. Hallelujah! Fucking great - at last, a Cup Final ticket...I looked up and caught a glimpse of the youths' heels as they legged it up the stairs. I looked back down at the ticket . . .

'Aaaarrrrgggghhhh!'

Everyone in the bar became quiet and looked in my direction. Knocking over the table and my pint, I ran after the youths. It was too late; they'd disappeared. And in the brightly lit upstairs bar I felt a complete fucking divvy. I could now see clearly the ticket I'd bought was only a barely credible forgery.

Cup Final afternoon; United versus Crystal Palace. Ripped off for £50, no ticket, I was taking my anger out on my car, which had broken down in the Peak District as I drove back from Manchester. After giving the car a damn good Basil Fawlty thrashing, I had to walk two miles to the nearest pub to phone the AA. It was 2.30 p.m. and I was still an hour's drive from home. There was no way I was going to make the kick-off. There was no television in the pub and my car radio didn't work.

3.40 p.m. I'd been sat on a stone wall in the middle of the barren Peak District next to my broken-down car for fifty minutes when the man from the AA turned up. By this time I was desperate for news of the Cup Final. 'It's 1-1,' he told me.

And what was wrong with my car . . . nothing a few squirts of WD4O couldn't fix.

Just gone half-past four and I'm a thirty-minute drive from home. I pull up at a set of traffic lights. In front of me a youth in a Ford Escort XR3 punches his fist into the air. Someone must have scored, I'm thinking, and the traffic lights are still on red. So I jump out of my car and run to ask the youth what's happening.

'Ian Wright's just scored for Palace,' he answers.

'Shit!...What's the-'

The traffic lights turn to green, the youth slams his foot down on the accelerator leaving me standing in the middle of the road.

'What's the score,' I shout after him, but he doesn't hear.

There's a blast on an air horn and a Grizzly Adams-like trucker sticks his head out of the window of his vehicle that's stuck behind mine.

'Shift that fuckin' heap or I'll do it for yuh,' he shouts.

'Do yuh know the Cup Final score?' I enquire.

Grizzly glares at me and starts climbing out of his truck. I hastily get in my car and drive off. Twenty minutes later down a narrow, meandering Peak District road, and I'm miserably thinking United must have lost 2-1. I pull up at a set of traffic lights. I'm still stuck behind the youth in the Ford Escort XR3. Again he punches his fist into the air. What's going on? The game should be over by now. The traffic lights are still on red . . . so I jump out of my car and run to ask the youth what's happening.

'Ian Wright's just scored for Palace in extra-time.'

'What's the-'

The traffic lights turn to green, the youth slams down his foot on the accelerator, leaving me standing in the middle of the road.

'What's the score?' I shout after him, but he doesn't hear.

There's a blast on an air horn. I turn around and Grizzly Adams is climbing out of his truck. I run back to my car, which has cut out, and turn the key in the ignition. It fails to start. Grizzly swings a boot at the back of my car, which I get going just in time, leaving Grizzly on his backside in the road.

Fifteen minutes later I finally arrive home. Dad and Benny Hill are sat on the settee. Mam's still out shopping. Refreshments are gone.

'Where you bin - down pub?' says Dad.

'Don't ask. What's the-'

Mark Hughes scores for United.

'Don't yuh know? Three-all; it's been a classic,' says Dad.

The match ends 3-3 and days later I'm back settled into my armchair (lucky 1977 Cup Winners' scarf around my neck) to watch Lee Martin score the winner for United in the replay and give them the FA Cup for the seventh time.

On the Monday after the first game a Radio 1 DJ said during his show, 'I've never been to a football match before, but a friend got me a ticket for Saturday's final. It was really exciting.' What a bastard. If you're a real football fan, doesn't it make you sick to see the close-up smiling faces (on television) of MPs, celebrities, and businessmen sitting in the stands at Wembley on Cup Final day, when most of them haven't been to a game all fucking season.

Italia '90: World In E-motion

World Cup '90. Every football-loving English person carries a mental scar from England's painful exit in the semi-final. It was especially hard for those of us not old enough to remember England's triumph in the 1966 World Cup, and who therefore have had to put up with the people who can remember, going on and on about it.

I watched every England game on the telly with my mates Copey and Chico, at Michelle's flat (Michelle was Copey's fiancée). Stocked up with cans of beer from the off-licence, we would settle into our seats for each match. There, was a growing belief that England could go all the way. The quarter-final opponents were the surprise team of the tournament - Cameroon, with ageless striker Roger Milla their danger man.

Eighty-one minutes of the match gone and we were sat in glum-faced silence. Roger Milla and Cameroon led 2-1; World Cup USA '94 seemed a long way off (France '98 even further).

'Penalty!' we all shouted.

England had a penalty.

'Lineker,' we all shouted, as he converted the spot kick.

Full time - 2-2.

Into extra-time.

'Penalty!' we all shouted.

England had a penalty.

'Lineker,' we all shouted, as he converted the spot kick. England won 3-2 and we were into the semi-final.

I've no need to go into the semi-final against West Germany. Everyone remembers Germany's goal, Lineker's equalizer, Gazza's tears, the penalty shoot-out, Pearce's and Waddle's misses.

Next day, everyone woke up with a World Cup hangover. I wasn't in the mood for work; I'd had enough of my warehouse job and knew for definite I wasn't going to spend the rest of my working life there. I was constantly clashing with my shift manager, nicknamed Ming the Merciless due to his striking resemblance to the *Flash Gordon* character.

He was a Forest fan and had had it in for me since the morning I'd gone into work wearing a Man United shirt the day after they knocked Forest out of the FA Cup. He was becoming obsessed with trying to catch me out, so that he could have me sacked.

I'd go to the toilet for a shit. Now who can predict how long the disposal of the brown stuff is going to take? If it's a Monday morning after a heavy weekend, then it can be a twenty-minute job. The Japanese start their working day with a vigorous aerobic session; the British like to start their working day with a cup of tea and a good shit, reading the newspaper at the same time and maybe smoking a fag. It's part of our culture. It didn't matter how long I'd take, when I came back from the toilet Ming would be standing at his office window looking at his watch and shaking his head disapprovingly. Then he'd always dash to the toilet himself. What was he doing I wondered, sniffing the toilet basin to make sure I'd had a no. 2?

There was one occasion when me and a mate had bought tickets to see The Jesus and Mary Chain playing at Rock City in Nottingham. It turned out the concert fell on a week when I was working a late shift. So I tried to book half a shift off to enable me to go to the gig. Ming refused, so I phoned in sick and had the whole shift off.

The following day back at work, I heard that an incensed Ming had phoned Rock City during the concert, with a message for a Tony Hill. Yeah, like the Mary Chain were really going to stop mid-set to see if I was in the building.

Anyway, it was the day after the World Cup semi-final. I was in no mood for Ming and the warehouse, but I went. Everyone was supposed to do 250 picks a shift to achieve the bonus, insisted Ming. Half a shift had gone and I'd done 10. I was called into Ming's Office.

'I want 250 picks a shift per person, half a shift gone and you've done 10. Why?' he demanded to know.

'Why not?' I replied. 'Anyway, I'm going home, I'm not feeling too well.'

'Why, what's wrong with you?'

'I'm suffering from PWCD

'Oh yes, and what is that exactly?'

'Post-World-Cup-Depression,' I explained, before walking out of the building.

A few months after Italia '90 finds me in Ostend, Belgium for the beer festival; a weekend trip into oblivion with a load of drunken, foul-mouthed punters from the back street Corner Pin pub in my village.

We were supposed to be staying at a 3 star hotel, just off the town square. 1 star more like, the only chance of seeing more stars there would be the ones swirling around your head after a drunken punch up in the bar. We were all allocated the top floors; my room was reached via a waterfall created by rainwater flowing down stairs, the source of which was a burnt out hole in the roof of the attic

181

room next to mine. We all complained to the proprietor, a big man with bushy black moustache and the personality of Basil Fawlty. Maybe he was justly gruff.

'It's your lot's fault. This hotel survived World War 2, only to get drink bomb damaged by English hooligans, ransacking rooms, one falling asleep drunk with a cigarette on.'*

*Many of our group were wearing England, Italia '90 shirts, not because we were hooligans looking for trouble.** We were actually proud of our national team for once. But, of course, such was the reputation of English fans back then that we all tarred with the same brush.

** OK a few of our lot liked a good scrap; I was out with two of them one night and was the only one not to have plaster over a bust nose in the morning.

'Yeah, well I reckon the wallpaper, fixtures and fittings have survived from World War 2 na'll, that tin'tin brochure is it Captain Haddock,' I put in with stupid, drunken bravado.

He looked down at me, glared at my Manchester United shirt, growled: 'Fer sure, a Manchester mouth.' Then lifted me off my feet with a grizzly bear hug and dumped me outside. 'We'll never forget or forgive the Red Army invasion of 74.'

For years I didn't know what this referred to, until I read in a fanzine about United's notorious 70's Red Army hooligans going on the rampage in Ostend.

This was a signal for some Belgium football supporters (still smarting from their late defeat to England at Italia '90) in the bar to get involved; several of our lads went into the fray. And this was supposed to be our hotel for the weekend, wipe your blood on the welcome mat on the way out.

182

The travel company made their apologies and as compensation upgraded us to another hotel: somehow they managed to wrangle it so we ended up in the best hotel in Ostend, the Thermae Palace, it had actually once been the residence of Belgium royalty. This fact and its palatial grandeur weren't the main things that impressed me, however. I couldn't believe my eyes and ears for different reasons, just a week before I'd seen it on TV: Channel 4 had showed the classic horror film *The Daughters of Darkness*, this was set in Thermae Palace. Then one of the waitresses told me The Cure were one of the rock bands to have stayed there, I was well impressed as an ex Goth.

So when our rabble arrived at the Thermae – about dinner-time – we'd already been drinking non-stop since being in the Nottinghamshire pub at 7.00 pm the previous evening (from there onto the coach to Dover, on the ferry all through the night, and then we were delighted to discover some pubs in Ostend were open 24 hours). Many attired in England shirts, now covered in all manner of stains: alcohol, food, vomit, kebab juice and blood. As we fell and stumbled through the doors some Belgian businessmen in suits, having meetings, fled in terror. The Hotel manageress rushed up, ashen-faced, and yelled about it being a 'respectful hotel.' I'm sure it was the scariest visitation at the Thermae since *The Daughters of Darkness* set up residence there.

The manageress exorcised these new demons by chucking a jug of holy water our way, shooed us from the hotel, and insisted we couldn't return until our rooms were available, about tea-time. Really, there wasn't a bad apple amongst us, our community was one were bullies weren't tolerated. We were just a group of pit village lads and men.

Yes, as stated, some were tough Arthur Seaton bastards who wouldn't shirk from a fight. Have the most razor sharp, uncensored sense of humour in the world, but are genuine, nice, salt of the earth people nonetheless. A culture that liked a drink and this time we'd over indulged. So add to that England shirts (the notorious football events of the previous decade meant England fans were looked on with revulsion, everywhere) and guess they saw us akin to some medieval English invading army, intent on rape, pillaging and destruction.

Our reputation wasn't enhanced any by old Fred – usually attired in a 1970's brown, wide-lapelled, leather jacket, yellow shirt and national health specs taped up with Celotape – coming down the stairs the next morning, then walking into the bar (where more business suits were gathered) and asking for a whisky. When he came to pay and tried to reach into his pocket for money realised he'd remembered his leather jacket but forgotten to put on his trousers, he stood there in his grotty Y-fronts.

I'd later get lost in town with Fred, until he spotted a porno cinema across the road and said he'd go ask the woman in the ticket kiosk for directions. Moments later Fred stuck his thumb up to me and shouted: 'I've found it.'

'Great,' I replied thinking he'd located our hotel. 'Are we heading back then?'

'Nah, bollocks to that, she told me where the red light district is, see yuh in t'morning yowf,' he said triumphantly with a wide toothless grin.

Later the hotel manageress had her head in her hands again, fearing the worse when a group of German lads came into the bar, wearing their World Cup winning national team's shirt. But we just shared a drink and exchanged good natured banter. Inevitably, though, the talk got around to that World Cup semi-final penalty shoot-out. To prove we didn't always bottle it in shoot-outs the matter had to be settled once and for all, it was agreed upon to have one right now, on the beach in front of the Thermae. The losers had to get a round in.

I was chosen to take the final penalty, by which time the score was 3-3 in penalties scored, but a German lad had missed their last one. My chance had come at last.

'Todsy...Todsy...Todsy,' the England fans chanted my nickname.

In my drunken head I believed the whole of England, the world, were watching me. John Motson was reeling off facts about my honours: at Subbuteo, Striker, back-street football. It was on my shoulders to restore the nation's pride. I tried not to be intimidated by their goalkeeper: a big, round, pink faced fellow with long arms spread wide. He looked like Mr Tickle from the Mr Men books and cartoon (now Arthur Lowe's voice was coming into my head: 'Don't miss you stupid boy').

I lowered my head to look at the ball and saw two instead, due to blurred vision, sending me cross-eyed. This, however, worked to my advantage, as it perturbed Mr Tickle when I glanced back up at the net, he didn't know which corner I was looking at to shoot the ball.

I took a few steps back, then fell in the soft sand back down onto my arse. The German's roared with delight. I jumped back up, brushed myself down, ran forward, and struck the ball sweetly with my black Converse booted right foot. Mr Tickle was going the wrong way, but his outstretched right foot caught the bottom of the ball, it soared upwards then landed in the sand, over the goal-line, surely? Not fully, argued the Germans. An exclusion zone was formed around it. A Russian linesman was called over...actually he was an elderly Belgian man walking his dog along the beach...his decision was final. He drew a line in the sand between the shell-suit top goalposts with his walking stick. Explosive chants of 'England..England..England' as he pointed to us and indicated a goal.

'Todsy..Todsy..Todsy.'

Good to their word the German's got the round in. I don't remember the rest of the day, but woke up in a strip joint, the madam of the place was laying into me and ordering me out of there: 'No one goes to sleep when my girls perform,' she screamed. A couple of Filipino strippers were down to their thongs on stage.

As I was being escorted out by two of her heavies, old Fred roared with laughter, he sat there, each arm around two scantily clad women, fag hanging out from nicotine stained fingers, toothless grin. 'I'm the one scoring t'naight, appen.'*

*Fred would be paying off the debt on his Eurocard for the next year.

Always Look on the Bright Side of Life

'DON'T LET THE BASTARDS GRIND YOU DOWN,' I'd scrawled it on the toilet wall of the warehouse in big biro pen lettering. Then - a'la Stan Laurel when imprisoned by Ollie down in the boat in *Towed in the Hole* - I jabbed the eye of the cartoon figure of Ming the Merciless. Hang in there, not long until Christmas and you're outta here, I told myself. I was just about to flush the chain, when I heard someone else come in through the main door into the Gents

186

lavatory; whistling fuckin' 'Chirpy Chirpy Cheep Cheep.' I knew that smell of after shave. Oh bollocks, Ming was out there. No good waiting, I knew that he knew I was skiving away in there. I'd have to face the middle of the road music, be squashed in the middle of it like a toad.

He was looking in the mirror, trimming his slick black goatee beard with a pair of little scissors (on a Swiss Army knife), his reflected eyes were on me, above a sadistic smile. 'Bryan Robson's in the wash today is he?'

'Huh?'

'Your United shirt, funnily enough you're not wearing it this fine morning. Washed out like your team is it?'

'Funny.'

'Stuart Pearce certainly hung you out to dry, ha, now that is funny.'

Stuart 'Psycho' Pearce's stunning free-kick at Old Trafford (in front of the Stretford End who'd been taunting him about his World Cup penalty miss), on the Saturday just gone, had been enough to give Forest a 1-0 victory. A few weeks previous to that I'd had to put up with his lapdog chargehand taking the piss, he was a Liverpool fan, and they'd hammered United 4-0.

I tried to wash my hands of Ming – before I wrung his neck – but the tap was one of those awkward press down things, and it wouldn't turn on or off properly. I slammed down my palm on the top, a jet of water gushed into my other cupped hand, then up and out, splashing the bottom of Ming's trousers and his polished expensive shoes. His usual scowl returned to his face, before he headed for the cubicle I'd just come out of.

Oh the sad bastard's not basin sniffing again is he? I thought. Then I heard a loud 'harrumph' as he bolted the

187

door. Fuck, the graffiti and cartoon, he'll know it was me. I tried to keep out of his way, taking the back road aisles on my pick truck in the vast warehouse. But it wasn't long before his abrupt voice came over the tannoy: 'Tony Hill to the office.'

Apparently a job had come in of 'utmost urgency' - 20 25kg bags of flour for a hospital (I know Thatcher was in power but surely the patients weren't that much on the bread line and near starvation?), and 20 x 20 packs of the huge tins of baked beans (beans on toast, yes this sounds about right for hospital meals under the 'Milk Snatcher'). I was just the man for the job, of course. Both these counted as just 2 picks, so I was certain not to make enough picks to share in the shift bonus.

I was usually knackered on the day's shift, especially on a Monday one after being on the beer the night before. So was dead on my feet after getting home from this one.

I climbed into my space capsule of a tiny bedroom, lay down, pressed buttons on the console at the side of my bed, an illuminated Technics stereo - 9 8 7 6 5 4 3 2 1, 'we have lift off,' the sounds of an Apollo rocket taking off, the voices of astronauts and Mission Control. I was off to see The Orb's 'Spanish Castles in Space,' then go 'Higher Than the Sun' with Primal Scream's *Screamadelica* trip, before 'Coming Down.' Chilling to Massive Attack's *Blue Lines* album, The Sunday's *Reading, Writing and Arithmetic*, The Cocteau Twins *Heaven or Las Vegas*.

As the week wore on and the weekend neared my music would become more up tempo and energised: Teenage Fanclub, Ride and The House of Love the bridge bands from the chill-out zone over to *Bleach* era Nirvana, Spacemen 3, some classic punk, The Stooges, Husker Du,

The Jesus and Mary Chain (definitely), the Pixies, Ned's Atomic Dustbin, That Petrol Emotion to the Wonder Stuff on waking up refreshed on a Saturday morning.

Next up at Old Trafford, United had Arsenal in the league. Time for the players to redeem themselves, lift my soul and reenergize me after another shit, draining week. I was pumped up for this one, Arsenal under George Graham were becoming fierce rivals to United on the pitch. This match would pour fuel on this fixture for years to come.

First Arsenal's Limpar put them ahead with a contentious goal. Surely it wasn't over the line, Les Sealey had clawed it way. Although there's no way we could see if that was the case from the Stretford End as it happened in the goal at the far end; behind which the Arsenal fans were celebrating wildly. In the second half, United's Denis Irwin went into a tackle with Limpar, Nigel Winterburn made a lunge on Irwin and all hell broke lose. All but Arsenal's David Seaman became involved in a mass brawl. Ince pushed Limpar into the advertising hoardings. Steve Bruce ran 80 yards to take out Winterburn (a month after the game, the FA fined both clubs £50,000 for bringing the game into disrepute and docked points). Great fighting sprit from United, releasing some of my own pent up anger, but we still lost 0-1, so I was even angrier and pissed off after that on that long journey home. Another 'Blue Monday' ahead.

United chaos seemed to reign everywhere - for the good: the Berlin wall and communism had come tumbling down, the Cold War thawed by the fire in the heart of people power, Germany united. Yet uncertainty of the future remained: Yugoslavia was on the brink of tearing itself apart, war with Iraq was looming, the IRA bombed London. I saw all this from the television window of my space capsule. Football was just a game, most people have shit jobs, but it was hard to feel positive about anything after watching United's recent performances after the weekly daily grind, living in crazy times.

I find safety and solitude and escapism in my bedroom bunker, or as the Jesus and Mary Chain had sung 'My Little Underground.' I tried to manage Manchester United better than Fergie, via a football game on my Amiga 500 computer. Only to get more frustrated and irritated at my United team getting worse results and are lower in the League than the real United. So I sacked myself, picked up my sword and sorcery potions to go slay enemies, dragons and monsters down in the dungeons. Only to continually get eaten or be blown up by magic bombs. Realising I was useless at these modern computer games I sold my Amiga and turned to Tolkien and his fellowship to take me into fantasy worlds and defeat evil for me, by reading *Lord of the Rings* (and *The Hobbit* and *Silmarillion*) for the first time.

I turn over from the bad news on Television, 'The Drug of the Nation' the Disposable Heroes of Hypocrisy, for *Snub TV* and more new alternative sounds. Then walk with fire in David Lynch's brilliant, dark, dreamy, weird and funny *Twin Peaks* world.

United improved with a 3-3 draw at City. Then beat Liverpool 3-1 in the Rumbelows League Cup. I was back on the Stretford End to see a 2-0 victory over Crystal Palace, followed by another 2-0 win at home to Sheffield United. They were also making steady progress in the European Cup Winners Cup. Ming was off work, on holiday – or on a mission to exterminate Flash Gordon. Lapdog was off sick too and their stand-in gave me cushier jobs. So I did some overtime, getting me closer to my escape fund target. Only for United to crash 2-3 to Chelsea at Old Trafford. Then on the Wednesday morning I left the house and discovered that the druggies on our estate had broken into my car to steal the stereo. I called the police. They told me someone would come and take a statement.

That night United were away to Arsenal in the Rumbelows League Cup. I was sat at home listening to the match on the radio; United were winning 3-1 despite Arsenal having one of the meanest defences in the country.

A knock came at the door. I opened it and there stood the policeman who had come to take my statement. We walked into the front room. He'd seen I was wearing a United shirt and could hear the radio with the match commentary.

'What's the score?' he enquired.

'Three - one to United.'

A frown came on to the policeman's face. 'I'm from London, originally. I support Arsenal.'

'Sorry about that.'

'Sorry! We were the Champions the other year, weren't we. You won't win 3-1 at Highbury; there's time yet.'

We sat down and I started to give him details of the car break-in, but really we both had one ear listening to the radio. Arsenal scored. A smile appeared on the policeman's face. 'There you are, we're coming back now.'

We continued to go through the statement. United scored: 4-2; then scored again: 5-2; then scored again: 6-2. A stunning hat-trick by Lee Sharpe, even on radio by the sounds of it. I couldn't contain my joy any longer. I didn't care about the car any more. I jumped out of my chair, punching the air.

'Six-two! Six-two! Arsenal - Champions? - not this season, matey!'

'It's a bloody fluke; 6-2. I don't believe it; it's a fluke,' he said.

I controlled my excitement.

'Do you want to go and have a look at the damage to my car, then?' I said.

'What do I want to look at your car for? It's the same as all the rest. I've seen hundreds of cars broken into,' he replied, with an edge to his voice.

He left the house. Walking down the path he shouted back, 'Your car tax is due; make sure you get it paid.'

Dad put the news on after the match, the so sad scenes of Margaret Thatcher in tears after leaving 10 Downing Street for the last time. Like a modern day Caesar her own trusted lieutenants and members of her inner sanctum had stuck the knife into her. My heart bled too, it really did. What goes around, Karma will get you my dear. And it may only be for a short time but I'm employed and you're an unemployment statistic. Get on your fuckin' bike.

At Christmas I resigned too, from my warehouse job, before I was pushed, a sweet moment: letting Ming inform me, with relish, that I'd only have 3 days off over the Christmas period, before giving him my notice. In panic he sent his lapdog chargehand lolloping after me, asking if I'd be prepared to postpone my departure until the New Year as they'd be short staffed. I kicked him in his dog's bollocks. I enjoyed a wonderful Christmas with family, friends, freedom and United beating Norwich 3-0 on Boxing Day.

In January United earned an away draw at Southampton in the quarter-final of the Rumelows League Cup. Free of afternoon shifts I was able to go up for the replay. I enjoyed the 3-2 victory on the night. But now with hindsight I look on it as one of those lesser known and half forgotten games that was very special to witness; one of those you'll tell youngsters about as an old man. This is mainly for the battle of now two legendary British football warriors: a young Alan Shearer scored 2 and Mark Hughes topped that with a second-half hat-trick.

Fergie was at last making us daydream believers. Now he'd steadily built United from the defence up, he'd started to develop that old United attacking flair: when 17-year-old prodigy Ryan Giggs made his debut against Everton, then was involved with the winner against City at Old Trafford, we had at last two quality wingers, with Lee Sharpe in great form. We had an attacking style again at last, good times surely lay ahead.

United lost in the final of the Rumbelows Cup to Sheffield Wednesday but had been on another Cup run; this time in Europe. They beat Legia Warsaw 4-2 on aggregate in the semi-final to reach the European Cup Winners' Cup Final. There they would face Barcelona.

I had to settle for watching it in a local pub. For once everyone wanted to see United win. Well, not everyone; but not bad for Jacksdale. Mark Hughes had once played for Barcelona; but it had never really worked out for him. Now he had the chance to show them what a great player he was.

Hughes (fast becoming a United legend) didn't disappoint, scoring both goals in United's 2-1 victory. His second a fantastic drive from an acute angle. I'm feeling The Stone Roses 'One Love,' Deee-lite – 'Groove Is in the Heart.'

The United supporters celebrating on the terraces in the pouring rain were singing a classic Monty Python song: 'Always look on the bright side of life.'

I wished I was there. The following season (from the cash I'd banked from the warehouse job) I would at last be able to afford a season ticket (LMTB to United supporters) and wouldn't have to miss a United game again.

On Ryan's Express

Season 1991-92:

I'd bought a season ticket for the Stretford End. It was the last season for the famous end as a standing terrace. The following summer it would be demolished and replaced by a new all-seater stand. The majority of United supporters were unhappy with the plans for the new stand: £500-plus season-club-class seats were to be placed in the middle section of the new West Stand; even the name Stretford End was to be dropped. But the biggest objection from United supporters was the proposed size of the new stand. When completed, the capacity of Old Trafford would be down to 43,500, nowhere near big enough for a club that had well in excess of 60,000 members.

United fanzines *Red Issue* and *United We Stand* started petitions against the plans and wrote article after article urging the United board to look to the future. Why not build a three-tier stand, taking the capacity of the stadium back to at least the 50,000 that was surely required for a club with such a huge following? The board responded by claiming that the foundations weren't solid enough for a bigger stand, and that there would be viewing problems.

A few years later, with the club membership well over 100,000, the board announced plans to rebuild the North Stand as a three-tier structure, taking the capacity of Old Trafford to 55,000.

There was a special turnstile for season-ticket holders, so I didn't have to queue for over an hour - often in the rain - to get into the stadium any more (luxury). United supporters had their usual optimism about the season ahead. Alex Ferguson had bought Danish international goalkeeper Peter Schmeichel and an exciting Russian international, Ukranian winger, Andrei Kanchelskis. The team was looking stronger all the time.

46,278 supporters packed into Old Trafford on the opening day of the season to see United beat Notts County 2-0. In the second half, Alex Ferguson brought on a seventeen-year-old substitute, Ryan Giggs. You could see straight away he was a rare talent: he gave his to soul to the Red Devils for his superhero powers to rule the world. A shooting star, a will-o-the-wisp dancing light of a footballer, tricking defenders to go the wrong way to their doom and his and United's victory, on a wing answering many a Red's prayer. Echoes - in skill and image - of a young and innocent George Best, the unfair comparisons.

Ferguson threw a protective blanket around him to ensure he neither burnt out nor faded away, a legend to be, who would endure. Anything or anyone deemed to be a bad influence removed. Like the unfortunate Lee Sharpe (eventually): a good-time boy, famously partying with Giggs until the spies in the wires tipped off Fergie, who rushed around there, stormed in to lay the law down and take Giggs into protective custody.

In the third Old Trafford game of the season, against Leeds, Giggs hit the post. He was already becoming established in the team and terrorizing opposing defences. The next home game, against Norwich, Giggs latched on to a ball, went around the goalkeeper and slotted it into

Norwich's net from a tight angle. To see the teenage Giggs at full pace, flying down the wing, was a sight to behold.

My crap Ford Escort car broke down in the middle of the A6 in Stockport on the way to the West Ham game. I had to endure abuse from drivers, being told off by the police for blocking the busy thoroughfare, wait an hour for the AA, then run like hell to make it into Old Trafford before the gates shut. Just as I'd pushed my way onto the terrace Giggs came flying into the box to latch onto a cross and fire home into the corner with a volley. A magic moment that made all the effort getting there worth it, forever. By Christmas he would be a household name.

October 6th 1991. United v Liverpool:
As always when these two Lancashire giants meet, there was a loud passionate atmosphere inside Old Trafford. The same old songs were being sung by rival supporters. United supporters would sing, 'Sign on, sign on; you'll never get a job. Sign on.'

Liverpool supporters would respond, 'You'll never win the League; you'll never win the League.'

Suddenly, one lone voice in the middle of the Stretford End shouted out: 'Hillsborough 89!'

Everyone - and I mean everyone - in the stand turned angrily towards the brainless dickhead. One youth grabbed him by the throat: 'Shut the fuck up, or get out.'

He was just one sad bastard, and it was the one and only time I'd heard the disaster mentioned at Old Trafford.

I decided to go and visit the Manchester United museum at Old Trafford. As I walked towards the stadium, four men sitting in a car shouted me over. I recognized their faces straight away; they were touts. You would see them in the streets around Old Trafford before every United game. I walked over to the car. I thought it best not to ignore them. There weren't many people about. A burly youth with a scar on the side of his face climbed out of the car.

'Are yer goin to the ticket office?' he asked.

'No, the museum,' I replied.

'Well, just go to the ticket office for us first. We can't go they know our faces.'

'All right,' I said.

I wasn't going to argue with him; I'd heard of a West Ham tout being stabbed near Old Trafford for selling tickets on their patch. The youth handed me several season tickets and membership cards, plus a wad of ten pound notes.

'Go in the ticket office and buy twenty tickets in K stand for the game against Coventry,' he said.

I did what he said, went to the ticket office, bought the tickets, returned to the car and gave them to the youth and returned the season tickets, membership cards and the remainder of the money.

'That's great mate,' he said.

I didn't wait for a tip.

At Christmas, United were top; Leeds were second. We dared to talk of winning the Championship. In March Leeds had gone top. United were out of the FA Cup but had reached the Final of the Rumbelows League Cup – they played Forest in the final. I was there, not my dream of an FA Cup final, and it wasn't a great game, but United won 1-0, leaving me none too popular with my friends back in Nottinghamshire.

So Near, So Far

Four days after beating Forest at Wembley, United faced Southampton in the League at Old Trafford. Victory would take them back to the top.

With the score stuck at 0-0 and time running out, United won a corner. The ball swung over and fell to Andrei Kanchelskis at the edge of the box, who connected with a blistering volley that flew into the corner of the net in front of the Stretford End.

Old Trafford erupted with noise; the relief was incredible.

'We're gonna win the League . . . we're gonna win the League . . . and now you're gonna believe us . . . we're gonna win the League,' sang the Stretford End.

Minutes later the final whistle blew; United were top, one point above Leeds and with a game in hand. There were only five games left. After twenty-five long years, could this be the season that United finally became Champions again? Would the enormous expectancy and pressure from the United crowd affect the players in the run-in?

I heard someone behind me in the Stretford End saying, 'I've got to be here for the last game of the season against Spurs; the last day of the Stretford End, when they parade the Championship trophy.'

One Mancunian entrepreneur had mugs and t-shirts printed with 'MANCHESTER UNITED CHAMPIONS 92' on them.

United's successful run in the Rumbelows Cup turned out to be their downfall in the race for the Championship. With a backlog of fixtures United faced the daunting prospect of playing the last four League games in seven days. While rivals Leeds had a well-spaced run-in, having gone out of both Cup competitions early (ironically to United).

Things didn't start too well. They could only manage a draw at lowly Luton, then everything went disastrously wrong: United suffered three straight defeats, first at home to Forest (1-2 there'd been a party atmosphere in the Stretford End until Scott Gemmill scored the winner for Forest, off all teams for me), then away to relegated West Ham, and finally at Liverpool; but by then it was already over. Leeds had beaten Sheffield United to become Champions.

A French man called Eric Cantona had been the inspiration for Leeds in the title run-in. For United the Championship was beginning to look like an impossible dream. United goalkeeper Peter Schmeichel was optimistic, though.

'I'm sure we will win the championship in the next two years,' he said during an interview.'

The last day of the season arrived. United, pressure off, were in top form, cruising to a 3-0 victory over Spurs, then with minutes remaining Gary Lineker (playing his last ever English League game) rose to head a goal for Spurs and the whole of Old Trafford stood to applaud him. 'Oh, Gary, Gary, Gary, Gary, Gary Lineker,' sang the Stretford End.

So the last few minutes of the last ever League game played in front of *the* Stretford End weren't spent celebrating United winning the Championship, but saluting the Spurs and England international hero.

Slacker

Soap for sore eyes
I need an intermission
If looks could kill
I'd kill your television
      'Kill Your Television' – Ned's Atomic Dustbin

'We were hearing from the psychiatrist earlier that laughter is a great therapy that also releases certain chemicals within the brain that are beneficial to our health. But unfortunately for little Benny Watson here (there was a shot of a sad-faced kid, sat in front of a television watching a *Tom and Jerry* cartoon) laughter is impossible because of a rare condition which causes pain, even if he smiles,' said Richard Madeley, with much sincerity during an episode of *This Morning*, catching my attention and bringing me out of my deep thought process.

I sipped my tea and looked away from the TV. What was I thinking about....? Ah, my future. I was now in the rut of long-term unemployment again. The kind of rut I'd been in for much of the 1980s. The kind of rut where I'd sit for hours staring at the television or the wall, or out of the window, planning my future. Which was easy to daydream about, but the reality of actually sorting my life out seemed much too like hard work. I'll do something creative, I'd think . . . Erm, something creative that'll make money . . . I'm not bad at art - I can draw daft cartoons that make people laugh - maybe there's some money in that; or I'll try to design some more t-shirts....Yeah, t-shirts with psychedelic or Celtic designs on them that'll sell thousands at Glastonbury. That's it - I've got the ideas; I'll start tomorrow. I could start today, but I've too important a schedule: *This Morning*, *Kilroy*, the News, dinner, *Home and*

Away, Neighbours, walk the dog, *Take the High Road, Doobie Duck 's Disco Bus,* tea, listen to spaced-out sounds: Spiritualized *Lazer Guided Melodies,* Aphex Twin *Selected Ambient Works,* chasing UFO's with The Orb, get pissed, get stoned, *The Late Show,* bed.

The thing was, I'd become comfortable with my apathetic, insular life. I'd sort of turned on, tuned in, and dropped down on the settee. It's the state of mind you get in when you've been long-term unemployed: all motivation goes, you become glued to an armchair for hours and mull over everything from the meaning of life (would United buy a decent striker and win the Championship before I die?) to which biscuit to dunk in my tea (Bourbon, custard cream or chocolate digestive?). The television becomes a hypnotic sedative.

I was twenty-six (with a mental age of eighteen) and still lived with Mam and Dad, who despaired of me. They'd come to accept the fact that their youngest child was a waster, but having two out of three children who'd turned out OK wasn't too bad. Elaine had become a knitwear designer, one of her designs appeared on the cover of *Vogue Knitting* magazine (yes Mam was incredibly proud) and had settled with a boyfriend in Manchester. Brian was now the signwriter for one of the big Nottinghamshire breweries and had even painted the lettering on 'the oldest pub in England', Ye Old Trip to Jerusalem, sited in front of Nottingham Castle. He had a lovely fiancée, Jo, a nice car and a nice house. I was expecting life to come knocking on my door.

If a job or girlfriend came along, then they came along. I had first refusal on a flat in the village when it became vacant, but I was in no hurry to leave home - how would a lazy bastard like me survive living alone? And, anyway, it seemed that most of the friends I had at school, who'd gone at a rush at life and got married with kids when they were too young, were now divorced or separated, with a mortgage around their necks and the CSA on their backs.

I lived for the weekends. If when Saturday (or Sunday or Monday night) came around and I could see United, get pissed, get a shag, then everything would be fine. Monday to Friday I could connect my brain back to the television set; unless United played midweek, or there was some other big football match, then those days became significant.

As for summers.....cricket, tennis, sweaty armpits; what a washed-out drag they were. I'd get serious football-withdrawal symptoms. At the back of my mind, though, I knew I couldn't get away with being a sponging Peter Pan forever.

In the dole office, signing on one day, I sat down to face Ms Cotteril. I looked forward to our games of verbal chess. This day I'd surprise her.

'Have you done any work in the last two weeks, Mister Hill?' she said, indifferently.

'No miss.'

'Sign here, then.'

'What training programmes are available to me?'

She looked at me quizzically, as if expecting a punchline. 'Doing what exactly?'

'I'm good with my hands. How about painting and decorating?'

'Well, you could go on a Training for Work course. It lasts six months, in which time you could achieve a NVQ qualification.'

'Wow.'

'You would attend college one day a week; the other four days are on-the-job work experience, providing a service to the community by decorating public buildings and homes, locally, of people on low incomes.'

'Lovely.'

'And you'll get ten pounds extra a week on top of your benefit.'

'You generous bastards. I'll take it.'

'You will,' she said, astonished.

'Yeah.'

A little tear seeped out of the corner of Ms Cotteril's eye. She went and told her colleagues, who then came over and shook my hand.

The training programme turned out to be a badly run scheme full of the unemployables: problem teenagers, ex-cons, slackers, alchies, hypochondriacs and over-fifties. Most had no hope of getting a real job, but - conveniently for the government - being on a training programme meant they weren't added to the jobless total.

There were three other people in my decorating gang. Wayne (problem teenager, future con), Bill (ex-con, alchie), and Alex (hypochondriac, over fifty). Wayne had been in trouble with the police for joyriding and criminal damage. He usually wore an LA Raiders t-shirt, baggy jeans with the arse at knee length, Reebok pump trainers and a baseball cap pulled so far down over his face that you rarely saw his eyes. He didn't speak much apart from the occasional 'yeah, right' and when he did talk he gesticulated, East 17-style. His hand movements made him a natural when it came to painting around windows.

Bill was in his mid-thirties. He'd been a bad lad in his younger days, doing time for burglary and GBH. Now he wanted to put all that behind him and settle down with his girlfriend and kid - only with his criminal record and tattoos (love and hate across his knuckles, a naked woman with a snake wrapped around her on his forearm, and a cobweb and spider on his neck) he couldn't find an employer who'd give him a chance. The back of his head went up into a sort of cone shape, which he attributed to the effects of his excessive drinking habits. He claimed that, midweek, when not drinking, his head flattened down again, but by the end of the weekend alcohol gave him a cone head.

Alex was fifty something, average height and average weight. He had a greying bubble-perm haircut, and a pair of gold-rimmed glasses rested on top of his bulbous nose. He wore a fine selection of bri-nylon 70s shirts, brown slacks and a pair of slip-on loafers. He looked healthy enough, but rarely turned up for work, having frequently been struck down with some obscure ailment. When he did show up he was like a talking medical encyclopaedia and loved telling us in grisly detail of the various operations, illnesses and accidents he'd had: 'The bone was sticking out of my leg, blood pouring out of me like a fountain, and the fucking head of the chap in the passenger seat was rolling down the hill,' etc.

Most of the houses we decorated were those of the elderly, or single-parent mums. There were occupational hazards. One day me and Bill were emulsioning the kitchen at an old man's house when he came into the room, took out his tadger, picked up a teapot and began to piss in it.

'Dunt mind mey, lads, jus gerr on wi tha wok,' he said.

He had difficulty emptying his bladder due to prostate trouble and stood there yanking at his prick, muttering away.

'Ooohhh bugger . . . let's ay it . . . come on, yuh bugger,' until there was a quick spurt of urine into the teapot.

This went on for about half an hour then, job done, he shuffled over to the sink to fill up the kettle.

'Dus tha want a cup a tea, lads?'

'NO!' we said in unison. 'We've brought flasks.'

One Monday morning, suffering from a wicked hangover, I arrived at a council house we were decorating to find that everyone else was off sick. The woman who lived there was a single parent in her late twenties. She had a plump figure and a mischievous face. She had four kids aged between 3 and 10, from four different men.

She left the house about 8.50 am to drag the kids to school and do a bit of shopping. I was upstairs painting her bedroom. With the house to myself and not feeling too well, I decided to lay down on the bed and chill out for an hour. I'd got my Walkman with me and put in a cassette of The Orb's *Adventures Beyond The Ultraworld* album, pressed play, turned up the volume, closed my eyes and headed into space. I was drifting through 'The Supernova at the End of the Universe' when there was a tug at the zip of my jeans. I opened my eyes and looked up. Two 38D flesh-coloured space craft hovered above my head. Before I could turn off The Orb and return to Earth, the mothership had docked with me.

So this is what they meant by providing a service for the community.

Cantona

'There's a lot of energy in Manchester, in football, music and culture. Maybe its because of the rain. Some cities you have beautiful things to see and visit; in Manchester, they have energy. I could feel something, the energy from the history of the city.' Eric Cantona.

The Stretford End was demolished. I had to transfer my season ticket to the Scoreboard Paddock on the opposite side of the ground. The opening home game of the season saw a huge open space where the Stretford End used to be. The disappointment of losing the Championship, plus the fact that United had lost their first game of the season at Sheffield United, left a three-sided Old Trafford with a subdued atmosphere. This surely must have affected the players as United crashed to a 0-3 home defeat against Everton. The crowd was so quiet at times that you could hear the players calling to each other on the pitch.

Two games gone; two defeats. The new season had started as badly as the previous one had finished. Some supporters had already given up on United's chances of winning the Championship.

The following Saturday's game at Old Trafford wasn't much better. Ipswich came for a draw, and got a draw.

New signing Dion Dublin finally gave United their first victory of the season, scoring a late winner at Southampton. Another victory followed at Forest, then Crystal Palace were beaten 1-0 at Old Trafford, but during the game Dion Dublin was badly injured, breaking his leg and damaging his Achilles' tendon, leaving him out for the season.

Was he a sacrifice of the Old Trafford Gods, making way for the new Messiah?

Three straight victories, and optimism was returning to the United supporters. The next opponents at Old Trafford were Champions, Leeds. Old Trafford may have been only three-sided, but the United supporters turned up the volume for this game. Revenge was needed, the players knew it.

The Leeds players, having finished their pre-match warm-up, left the field. All except one player, Eric Cantona, lying on his back in the sun, continued to do his leg-stretching exercises. 'United....United,' thundering from the stands. Cantona rose to his feet and looked around at the three sides of Old Trafford; the atmosphere and surroundings appeared to have made an impression on him.

There was only one team going to win that day and United were 2-0 up by half-time, with goals from Kanchelskis and Bruce. In the second half Leeds's Chris Fairclough floated over a ball from the wing into Man United's penalty area. Cantona connected with an acrobatic overhead volley that Schmeichel did well to smother. The United supporters applauded the Frenchman's effort; Cantona's skills had made an impression on us.

United beat Everton 2-0 away for their fifth straight victory, but the supporters' optimism was short lived as United went over two months without a single League victory, scoring only four goals.

Mark Hughes, always the player for the big occasion, got us out of the shit at home to Liverpool. Two-nil down with less than fifteen minutes to go, Hughes scored two classic goals to grab United a draw.

'Superb vision. He has a quick look...there it is....sees Grobbelaar off his line, and thinks, I'll have some of that.' Sky Sports Andy Gray described the goal, thus, as I watched the game again later on video.

In the pub I was talking to a local Leeds United supporter called Ginner, who was banned from Sunday football for life for attacking a referee, and banned from

Elland Road for being named on the page three of *The Sun* newspaper for rioting with other Leeds fans at Bournemouth. Neither of us was happy with the way our respective teams were playing.

'United never look like scoring again just lately,' I told him.

Three weeks later, every United fan anywhere will remember where they were and what they were doing when they heard the news.

I heard it on Radio 1's *Newsbeat*, but I still didn't believe it so I put the teletext football news on the television.

'Cantona signs for Man United.'

I rang United's clubcall just to confirm it. I still wasn't sure. Cantona would make his debut for United in the local derby against City at Old Trafford. Appropriately for a Manchester derby, it pissed down that day and United beat City 2-1 (one from Ince; Hughes getting the other). That was great, but the special event of the match was Cantona coming on as a substitute.

'We've got Cantona - Say - We've got Cantona,' sang the United fans.

With one of his first touches, Cantona on the halfway line pulled off an overhead kick/pass to Mark Hughes. At that moment every United supporter knew great days were ahead. The fourth dimension had arrived; the team was complete. A Cantona-inspired United beat Coventry 5-0 at Christmas to go second in the League.

Legends

Late February. The 1992-93 Championship was becoming a three-horse race between United, Aston Villa, and Norwich. I'd stayed at Elaine's flat in Manchester the night before

United played Middlesbrough at Old Trafford. I wanted to get to the ground earlier than usual on the Saturday. George Best was appearing at the souvenir shop. It was a chance for me to meet my childhood hero.

At the ground I queued with other United supporters for about an hour. There were plenty of females in the queue. Lucky bastard, he still had plenty of women wanting to get near him. It finally came to my turn in the queue to meet the charismatic footballing genius. We talked and talked about United's glory days, his great goals, the women he'd shagged, getting pissed, etc. Well, no we didn't. He smiled, said hello; I smiled, said hello. I shook his hand, handed him my pen and an issue of the *United* magazine with himself pictured on the cover, which he autographed - only he forgot to hand me my pen back.

'Er, thanks George. That's my pen....but you can keep it if you want,' I said to Best, embarrassingly.

'Oh, sorry. This is yours, is it? Here you are,' replied the United legend, handing my pen back, smiling.

Not a very scintillating conversation, but there were other people waiting impatiently in the queue, and my thirty seconds were up.

The game against Middlesbrough produced another fine performance from United, who won 3-0. An in-form Giggs scored a scorcher.

After the game I was standing in the forecourt in front of Old Trafford waiting for my mate Ed, who sat in another section of the ground and had gone to the souvenir shop. I had earlier bought a copy of the 1968 European Cup Final programme between United and Benfica, which I was flicking through. I looked up from the programme. An old man emerged from the Main Stand and was walking towards me. I looked back down at the programme, then I clicked. My head shot up and looked in the direction of the approaching old man. I couldn't believe it; I'd always wanted to meet him, but I'd never even seen him in real life. There had been times inside Old Trafford during a game when I'd looked over to the directors' box to catch a glimpse of the legend, but I never had. Now here he was, a few yards from me: Sir Matt Busby.

I walked over and shook the great man's hand, then he autographed my copy of the 1968 European Cup Final programme. It was a cold day and I realize now that Busby (then in his eighties) couldn't have been in the best of health, but he still had time to sign autographs for the fans.

Ned Kelly, United's head of security came over and put his arm inside Busby's.

'I'll walk you to the car Sir Matt,' said Kelly.

Touched by the hand of God, I stood in reverence and watched 'Mr Manchester United' walk away into the distance.

I looked back towards the Main Stand. A bald-headed middle-aged gentleman was walking in my direction. One of the most famous bald-headed gentleman in the world, one of the most famous and greatest ever footballers in the world: Bobby Charlton himself. I shook his hand. The United and England legend autographed my copy of the '68 European Cup Final programme.

One sixties legend left to meet and it was only a few minutes before striker supreme Denis Law came along. I shook his hand and he autographed my copy of the '68 European Cup Final programme, putting his name alongside Busby's and Charlton's. Law didn't play in the '68 European Cup Final. Injured, he lay in a hospital bed getting pissed at the time of the match, so I don't know what he felt signing the programme, but he did it anyway. The programme is now framed and displayed on my wall.

A few weeks later I met Alex Ferguson and all the current first-team players at one of these supporters' club do's. I was a member of the Mansfield Branch of the United supporters club at the time. It was one of those do's where the players sign autographs and mix with the supporters for a while.

I was in the toilet having a piss. In walked Paul Parker (who was having his best season so far for United). The England squad would soon be named for an upcoming international.

'Have you heard anything from Graham Taylor yet?' I asked Parker.

Did he not like that.

'Don't talk to me about that arsehole,' he replied.

Norwich Away

I usually went to United games in the company of my mates Ed and Rob, who I'd got to know through the Mansfield supporters' branch. Ed, aka DJ Doom, hosted the breakfast show on hospital radio, easing the fears and aiding in the recuperation of the patients by waking them up to 'Death Disco' by PiL and 'Atmosphere' by Joy Division. He was in his mid-twenties and had only become interested in football when he moved to Manchester to attend college, studying economics. A friend took him to Old Trafford to see United play. He was hooked, and has been a season-ticket holder ever since.

Rob - in his mid-thirties and a United die-hard from the 1970s - he liked a drink or two or ten, and he'd often travel to games with a flask of vodka and a tin full of spliffs. Be in Rob's company before a match and you'd be out of it by kick-off time.

United, Villa, and Norwich continued to exchange places at the top of the League. Early April and United, away to League leaders Norwich, were in a must-win situation, after just having their worst League run since the autumn, drawing three and losing one, leaving them in third place. If Norwich were to win this one, United would be five points behind with only six games remaining.

I'd managed to get a ticket for the game and travelled down on a supporters' bus, reaching Norwich about an hour before kick-off.

Ed and Rob couldn't make it for this game. To kill time on the long journey and relieve the tension I put my headphones on to listen to Radiohead's *Pablo Honey*. But the guy sat at my side kept nudging me; full of nervous energy he kept asking me to reassure him we wouldn't fuck up again. I felt confident I assured him, not sure that I was. He seemed all right, an average thirty-something red. It wasn't until later that I discovered I was in the company of Hector the Collector, whose house was crammed from top to bottom with United souvenirs. He had apparently once tried to strangle his best friend, who had accidentally sat on and broken Hector's signed and framed George Best picture that he'd bought from a stall near Old Trafford.

We got off the bus near Carrow Road. I walked with Hector towards the stadium. On the way we stopped to buy a match programme. Hector held his programme carefully in his hands and eyed it admiringly.

'I've got all United's programmes going back years . . . all in mint! condition, you know,' he said.

212

'You must have hundreds, then.'

'Yes hundreds, and all in mint! condition. Do you know how I keep them in mint! condition?'

'No,' I replied, starting to get a bit worried.

From an inside coat pocket he whipped out a small rectangular-shaped clear plastic bag.

'First I place the programme inside this plastic bag. It's a smooth, soft plastic bag, which will protect the programme but won't scratch it. Go on, feel it,' he said, pushing the plastic bag towards me.

I felt the bag.

'Yes ...it's... er...smooth and soft,' I said.

He carefully inserted his match programme into the plastic bag. 'Then!' he said, whipping out another plastic bag from his inside pocket. 'I place the programme inside the soft and smooth plastic bag inside this plastic bag. This plastic bag is tougher and stronger and will give added protection to the programme. Go on, feel it.'

I felt the plastic bag.

'Yes it's definitely tougher and stronger.'

He placed the programme inside the smooth and soft plastic bag inside the tougher, stronger plastic bag. From his inside coat pocket he then whipped out a Man United souvenir shop bag.

'For that little bit of added protection, and for me to be able to carry it along safely, I place the programme inside the two plastic bags inside this plastic bag.'

'What happens if they do get creased?' I asked.

'Oh, earlier in the season I couldn't get a ticket for Man City away, but my mate went and brought me back a programme. I accepted the programme and paid him for it, but [a look of horror filled Hector the Collector's eyes] 'there was a big crease right down the back cover,' he said.

'You wouldn't want that, then,' I said, without a hint of sarcasm.

'No, I had to bin it when I got home.'

I left Hector and headed for a pub for some pre-match beers. I entered a pub near Carrow Road, no canaries to be seen or heard chirping anywhere, the place was packed with roaring Red Devils, several up on tables chanting: 'We'll keep the Red flag flying high cos Man United will never die.' That old fighting Stretford End spirit, exorcising haunted memories of Championships thrown away. Yet the nervous tension prevailed. After sinking several pints of lager I walked to a chippie to get something to eat. There were doubters in the queue outside the chippie.

'I think we've already blown it,' one of the United supporters said. Pessimistic bastard, I thought. That's just what you want to heat before a match of such importance.

Inside the stadium I quickly realized the ticket I'd been given was for the Norwich end of the stadium, and sat there quietly until the players ran out. It then became obvious that there were a few hundred other United fans in there as the chant of 'United! United!' broke out from different areas of the stand, much to the annoyance of the home fans. Scuffles soon broke out.

On the pitch Alex Ferguson opted for all-out attack instead of playing it safe, employing Ryan Giggs as striker in place of the suspended Mark Hughes, and Kanchelskis and Sharpe as wingers.

Ferguson's gamble paid off gloriously. United were 3-0 up and had the game won inside the first thirty minutes, having played some scintillating football, the pace and passing of United's attacks ripping the Norwich defence to shreds.

At half-time in the refreshments area under the stands, fighting broke out between United and Norwich supporters. I saw a youth who'd travelled down on the same bus as me. 'This is brilliant. I didn't realize there was so many United fans in here,' he said to me before pulling out his hidden United scarf from the inside of his coat, wrapping it round his neck and then heading into the midst of the action.

Ex-United player Mark Robins pulled one back for Norwich in the second half, but United were cruising to victory with Kanchelskis and Ince both hitting the woodwork.

United were now in second place just a point behind leaders Aston Villa, and with a superior goal difference.

On the journey home we dared to talk about the possibility of winning the Championship.

We Are the Champions

The next game was at Old Trafford. The talk of winning the Championship had been premature: there were just five minutes of the match remaining and United were trailing 0-1 to Sheffield Wednesday. That old feeling of déja vu had returned to the United supporters; it was looking like we were going to blow another League title. We'd done our bit in the crowd, turning up the volume and getting behind the team, but United had missed chances.

Giggs floated over a corner, and there was Captain Braveheart, Steve Bruce, to head the ball into the back of the net. We celebrated with relief, but a draw at home in the Championship run-in wasn't good enough. Minutes ticked by. I looked at my watch. Time was up, but the game

215

continued. Time went on and on. United attacked and attacked. The fans urged them on. I looked at my watch. 4.55 p.m. United attacked, Pallister crossed the ball into Wednesday's penalty area; the ball came to Steve Bruce who headed it into the corner of Wednesday's net. Unbelievable: 2-1 United in the seventh minute of injury time. The ground exploded with one of the loudest and wildest celebrations of a goal I've heard at Old Trafford. It was as if at that moment the twenty-six-year-old burden of not winning the Championship was lifted; there was a real belief the team could do it. There would be no fuck up this time. United had gone top with five games remaining.

The following Monday (Easter) United were away to Coventry. Outside Highfield Road there was hardly a Coventry supporter to be seen. Inside the stadium it must have been 70 per cent United, with red and white to be seen in every section of the ground. United scraped a 1-0 win, Denis Irwin scoring the goal.

United won their next two games - 3-0 at home to Chelsea, and 2-0 away at Crystal Palace, their fifth successive victory - leaving them four points ahead of second placed Aston Villa with only two games remaining.

Villa played their next game on Sunday; United weren't to play till Monday night. Everyone expected Villa to win, they were at home to Oldham, who were in the relegation zone. The game was on telly, but I wasn't bothered about watching. I turned on the radio in the second half. Oldham were leading 1-0! If the score stayed the same United would be Champions. It suddenly dawned on me United could only be twenty minutes from the title, but surely Villa would come back and win. I carried on listening to the commentary of the game on the radio, as nervous, if not more so, than when I listened to United on the transistor radio as an obsessed Man United daft kid, a life time away it seemed, yet even back then United winning the Championship was beyond my memory, something written about in the book of legends, almost mythical, grainy black and white footage, another 60's make-believe dream.

With only a few minutes left, the score was still the same: 1-0 to Oldham. My heart began to thump. I put a blank audio cassette in the stereo and began to record the commentary. If this was going to be the moment United won the Championship for the first time in twenty-six years, I wanted it on tape so that I could hear it again and again.

'The final whistle blows....twenty-six years of waiting....an entire generation is over....Manchester United are Champions.'

What a feeling. I just wanted to go out and celebrate, but the pubs weren't open for an hour. I phoned Ed.

'We've only gone and bladdy done it,' I said.

I'd borrowed some CDs from my brother, one was a rock compilation, on it was Queen's 'We are the Champions'. I don't really like Queen, but I was off me head, and this was the only song for the occasion. I put it on, turned up the volume and opened the windows, then I pulled out a single from my old vinyl record collection: Sham 69's 'If the Kids Are United'. I blew the dust from the surface and stuck it on the turntable. I especially turned up loud the last bit of the record where there's a crowd chanting, 'United . . . United. . . United.'

As soon as that had finished I put 'We are the Champions' back on, followed by the cassette recording of the radio commentary describing the moment United won the Championship, then 'If the Kids Are United' again. This carried on until it was pub-opening time.

A funny thing in the pub that night: there were people who I had known for years wearing Manchester United t-shirts, and I never even knew that they supported United.

United were to be presented with the Premier League trophy after the final home game of the season against Blackburn the following night. The pressure was off now, we could party.

We knew the atmosphere was going to be special that night, but as we approached Old Trafford we began to realize it was going to be extra special. Red, white and black waves of United supporters were heading towards the stadium, carrying flags, banners, scarves and drums.

Ed and me went to the off-licence for a few cans of lager, then each bought a Manchester United Champions flag and joined the thousands of flag-waving, singing United supporters on the grass bank across from Old Trafford. One United fan had celebrated a bit too much and had fallen off the bridge over the railway line at the side of Old Trafford, landing on the tracks below. The fire brigade were lifting him to safety.

I held on tightly to my season ticket in my pocket. I wasn't going to have ruined one of the best nights of my life by having it pinched and not being able to get inside the stadium.

Unless you are a United supporter and unless you were inside Old Trafford that night, you could never imagine how great the atmosphere was. You had to experience it (sections of the new Stretford End were now open). I think the players were enjoying it a bit too much as well.

Blackburn went 1-0 ahead to turn down the volume slightly, but thirteen minutes later, up stepped Giggs with his party piece, firing in a stunning, curling, twenty-five-yard free-kick into the top corner. Party on.

Except for a few hundred Blackburn fans the whole crowd was singing. All around the stadium thousands of flags were being waved; red, white and black scarves were held aloft: 'We'll never die . . . We'll never die . . . We'll keep the Red flag flying high . . .'

I wondered what the feelings of Sir Matt Busby were, sat up in the stands. Paul Ince and Gary Pallister scored two second-half goals and United won 3-1. After the final whistle Bryan Robson and Steve Bruce jointly held aloft the Premier League trophy.

The special moment of the night for me was when the team, on a lap of honour with the trophy, came in front of the Scoreboard Paddock, where I stood, just as the supporters began a roof-raising rendition of 'Glory, Glory, Man United'. I'll never forget that, never forget that, never forget that.

On the journey home that night, I turned to Ed. 'That's it, then. I can get on with the rest of my life now,' I said.

One ambition remained to be fulfilled with United, though: seeing them play in an FA Cup Final at Wembley.

There was still one United game to attend that season. Thousands of United supporters (myself and my mates included) had bought tickets for Wimbledon away on the last day of the season, thinking the Championship would go to the final match.

A road runs up a hill at the side of Selhurst Park. At the top of this hill, thousands of United fans had gathered, celebrating the Championship. Myself and Rob stood on a wall, sharing a spliff and sampling a few cans of lager. Back down the road as far as you could see flowed a red river of United fans, we must have stood there for forty minutes and in that time the broad line of United fans coming up the road was unbroken. All decked out in red, white and black, with flags flying. They looked like some medieval army marching triumphantly back from a battle, singing songs of victory.

We had tickets standing on the huge terracing behind one net. Inside the stadium it was like days of old, the terracing was packed. I couldn't be bothered to push my way through the crowd to get a decent view, so I ended up climbing up the side of a floodlight pylon. I stayed there until my arms ached, then went and joined other United supporters on top of a refreshment hut at the top of the terracing, until police made us get down.

Wimbledon's Vinny Jones tried his best to find out if there were any Wimbledon supporters in the ground by shaking his clenched fist before kick-off, then afflicting GBH on Paul Ince as the game got underway. In the second half, Giggs introduced himself to Jones, dribbling the ball past him, leaving Jones on his backside. United won the game 2-1, with goals from Ince and Robson. The team was supposed to do another lap of honour at the end of the match for those fans who didn't have a ticket for the Blackburn game, but overeager cockney reds kept invading the pitch, so the lap of honour was cancelled. I didn't mind, I'd had my night of glory the week before.

Even Better than the Real Thing

The opening day of the 93-94 season found me in Leeds, and the lovely supporters of the team of that fine Yorkshire city buying me a pint. I'd left my mates in Roundhay Park to go to the nearest pub to get a beer in, and here was one gifted to me from the most unlikely of sources. I'd asked them for the football results and had a quick chat about the beautiful game; they seem to take to me, hence the Carling in my hand. Yorkshire people tight? Nonsense. But I did feel a bit guilty.

'Maybe I should be the one getting you lot a round in, as a thank you for gifting us Cantona,' I told them, pissed and merry, after an afternoon of drinking.

Their demeanour towards the little upstart immediately changed, Harry Enfield's George Whitebread disgust and scowls on their faces. 'Can't believe we've been talking to scum.'

'And bought him a pint! Cheeky cunt.'

We'd just watched Stereo MC's on stage, 'to the left, to the right,' I weaved through the crowd and was out of there.

Now for the big event in Roundhay Park, 'the greatest show on earth,' U2's *Zoo TV* tour. A multimedia extravaganza (ironic that a group that care so much for the state of the planet should use enough electricity to light up a city); life-affirming anthems, Bono full of swagger, the greatest rock star on earth at the time. A fantastic night of live theatre. For me, though, the greatest show on earth was about to take place in the Theatre of Dreams that season; raise the curtain, raise the roof. First up the ring master, Cantona, with just as much swagger, charisma and rock star appeal as Bono. Looking like a tough bastard brother of Elvis: turned up collar, army haircut quiff, pot on his arm. A Red rebel with a cause. Stepping off his throne, in the United Hall of Fame, to fire a thunderbolt into the top corner of Arsenal's net; another magical moment to ensure immortality.

The whole team in sublime form nearly all season long (apart from in the European Cup were the anti-English club three foreigner rule - including Welsh, Scots and Irish - meant the team couldn't turn out in that competition). Robson playing his farewell games, stepping aside for Keane to fittingly fill his boots; a new midfield, die-hard, powerhouse. Alongside Keane the rampaging Ince. Three young fast paced wingers – Giggs, Kanchelskis and Sharpe – almost unstoppable. The swashbuckling Mark Hughes linking up brilliantly with Cantona. The loyal McClair coming off the bench to give his all. A solid settled defence – Bruce, Pallister, Parker and Irwin, the last two as good as wing-backs. Behind these Schmeichel, the best goalkeeper in the world, and as good as a quarterback in his distribution of the ball.

The beautiful game as beautiful as I've ever seen played in the English league, Red poetry in motion. Watched from the terraces (in the East Stand Lower, the new Stretford End was an all-seater) for the last time. Without doubt my favourite ever season watching United, with hindsight. I couldn't get enough of it, in fact I couldn't get enough of football in general this season, perhaps I had an instinct that the old game would never be the same again?

Even though I was going to every United home game and as many away games as possible, I still couldn't turn down the invitation to go to other football matches. A Forest supporter friend of mine asked me if I wanted to go to a match with him; someone else asked me to go and see Mansfield Town with them, another to Derby County. I told them all I would go if United weren't playing. Ed couldn't understand.

'I thought you were a Man United supporter,' he said.

'I am,' I replied.

'So why are you going to see Forest and Mansfield?

'It's football. I need it.'

I told him about my passion for football and about my Sundays. I would get up with a hangover at 11 a.m. and watch a video recording of the previous night's *Match of the Day*. At 12 p.m. I'd turn on Sky Sports' *Goals on Sunday* and watch that for a few hours until Italian football came on Channel 4. From then on I'd flick between channels to see the regional match on ITV. I'd watch these matches until the big Premier League game started on Sky, before again watching a re-run of Saturday's goals on Sky to finish my football-watching marathon at 7 p.m.

'You need help; your going to OD if you're not careful,' he said.

Ed began to give me counselling: 'Man United should be enough. You don't need to go and watch other clubs; you'll have to try something else to reduce your excessive intake of football.'

'Like what?'

'What about alcohol? On Sundays, why don't you come down the pub and have a drink with your mates?'

'There's a telly in the pub; I'll just turn that on, get drunk and watch football.'

'Well, there's a pool table in the other room. Go and have a game on that.'

'But the set of pool balls are red and yellow. I'll only want to win if I'm red; if I break off and pot a yellow first I'd deliberately lose,' I explained.

223

'What about trying drugs to get you off football?'

'I took some magic mushrooms once, but I just started imagining I was playing football on Mars with a load of Clingons.'

'What about sex?'

'She has to be a football fan, but I keep having this recurring nightmare where I'm with this beautiful woman. I get her back to my place, she starts getting undressed only to reveal that she has a tattoo of Jimmy Hill's face on one tit, and "Leeds United - Champions 1992" on the other. It's a right turn off.'

I've no regrets, though. My football addiction had led me to actually be there, to witness just about everything there was to see in late 20th century English club football: the league won in every division, League Cup finals, a Simod Cup final, the Freight Rover Trophy final, great players, great goals, hooligan battles. Regrets I have a few: the darkest day in football history, the last days of the terracing. One big occasion alluded me however, in those days the biggest game in English football, as it had been ever since the days Lord Kinnaird did battle with Royal Engineers in Victorian England, loved the world over ever since, the FA Cup final.

January 1st 1994:

Somebody in their wisdom decided that Man United v Leeds should kick-off at 1 p.m. on New Year's Day. I knew I would still be over the drink-driving limit on New Year's Day morning, so I had booked a taxi to take me to the nearby town of Kirkby-in-Ashfield in order to catch the United supporters' bus from there.

I was still out partying at 4 a.m. When the taxi picked me up at 7 a.m. I was still well pissed up. It was a freezing cold morning, but being drunk I didn't notice, and left the house without my coat and scarf. I'm surprised I remembered my season ticket and money.

On the bus I fell into a drunken slumber. I woke about an hour later, as we were crossing the Derbyshire Peak District. The pleasant effects of alcohol had now been replaced by the 'I'm never going to drink again' effects. I had pains in my stomach, felt sick, had blurred vision, and it felt like there was a woodpecker inside my head. I was shivering from the cold; I started looking for my coat and scarf before realizing I'd left them at home. I thought I knew what was needed. Hair of the dog. I'll get a few more pints down me; that'll make me feel better.

We were in the Gorse Hill, a pub not far from Old Trafford, our usual place for pre-match drinks. I took a few sips of lager and then rushed to the toilets and threw my guts up. I came back from the toilet and tried again to have a drink, but my body was having none of it. We just sat in the pub like zombies, no one speaking until it was time to go to the stadium.

United versus Leeds; the atmosphere for this game is usually electric, but it was Old Trafford unplugged that day.

A group of hangover-free young lads starred chanting, 'United,' and thousands of bloodshot eyes turned in their direction, their owners thinking, Oh God, we haven't got to sing, have we?

But we had, and a lacklustre version of 'Alex Ferguson's Red and White Army' began and quickly faded away. There was just a wee bit of suspicion that both sets of players had been celebrating the New Year as well. The game was a boring 0-0 draw, with hardly a shot on goal. Shivering with cold, suffering from alcohol poisoning, and watching a drab game, I wished I'd stayed in bed. But you have to make these sacrifices, and it was something that us football supporters were going to have to get used to. The last words of Duncan Edwards had been to ask Jimmy Murphy: 'What time is the kick off for the next match?'

'Usual time, three o'clock,' had been the reassuring whispered reply, as if to comfort Edwards that all was well and as it should be in his world. For over a hundred years it had been a sacred time for football fans, set in a stone dial, until smashed by TV contracts. Us loyal supporters were no longer the chief source of income, we have to obey an overseas media mogul's schedule, forget tradition and our views. During one of my last seasons as a Stretford Ender, as a season ticket holder, United didn't play a game at three o'clock on a Saturday, at all, from about mid October to February.

Busby R.I.P.

January 1994. United were fifteen points clear at the top of the League, playing exciting, attacking football. And although United had been knocked out of the European Cup in the 'hell' of Galatasaray's Ali Sami Yen Stadium, they were off on two more domestic Cup runs.

Driving home one Thursday night, I heard the news on the car radio. Sir Matt Busby had died, aged 84. The following Saturday, United were at home to Everton, it was one of the most moving occasions I've ever experienced.

After the news had broken of Busby's death, floral tributes began to build up in front of the Munich disaster memorial at Old Trafford. On the Saturday before the game against Everton there was a reverential hush among the supporters outside the ground. By now the tributes placed on the ground to Sir Matt covered a huge rectangular area, cordoned off by metal barriers, with a clear path running down the middle to the doors of the Sir Matt Busby Executive Suite.

Ed and me bought flowers and placed them with the rest. There was more than flowers, though; supporters had given up their treasured United mementoes - old scarves, autographed footballs, photographs and programmes - to pay their respects to the great man.

It wasn't just United supporters; there were also tributes from Man City, Liverpool and a host of other clubs' supporters.

We walked up the steps at the side of the Munich memorial to look down on the scene below. There were now thousands of United supporters around the metal barriers protecting the temporary shrine; so many that not everyone who wanted to could get to the front of the crowd.

It started with just a few supporters at the back, but then thousands of United fans began removing their lucky old scarves and throwing them into the area of Busby tributes. It was like a torrent of red, white and black scarves was falling from the sky. I wished I'd brought mine with me.

Inside the stadium ten minutes before the kick-off, the DJ gave the announcement to confirm there would be a minute's silence. Everyone mistakenly thought that this was the cue to start the minute's silence, so for five minutes (before the players came out) all 44,750 supporters - Everton fans, to their credit, included - stayed totally quiet. Then a lone Scottish piper led the players out. For another two minutes, as the players and ex-players stood along the centre-circle, not a sound was heard from the crowd until the ref blew his whistle and the ground erupted with the chant of, 'Busby! Busby! Busby!'

You had to feel sorry for the Everton players and fans. Everyone knew United would turn on the style and win the game, and turn on the Busby style they did. If it hadn't been for the Everton goalkeeper Neville Southall and a bit of bad luck United could have won 6 or 7-0. Cantona hit a post; Kanchelskis hit the bar; Giggs scored the only goal of the game with a header. There was one piece of breathtaking brilliance from Giggs: he collected the ball on the halfway line then, reminiscent of George Best's famous goal against Sheffield United, set off on a mesmerizing run past several Everton players, but just couldn't find the finish in the area.

The ghost of Busby up in the stand would have enjoyed that.

Hardly anyone spoke on the journey home after the game that night.

Blues Run the Game

Mid-March 1994. United were clear at the top of the League, had reached the Final of the Coca-Cola Cup and were in the semi-final of the FA Cup. There was talk of winning an unprecedented Treble; certainly, with the football they had been playing, everyone had a belief they could pull it off.

Sheffield Wednesday had just been humiliated 5-0 at Old Trafford in the League, with United producing one of the best performances of the season; every goal was a stunner. I remember it being a bitterly cold night. A blizzard swept around Old Trafford as United stormed into a 4-0 half-time lead. I was wearing three t-shirts, a jumper, a scarf

228

and jacket, and was still cold. I looked over towards the Sheffield Wednesday fans, and there sat Tango Man, bare chested.

'Tango, what's the score....Tango, Tango, what's the score?' chanted the United supporters.

Tango Man got up out of his seat and started slapping his bare belly to the applause of the United supporters.

The Coca-Cola League Cup Final. Villa beat United 3-1; the Treble dream was over. United, as a team, never turned up that day, but Mark Hughes scored his second Wembley goal of the season.

The following Tuesday I walked into a chemist in the nearby town of Eastwood, wearing a United shirt. A woman sat with her little lad, waiting for a prescription.

'Aye-up, a Man United supporter. What's he come in for: some anti-depressants? she said loudly to her son.

'We'll still win the Double,' I said confidently, and with a smile on my face.

A few weeks later, sat in the stands at Wembley, my confidence was crushed. With just a few minutes of extra-time remaining Untied trailed 0-1 to Oldham in the semi-final of the FA Cup. The season looked like falling apart for United: they'd lost in the League Cup Final; Blackburn were putting on the pressure in the League; and now they were just a minute away from going out of the FA Cup.

All the years of false promises and disappointments of not getting a Cup Final ticket came back to haunt me. I was a season-ticket holder now; I'd not missed a home game all season, I would be guaranteed a ticket if they reached the Final. But now, with just a minute left, my dream was slipping away....

In these moments I felt utter despondency, was this the final nail in the coffin of a lousy week? The two great passions in my life, music and football, the two great escapes I could turn to, get lost in, find myself in, look forward to when I felt lonely and my life meant nothing at all. Jump up on and be inspired by an inspiral magic carpet or Spiritualized or be spellbound by wizard Cantona and his magic ball of tricks on a green carpet. The rush of euphoria when the ball hit the back of the net against the bitter blues and your biting blues vaporized by an atomic endorphin bomb crowd explosion.

Those sublime Saturdays when I was driving to Old Trafford and my main music dealer, John Peel (via an as yet unheard C90 cassette recording of one of his recent shows in my car stereo) delivered a new music drug: like I'll never forget the time he first played PJ Harvey's 'Dress' single. I was so stunned by it that I'd didn't notice the traffic lights had turned to green - and the honk of car horns - in Didsbury, Manchester, as I was desperately rewinding the tape to hear it again. It firing me up with even more adrenalin before United's match against Liverpool. Always on my stereo at this time, the Red Devil blood pumping sound of the season, Leftfield and Lydon 'Open Up,' the 8.30 minute version, followed by the 'Dervish Overdrive' 13 minute mix. Then driving back from a United victory with new records - vinyl and now CD's - on the passenger seat. Listening to these before going out for the night, feeling on top of the world. If United won and there was a live gig to go to the same weekend I'd be on cloud 9, or 10, 7 or 11 (depending which United star scored) for days. Even if United lost (which they rarely did this season) I could find Nirvana, turn them up to 11 to exorcise my Red Devil

230

demons and recharge my batteries before going out, *Nevermind* – 'Come As You Are', another match will be along soon, go out and get pissed.

This week, however, in the space of five days, music and football were ripping out my soul, I felt, momentarily. Isn't it strange the things that pop into your head at these moments: a track I'd heard - and been moved by - on a late night radio show a few nights previous, 'Blues Run the Game' sung by Nick Drake. I shook my head and gave one of those dark huh huh laughs at the ironic title of the song. Yes the blues are running the fuckin' game are out there, then felt sad again at the lyric's meaning and another one who'd suffered heartbreak end game blues.

Sat there at this moment, a cold April day, I shivered in the shadow of the Wembley roof. Five days earlier my blood had gone cold, in the shadow of death: Kurt Cobain had committed suicide, chose to burn out rather than fade away, joined the legendary 27 Club, or what his mother called 'the idiot club.'

Cobain was one of the few 'rock stars' whose interviews I read and thought his words and views had actual substance to them. He was near my age. I felt I shared – and could relate to – his outlook on life, his sensitivity, isolation, not wanting to join the rat race or flow with the mainstream. Yet he still felt the need to bare his soul with a guttural rebel yell that could be heard by the masses.

Nirvana's music and Cobain's lyrics definitely spoke to me and thousands like me; outsiders in our milieu. Until millions tuned in who didn't care what it was all about, the riffs sounded good, 'it rocks man!' And Cobain no longer cared. The hype and heroin had sucked out his soul, nothing mattered anymore, not even the love of - and for - his wife and baby.

I came in from Woody's club that night and sat up into the early hours, watching the news reports, the history, the videos, the broken hearted fans, on *MTV*. For the first few hours Dad had stayed up past his usual bedtime to watch it all too. Until he realised I was giving him a freezing cold shoulder and didn't want him there. He didn't like Nirvana's music, Kurt Cobain meant nothing to him. I'd say it wasn't morbid curiosity on Dad's part, he was actually trying to understand it, how I was feeling, and empathise. But this was something I wanted to watch and get my head around on my own, so ignored his questions.

I know you can't compare the death of a rock icon to a football team losing a match in the bigger picture, but United were playing on in the memory of the recently departed Sir Matt Busby; to achieve something his Busby Babes never did, but surely would have - and much more - if circumstances had been different, The Double. For a man who almost lost his life following a United dream, most of his young team did of course, then gave the rest of his life to United to honour their memory; there'd never be a final curtain at the Theatre of Dreams.

But this was personal too, United were playing for me, just for me. Forget the thousands of Red's in the stadium and millions watching worldwide. They had to win, for me, I had to have at least a few dreams come true in my life; seeing United in an FA Cup Final was high up on the wish list.

I looked at my watch, there's time yet, this is UNITED. We NEVER give up, 'we keep the Red flag flying high because Man United will NEVER die'.....

Don't you always have to get an annoying bastard sat behind you now that the stadiums are all-seaters?

'Oh, poor lads. They're tired. Blow the whistle and let them get off the pitch,' said a woman behind us.

Brian McClair flicked the ball overhead into Oldham's penalty box and there was (who else) Mark Hughes, leaning back to magnificently volley into the corner of Oldham's net . . . Dream on. Me and Ed went crazy. Ed went a bit too crazy, ripping my jacket.

'Oh, poor lads. They're tired. Blow the whistle and let them get off the pitch,' we both said loudly.

The ref blew the final whistle.

The replay took place at Maine Road the following Wednesday. We'd got standing tickets for the Kippax Stand. As we approached the stadium there was no police cordon checking to see if supporters had tickets for the game.

Oldham were swept aside by a United side firing on all cylinders. Bryan Robson was back in midfield to give one last great performance for United before becoming manager at Middlesbrough. Mark Hughes, probably having his finest season in a glittering career with United, was in top form. Everyone knows about his volleys, but I've seen no finer player who can drop deep, control and hold the ball up and then spread it out to the wings. The main recipient of Hughes's passes that night was Kanchelskis, who gave one of the best individual performances I've witnessed, ripping the Oldham defence to shreds. Kanchelskis hadn't signed a new contract for United, and there were rumours he would be leaving in the summer.

'Andrei must stay . . . Andrei must stay,' chanted the United fans.

The ever-reliable Denis Irwin scored a great first goal, playing a one-two with Robson before volleying into the net. Kanchelskis scored a stunning solo goal for the second, weaving his way past defenders on the edge of the box, before turning and firing in a shot from twenty yards that flew into the top corner.

Oldham made a brave fight back, scoring a goal six minutes before half-time, but second-half goals from Robson and Giggs finished them off.

Who'd have thought I'd experience the best atmosphere and watch the best football of the season on City's Kippax. It was also a couple of extremely bitter blues brothers that had re-ignited my passion for music: like Nirvana before them, new Manc band Oasis mixed elements of The Beatles and the Sex Pistols. They'd just released their debut single, 'Supersonic.' I was feeling it, I believed, especially when I later heard 'Live Forever.'

United and me were heading for Wembley, and in this form I was sure United would be playing in the Cup Final for the Double.

Cup Final '94: The Best Week Ever

I thought my best days had left
My best years had left me behind
Then I watched them come back
Then I watched them come back to me
        'Already There' – The Verve

In the League run-in United had consecutive wins against Man City, Leeds, Ipswich and Southampton. Nearest rivals Blackburn lost at Coventry and United were Champions for the second year running. We still had one home game remaining, which now (as with the previous year) could be used as a celebration party. I was there, on the Sunday at Old Trafford with my mates, pissed and happy, watching United crowned Champions. Then, just six days later, I was....

Cup Final afternoon. Dad and Benny Hill were sat on the settee. Refreshments were sorted; Dad with his bottles of brown ale, a pork pie, and cheese and pickle sandwiches; Benny Hill with a bowl of water and three Boneos. The armchair that I'd ended up sitting in to watch every Cup Final since 1976 (well, not exactly the same armchair; Mam and Dad had changed their three-piece suite a few times over the years) was empty. I was sat on a United supporters' coach a few miles from Wembley, transfixed by my FA Cup Final ticket. I'd been staring at it in the same hypnotic gaze for the last two hours on the journey down from Nottinghamshire.

Ed sat at the side of me and had hardly been able to get a word out of me. I was too busy thinking back over the years . . . back to 1976 when I thought Gordon Hill was my cousin and would pick me up in his sports car and drive me to Wembley. All the disappointments, the false promises, the lies . . . now, after eighteen years of trying, I actually had a Cup Final ticket.

It had been so easy to get, as well. I'd not missed a home game all season, I had a bit of money in the bank, and I was a member of the United supporters' club in Mansfield. All I did was hand over my token sheet to Peggy (who runs the club) and she sorted it all out for me.

But what if, after all these years, the Cup Final turned out to be a massive anticlimax. The prospect of United losing to Chelsea didn't bear thinking about.

235

I'd brought my lucky 1977 Cup Winners' scarf with me, of course. And as we walked down Wembley Way enjoying the pre-match atmosphere, rain started to fall from grey skies. I thought this a good omen for United. It was like many a Saturday afternoon in Manchester.

There's something I've noticed over the years: whichever set of supporters are more up for the occasion before a big match, their team always seems to win. I could feel the confidence among the United supporters that day, and it filled me with optimism.

A few months earlier before the Coca-Cola Cup Final, the United supporters seemed lacklustre compared with their usual support, and were out-sung by Villa fans. It's as if football supporters have a collective sixth sense about the outcome of a match.

Inside the stadium the United supporters were in great pre-match singing mood; thousands had gathered in the corridor underneath the stands. Hanging from the top of the corridor that runs all the way around Wembley, hung banners representing all ninety-two Football League clubs, each printed with a badge. I think the Wembley officials must have deliberately hung a Man City banner in United's half of the stadium, just for our amusement.

A youth scaled a wall at the side of the corridor, then edged along an iron girder to reach the banner. He then began tearing a hole in the Man City badge before dropping off the girder into the cheering United supporters below, bringing down a large section of the banner with him.

'City is our name; City is our name - eighteen years and won fuck all - City is our name,' chanted the United supporters. As I soaked up the atmosphere, a feeling of exhilaration swept through me.

'This is it, this is what it's all about,' I said to Rob. Everything was falling perfectly into place for me to have the greatest football-supporting day of my life.

'No, no, no....yuh had enough time to tek lace out on it...wing...Giggsy's free on yuh left....pass it....gi'e it him....tek him on,' I shouted, venting my frustration.

It was midway through the first half and United were being out-played, out-battled and out-thought. As in the League Cup Final and the first match against Oldham in the semi-final at Wembley, the seemingly unstoppable United express had come off the rails. This time, though, we were up against a team that had beaten us twice in the League. A poor clearance by Pallister fell to Gavin Peacock at the edge of the area, who then let fly with a left-foot volley that dipped over Schmeichel and thudded against the crossbar. Me and Rob lowered our heads dejectedly. I could imagine my Dad back home turning to Benny Hill and saying, 'Our Tony's waited eighteen years to watch this crap.' And the dog barking in agreement.

'I feel sick,' I told Rob. And fifteen minutes before half-time I left my seat and went down beneath the stands. Chelsea weren't reading the script - this was supposed to be mine and United's day. I walked down the corridor a short distance, then went over to an opening in the outer wall at the top of some steps to get some fresh air. Outside the stadium groups of ticketless fans drifted through the pouring rain. A man sat under the shelter of a tree, listening to a transistor radio. A few yards away, what I guessed to be his young lad stood out in the open, unconcerned at getting wet. He had a red scarf wrapped around his neck, his hands were thrust deep into the pockets of his jeans and, glum-faced, he was staring straight up at me. I felt like I knew him so well.

Ten minutes into the second half and the game still goalless, I decided divine intervention was needed. Tightly grasping my lucky 1977 Cup Winners' scarf I closed my eyes and prayed to Sir Matt Busby. Several minutes later Giggs (at last) showed some of his usual form, going on a mazey run to the edge of the Chelsea penalty area before toe-poking the ball to the advancing Irwin, who was upended by a late tackle from Eddie Newton. An ice-cool Cantona slotted home the penalty, sending Kharine the wrong way.

Nine minutes later, any doubts I'd had about the outcome of the match seemed like a distant memory as United, now 3-0 ahead, had the Cup and Double won. The second goal had also come from the penalty spot after Kanchelskis had been bundled over by Frank Sinclair just inside the eighteen yard box. Again Cantona strode up to outwit Kharine.

Minutes later, with me and Rob still out of our seats celebrating, 'Wembley warrior' Mark Hughes capitalized on a slip from Sinclair to fire home United's third.

Although I'd made a conscious decision to remember as much of the day as possible (keeping myself down to a couple of pints before the match) most of the last twenty minutes of the game is now just a joyous blur.

In the last minute Paul Ince (with a chance to score himself) unselfishly pulled back for Brian McClair to side-foot home United's fourth goal. The ref blew the final whistle. Steve Bruce lifted the Cup and the players went on the lap of honour. The last player to leave the pitch that day was Eric Cantona, carrying the FA Cup. Before he disappeared down the tunnel he stopped and lifted the trophy to the cheering United fans in the stands above him. I like to think he did this for my benefit and that he was saying, 'Here you are, Tony, this is for you - you deserve it.'

Losing My Religion

In the summer of 1994 I made another visit to the Man United museum at Old Trafford. The FA Cup and Premier League trophy were on display inside a glass cabinet. As I stood looking at the trophies, two Mancunian kids were arguing at the side of me.

'They're not the real trophies, they're just copies,' said the first Manc kid.

'Don't be daft...course they're the real trophies,' responded Manc kid 2.

'They're not.'

'They are...I'll bet you a tenner.'

'They're not....they wouldn't put the real trophies in here 'cos all you'd have to do was smash the glass and you could just walk away with 'em.' Manc kid 1 seemed to win the argument.

How was the new season going to live up to the last: win the European Cup? Do the Double again?

In truth, I was becoming a bit disillusioned with the Old Trafford experience; it was becoming something like a trip to a theme park, a family day out. Take the wife, take the kids, take Gran, take a month's wages, take out a loan. A visit to Old Trafford these days will cost you a fortune. If you're not lucky enough to possess a season ticket (you can put your name on a waiting list, and your great-great-grandson could receive one in the year 2126) or get tickets from official sources, then you can expect to have to pay five times over face value from a tout. I'd actually seen a new breed of tout down in the plush new bars of Salford Quays willing to accept a cheque from a parent of a middle-class family.

So you've purchased the tickets. Great, you're in. But don't be in a rush to put away that wallet; keep your Goldcard handy. Next the kids will drag you to the Megastore and refuse to come out until you've bought them the new kit, a signed picture of Ryan Giggs, or anything else that takes their fancy from the multitude of souvenirs emblazoned with United's colours and badge. These include: mugs, scarves, teddy bears, watches, hats, curtains, wallpaper, pencil sharpeners, duvet covers and table lamps. And why not treat Gran to a pair of carpet slippers and a set of musical heated rollers that play the *Match of the Day* tune.

I thought my mate (I won't name him to save him embarrassment) was losing it when, in a mad spree, he bought a United wallet, book, video, signed painting and two watches, all in one day.

'You've already got a watch. What are you going to do with the other two? Wear one on each ankle? Or strap them to the inside of your coat and sell them to tourists?' I asked him.

'Why didn't you stop me?' he replied.

You finally emerge from the Megastore laden down with bags full of United goodies and head into the stadium, where you might have just enough money left for a programme and some refreshments: Champs lager, Champs cola, Champs chocolate bar and Champs meat pie, etc.

For me Old Trafford was no longer the hotbed of passionate atmosphere it used to be. It pissed me off every time I looked across to the Stretford End, to the spot where I used to stand - now a £700-plus, season-club-class seat. So, OK, these seats generate huge income for the club, and there has to be a place for them; but why not in the Main Stand or some other area of the ground, not slap bang in the middle of what once used to be the heart of the Old Trafford atmosphere?

Many of the real loyal supporters were getting priced out. I thought about the two kids I'd seen arguing over the trophies in the summer, and wondered how often they got the chance to attend matches. Probably never. The club was showing little interest in accommodating young people from suburbs of Manchester. The PLC were turning their back on the descendants of the supporters who helped make the club great, in favour of the executives and bag people (daytrippers laden down with merchandise). Well, the PLC had better hope that the trophies don't dry up and the team drop to levels of mediocrity, because the glory hunters will soon lose interest. And then they might regret isolating the kind of supporter who would stick by the team through thick and thin.

By Christmas the European Cup dream was over; United had finished below Barcelona and Gothenburg in the Champions League, and failed to qualify for the later stages.

In January the infamous game at Crystal Palace took place, with Cantona kung fu kicking a bigot, resulting in him being suspended for the rest of the season.

The season was falling apart. Blackburn were starting to run away with the title.

Everybody Hurts

My thirtieth birthday was just months away and I was going through a late-twenties crisis. Even though I only looked about 19, the thought of being thirty filled me with dread: the end of my young life . . . the start of a slow downward slide towards old age . . . my dreams of becoming a professional footballer would finally be over, there would be no hope left of a passing United scout seeing me kick a tin can down the street and sticking his head out of his car window and shouting, 'Nice control, son. Come and play for us.'

What did I think was going to happen to me on my birthday? That I'd wake up in the morning, look in the mirror and discover I'd developed a beer gut and gone bald overnight? Would I suddenly start moaning about pop music being a tuneless noisy racket?

So when the pretty, curvaceous teenage girl I'd been chatting up in a local pub gave me her phone number with 'Call me any time' written underneath, it was just the boost my flagging ego needed.

I'd remained a dedicated bachelor; relationships scared me. I didn't want any commitments or responsibilities. When, in my early twenties, a girl whom I'd only been seeing for a few months mentioned the word engagement,' I was off: engagement! marriage! settle down with a wife and two kids . . .have to support them by doing a factory job I hated . . . no more regular trips to see United. Yeah, I know it's a selfish attitude, but I didn't want to lose my freedom.

A date was arranged, I'd take Tina to the cinema; not expecting two of her friends to tag along as well. The film we were going to see was *An Interview With A Vampire*. Tina rang me up half an hour before I was due to pick her and her friends up.

'A warning to yuh, Tony,' she said.

'What's that?'

'We're getting Gothed up for the film. We can do you as well, if you want?'

'Er, no. You're all right; been there and done that,' I replied.

Tina lived twenty yards from one of my local pubs. It was a Saturday afternoon and I knew many of my friends would be in there. I pipped my car horn and Tina and her friends emerged from her house. They were dressed head to toe in black; white make-up covered their faces. Shit! If any of my mates looked out of the pub window and saw this spectacle - me picking up three teenage Goths - I'd never live it down. I stuck a Siouxsie and the Banshees cassette in the car stereo and turned up the volume. This will impress them, I thought. I know me Goth music.

'Who's this?' asked one of the girls in the back seat.

'It's Siouxsie And The Banshees. You don't know who they are?'

'No. Haven't you got anything by The Offspring?'

Jesus! Now I did feel old; they were Goths and they didn't know Siouxsie Sioux was their queen. We'd got the times wrong for the showing of *An Interview With A Vampire* and went to see *Forest Gump* instead, sitting near the back of the half-full cinema. A woman two rows in front of us turned around, then fled in terror after seeing three ghostly faces peering at her out of the gloom.

Stupidly, I let myself fall in love with Tina, but, with the age gap, it was never going to go anywhere between us, and, anyway, she wanted a different boyfriend every two weeks. We remained 'friends', though, and would occasionally see each other.

I'd not missed a United home game for over three seasons, but Tina wanted me to take her out on a Saturday

243

when United were at home. She asked me if I wanted to take her to the cinema and then on to Rock City in Nottingham, where there was an 'alternative all-nighter'. United were only at home to Ipswich Town, and the most boring games of the last two seasons had been against Ipswich: 1-1 and 0-0. They always came to Old Trafford to defend. I can miss this one, I thought.

I wasn't picking Tina up until five o'clock, so I went for a couple of pints with my mates at dinner time. When I came in from the pub, I switched on the television to check the latest football scores on BBC's Ceefax service. They'd be into the second half by now.

'Manchester United 4 Ipswich Town 0.'

That's just typical, I thought. For the last two seasons the game's been a boring draw. I don't go and United are winning 4-0! I went into the kitchen to make a cup of tea, then walked back into the front room and looked at the TV screen.

'Manchester United 6 Ipswich Town 0.'

No, this can't be happening. I sat there drinking my tea staring at the Ceefax latest scores.

'Manchester United 7 Ipswich Town 0.'

I mouthed the word seven, but no sound came out. Minutes later the screen flashed and the score changed again.

'Manchester United 8 Ipswich Town 0.'

Then again.

'Manchester United 9 Ipswich Town 0.'

I was thinking, Please God, don't let them score ten; they can't score ten. United's record victory is 10-0, achieved by the Busby Babes against Anderlecht in the European Cup; their record League victory is 10-1, and that was over a hundred years ago, when United were called Newton Heath. I was convinced United were going to win 10- or even 11-0, and I'd be watching their record victory on Ceefax. The match ended 9-0. Andy Cole had scored five of the goals.

I picked Tina up in the car. As she was getting into it, I was banging my head on the steering wheel, muttering away like Dustin Hoffman in *Rain Man*, 'Nine-nil. I wasn't there. Cole five. Nine-nil. I wasn't there . . .'

She didn't understand. 'You're obsessed,' she said.

Hours later, sat in Rock City with Tina, things seemed a lot better. A spliff or two had eased my troubled mind. I was enjoying her company and I thought she was enjoying mine. But at the end of the night Tina had fallen for a 14 stone, 6ft 2 tall, thrash metal beast, his frantic digit dexterity air guitar display and flailing long oily black-haired mane on the dance floor. Where I didn't look good: in my old punk biking jacket and jerky moves that somehow mixed pogo with shoe-gazing. I did try thrash metal head-banging, but only succeeded in slightly head-butting Tina instead. She had arranged to go back to his flat in Nottingham. I even drove her there to make sure she arrived safely, I was worried about her, I'd overheard him say he had 'Anthrax.'

Six-thirty, Sunday morning. Driving back from Nottingham, the rain was beginning to fall. I'd missed United winning 9-0 and the girl I thought I loved was back in town being ravaged by a thrash metal monster. I was feeling slightly pissed off. I turned on the car radio for some music. The Boo Radleys were singing 'Wake up it's a beautiful morning.'

I turned it off and drove home in silence. When I got in I just wanted to go to bed and sleep until it was time for the pubs to open, when I could go and drown my sorrows.

I'd recorded the previous night's *Match of the Day* on the video. I thought I might as well watch United's goals before I went to bed. I sat there bleary eyed as United's sixth goal hit the back of the net. I was watching my team thrash the opposition, but seeing each goal was a painful experience.

My season ticket seat at Old Trafford was now situated in the East Stand, lower, just behind the top right-hand corner of one net, next to my mate Ed. Being sat behind the net I always looked to see myself on television when watching a recording of United's goals. But I never had.

As they showed United's eighth and ninth goals there was a close-up of the crowd behind the net. There, right in the middle of the screen, was Ed, deliriously celebrating. At the side of him was one sad empty seat, the only empty seat in the entire stand.

At the end of the highlights they interviewed Alex Ferguson. 'Those of us lucky enough to be here today have witnessed a once-in-a-lifetime performance,' said the United manager.

I turned off the telly and trudged upstairs to bed.

Cup Final '95: Wembley Nightmare

Fergie got his Cantona-less team sorted and United began to chase Blackburn in the League and set off on another Cup run.

United beat Crystal Palace in the FA Cup semi-final after a replay, to set up a Final against Everton. In the League Blackburn began to falter at the top, and United put the pressure on and drew ever closer. Suddenly United were in with a strong chance of winning a second consecutive Double.

The final day of the League season. If Blackburn were to lose away at Liverpool and United to win away at West Ham, then United would snatch the Championship at the death.

Liverpool - off all teams - did their bit by beating Blackburn, but despite United's pressure they couldn't find the back of the net against West Ham. Andy Cole came close in the final minute - if he'd have scored it would have been enough to win the title - but it wasn't to be.

Ah well, there was still the FA Cup. I handed over my token sheet to Peggy at the Mansfield branch of the supporters' club. Peggy and coach driver Norman always sorted out the tickets for the big games. I told her that I could afford only a cheap ticket for the Final. I wasn't bothered what seat I got as long as I was there.

I got a cheap seat all right - £10 it cost, and printed on the bottom it said: 'SEVERELY RESTRICTED VIEW.' Not restricted view, but 'SEVERELY RESTRICTED VIEW.

I wondered for hours what would be causing my 'SEVERELY RESTRICTED VIEW.' Behind some great big fat bloke, perhaps? Or stuck behind one of the giant scoreboards that hang from the Wembley roof?

Cup Final afternoon. Refreshments sorted; £3.70 for burger and chips.

Inside Wembley Stadium I discovered the severely restricted view was one of the bloody great columns that hold up the roof. I could see only half of one net. So English football's showpiece occasion, and I spent most of the match half in and half out of my seat, my body bent forward and my head on one side, so I could get a decent view of the pitch.

Good old Wembley Stadium, the biggest public toilet in the world. The whole place reeks of urine for a big Cup Final; that's because not everyone can fit in the crumbling old toilets before kick-off and half-time. It's the game of Wembley roulette, as you sit there in the stands with your bladder bursting during the game, thinking, Should I go to the toilet now and take a chance of missing a goal or a piece of exciting action, or wait till half-time and have to piss up against a wall (and you still have to queue to do that)?

Everton scored. United didn't. Everton won the Cup. That was that. Every football supporter from up t'North that's seen their team lose in a Cup Final knows the horrible long journey home up the motorway. First you've got to sit on the bus for ages, as it makes agonizingly slow progress along the tight road through the industrial estate around Wembley, all the time having the piss taken out of you by victorious opposing supporters on the coach that's at the side of yours.

All you want to do is get back to your local pub for a drink, but, of course, this is England, with the fucked-up licensing laws, so you keep anxiously looking at your watch, wondering if you are going to make it back for last orders.

After this Final we saw something to cheer us up as we walked out of Wembley Stadium: bus spotters. I couldn't believe my eyes. I didn't know they existed. There they stood in a group, excitedly jotting down the details of buses in little notebooks. Some were taking photographs, and one had a video camera.

'We've got to go and mingle with them for a while, to see if they're for real,' I said to Ed.

We started talking to a bus spotter called Norris, who looked like a dishevelled bank manager and said he was on some sort of mission. Norris took out a photo album from his briefcase and opened it to show us. On the two open pages were eight photographs, each the same, with Norris standing next to a Norris look-a-like in front of a bus. Norris pointed to each picture in turn.

'This is me and Ralph in front of a bus from Derby.'

'This is me and Ralph in front of a bus from Colchester?

'This is me and Ralph in front of a bus from Glasgow.'

'This is me and Ralph in front of a bus from Bristol.'

'Now this is a special one, this is me and Ralph in front of a bus from Italy.'

'You've had a good day, then, with all these buses?' I asked.

'Oh yes. Paradise - absolute paradise,' answered Norris.

Well, at least he'd had a good day.

The season over, United had won nowt. A year ago I'd seen them win the Double in the space of a week; this year I'd seen them lose the League Title and Cup in a week. The best game of the season had been United beating Ipswich 9-0, but, of course, I'd missed that. And Cantona would be banned well into the next season.

I was struggling to find the money to renew my season ticket and could expect a summer of having the mickey taken out of me for being a United supporter by local Forest and Derby fans. Time to climb back into my space capsule, headphones on, Portishead, *Dummy*, feeling like one, 'Sour Times' 'Numb' off on a 'Wandering Star' in blackness of darkness, hopefully not forever. 'It Could Be Sweet' again.

Therapy

No longer being a United mad kid or feeling like a teenager in love with them, not getting a kick out of the Old Trafford experience like I used to, longing for the old Stretford End, and an enforced trial separation anyway (I was having to loan out my season ticket for matches to pay the bills and keep the wolves from the door), disillusioned with what Fergie was doing with the team, all added to my depression.

Cantona was still suspended until October. Then three other of my favourite players left: Kanchelskis, Ince and Hughes (who is probably my favourite ever player in my time following United live).

The opening game of the season and United lost 1-3 to Aston Villa. Alan Hansen ripped into them on *MOTD*, Fergie was losing the plot he suggested, famously stating: 'You'll never win anything with kids.'

We can all laugh and mock Hansen now, with hindsight, but I'm putting my hand up here, I thought he had a point at the time. Whereas Giggs was already an outstanding talent, established as a great player, I didn't look upon the rest of 'Fergie's Fledglings' as worthy enough to be talked about in the same breath as the legendary Busby Babes. They'd been beaten by Leeds 4-1 (over 2 legs) in the Youth Cup Final. And I'd seen Gary Neville, Butt and Scholes (Beckham didn't even make the squad) play for the young England team in the European Under 18 Championships (I went to the final at Forest's City Ground), and none seemed outstanding. All of them appeared adept and good squad players but I honestly didn't see them – initially I say here – becoming legends of the game, develop into such great players and be part of a team as great as any United has ever seen.

This is why I'm a humble football fan and Alex Ferguson is a great manager, the genius creator of Red machines that can conquer the world. He spotted them as vital new components of power and ability at an early age; fine tuned them, until the moment came to engineer a new United team and fitted them seamlessly in.

*

It was all my own fault, the situation I was in. I'd never I wanted to settle down, join the rat race or be a stereotype. So where had this attitude got me by the age of thirty? Living in a flat above a shop, permanently overdrawn at the bank, feeling depressed, occasionally lonely, living on 10p cans of beans from Aldi (I would sometimes treat myself by splashing out on a 15p can of hot-dog sausages). By now I'd spent so many years unemployed that I'd graduated and become a Professor of Doleology. And in exchange for a few beers in a local pub, I would give advice to people who found them selves out of work for the first time.

I discovered a therapy for my depression: writing. And what did I write about? Well, the only things I knew: football, United, music, my life. I'd been reading D.H. Lawrence's *Sons and Lovers* for the first time since I was at school, and decided to go and take a female friend to look around his birthplace museum in Eastwood (just a few miles from Jacksdale).

There were a couple of American tourists in there. 'Gee this is so quaint,' one of them said, earnestly, as the guide showed us around. I couldn't see what all the fuss was about. To me it just resembled my grandparents' house in

251

Selston. That was an end terrace with a coal fire, an outside toilet, and pit paraphernalia dotted about. I told the Americans so, laying on the local accent as thickly as possible, showing off as I fancied my 'friend' really.

'Ey up, mi ducks, dus tha' know this jus' reminds mey o' mi granma and grandad's ouse when ah worra young un?'

'You're a local guy, right?'

'Aar.'

'You're a coal miner?'

'Oh aar. Ah was down pit when ah were ten.' (This was my chance to do a take on Monty Python's 'Four Yorkshiremen' sketch.)

'Ten!?'

'That's raight. Ah 'ad t'tek ponies down in t'mine. We ad a family pony that we kept in back garden: Billy Big Ears,' I said, wistfully, lowering my head. 'It worra sad day during t'strike, that we were that 'ard up we ad to av 'im in pot.'

'Oh my gahd,' the American gasped.

There were also several Norwegian tourists in there. One wearing a Manchester United shirt was listening to me intently. Dropping the pretence I began chatting to him. He was a big fan of Man United and English football and had visited Old Trafford. He listened enthralled as I told him about my football experiences. It was then that I decided to go home and write a book, like you do from my background!

Why not, though? I'd recently read Nick Hornby's *Fever Pitch*, a good book, but over hyped by the sophisticated press, and the new middle-class football fans it catered for. The light bulb blew inside my head as I dipped into

Hornby's stories, in my bedroom - aptly Pulp's *Different Class* album was spinning on my turntable, 'you want to live like Common People' - and I realised I'd seen far more momentous times in football than Hornby and my life was as entertaining too.

I called in at W.H. Smiths in town and bought a pack of English GCSE pass cards (priced £2.99) to brush up on my writing skills. It was a bit of a wrench parting with such a substantial sum of money. I could have bought two pints of lager or enough food from Aldi to keep me going for weeks.

At the back of a wardrobe in my old bedroom at Mam and Dad's house I found a box full of my old football programmes. And up on a shelf were the books from my childhood: *Knock-out, Whoopee, TV Comic* annuals 1973-76, *The Manchester United Story* by Derek Hodgson, *Shoot!* annuals, THE KEVIN KEEGAN ANNUAL, 1977! (which sadistic relative had given me that as a Christmas present?), and *The Topical Times Football Book*, 1976, which contained a cartoon strip called 'Mr Leather Lungs - his voice rescued his club from relegation'. It was about a supporter who's team needs to win their last game of the season to stay in the First Division. With the score still 0-0 and only ten minutes left to play, Mr Leather Lungs gets up out of his seat and incites the crowd to give vocal support. Sure enough his team - inspired by their fans - grab the winning goal. At the end of the match the victorious manager goes over and personally thanks Mr Leather Lungs for saving the day. Fine in 1976, but today Mr Leather Lungs would probably be arrested, ejected from the stadium, and have his season ticket confiscated. Consequently his team would be relegated.

As I flicked through the books and programmes, I could hear James, the young lad next door, in his bedroom, doing a commentary as he played a football game on his computer. The memories came flooding back. I picked up a pen, opened a pad and began to write.

I completed the first version of *If the Kids are United*, in handwriting. I can't type, and certainly didn't have access to a word processor or computer. The nearest I'd ever got to computers was playing space invaders on my Atari games console or failing on the Amiga. Soon I was getting better-than-expected feedback from friends who read my football stories. What was I to do next . . . try to get them published? This was all new to me. I still listened to the John Peel show on Radio 1. He's a passionate football fan and regularly had fanzines sent to him. He's a genuine person, so hoped he'd take a look and give me an honest opinion. So I packaged it up and sent it off to Broadcasting House, and waited for his response.

*

The results started to come for United. Yet a vital spark in the machine was still missing, Cantona, did he still have the fire? Would he be too fired up and blow up his career and United's hopes for the season?

In his first game back, fittingly against Liverpool, he answered his critics and doubters, and relit the fuse in United's title challenge and my passion.

A man possessed, foot down to the floor behind the wheel of Fergie's turbo charged juggernaut, driving everyone on, back to United utopia over the horizon, catching Newcastle in the race. Keegan was looking nervously over his shoulder and started to crack, his team's wheels came off, sending them crashing out.

*

It was the time to attend a Restart Course, a scheme to help the long-term unemployed get back to work. You were taught how to write letters, interview techniques, advised on the various training programmes available, and given one free cheese cob.

I'd been on a Restart many times before. It lasted a week. About ten unemployed people sat around a big table listening to the course leader, who this time was an ex-manager of a now closed factory that had mixed toxic chemicals.

'I know all about unemployment because I spent three months out of work myself before getting this job,' he informed us.

We were shown an out-of-date video of the wrong way to conduct yourself at a job interview. It showed a stereotypical punk circa 1983 (orange mohican, earrings, Sid Vicious t-shirt, ripped jeans) slumped in a chair mumbling incoherently to the questions being asked by an agitated interviewer.

'Now what was wrong with him?' said course leader.

'Yeah what was wrong with him?' I enquired.

'His appearance, his attitude, his body language, his unclear speech.'

'So what your saying is, if everyone dressed smart and spoke like a newsreader there'd be full employment and a smile on the face of society.'

'He'll never get a job looking like that,' he said.

255

'How do you know he's not some brilliant guitarist whose band are about to hit the big time?' I protested.

I filled in a c.v. then switched off and sat there writing some more of my book. The course leader interrupted my creative flow.

'Mr Hill.'

'Yes, course ceader?'

'On your c.v., under personal achievements, you've put, "Eating a curry when pissed without getting any on my clothes. Correctly filling in a community charge form first time. Getting through the express lane checkout at the supermarket with more than the eight items allowed." And then you've put "writing a book".'

'Yeah, I'm writing some new material right now.'

'It's going to get published, is it?' he said, scornfully.

'Who knows, maybe.'

He rolled his eyes to the ceiling, shook his head and then looked at everyone else in the room. 'There's going to be some interesting reports go back to the DSS about some people in here,' he said.

I'd needed some more writing paper, only course leader wouldn't give me any 'for personnel shenanigans.' But I knew where I could get some (it would have text on one side but I could use the blank back), the course leader's assistant: a large computer console that asked you questions; then told you what job you're suited for and printed out the relevant information on a piece of paper. Yeah, people no longer helped you sort out your future anymore, computers did.

It asked something like: 'Do you like working outdoors?' And you had a choice of answers: 'Oh yes please' or 'Like very much' or 'Don't know,' 'Dislike,' or 'Get the fuck out of here.' There was about fifty fuckin' questions, so I put 'Like very much' for every one. I.e. 'Would you like to be a Lumberjack?' – 'Yes, I've always wanted to be a Lumberjack.' The computer told me I was suited for over five hundred jobs and did I want the jobs printing out. I put – 'Yes and details'. It took the computer fifteen minutes to print it all out on a paper as long as an Andrex bog roll. I pulled it out so it stretched right across the office, singing: 'I'm a Lumberjack and I'm ok....' Course leader scowled at me over the top of his glasses.

Some pinheads had attempted to break into my flat. They'd failed, but I'd been tipped off they were going to try again. A few days later I was drinking in the Portland Pub, just thirty yards from my flat. Someone told me they'd seen a couple of youths hanging about outside my door. I left the pub to go and check everything was OK. British Telecom had just brought in the service where you dial 1471 to find out if anyone has rung while you were out. Someone had rung me, but I didn't recognize the code or number. I'll bet it's those thieving bastards ringing to see if I'm out, I thought. I rang the number. Someone answered. I'd had a few beers and was feeling on edge.

'Who's this?' I demanded to know.

'Have you dialled the right number, we're down here in Suffolk,' the somehow familiar male voice replied.

HAH! Suffolk, lying bastard. Is that the best excuse he can come up with now 1471 has caught him out? 'I've just got in and dialled 1471 and your phone number's on there,' I said.

'Oh, right. Who's speaking?'

Shit! I knew that voice. I'd been listening to it on Radio 1 for the last fifteen years. 'Er...that's John Peel, isn't it?' I spluttered. I felt such a twat. John Peel's been nice enough to ring me up about my book, and I'm pissed and paranoid. 'It's Tony Hill. I sent you some stuff I wrote about football.'

I sat there and listened in a bewildered drunken state as John Peel told me he'd enjoyed my book and gave me advice on what to do next. Like, to keep writing, and had I thought of contacting the United fanzines for help. I wasn't expecting this phone call and was struck dumb, not being able to think of anything to say.

'Well, I've got to go and walk the dogs now. Best of luck and stick with it,' he said, and was gone.

What a missed opportunity. John Peel would be up there in my top five list of people I would like to meet. And he'd just been on the other end of the phone line and I'd hardly said a word. He's been such a major influence on my musical tastes. I could fill pages with the names of great groups I first heard on his show (New Order, Echo and the Bunnymen, Nirvana, P J Harvey, Orbital, The Verve, etc.).

As soon as I put the phone down, I could think of loads of questions I could have asked him. Ah, well at least he'd given me the encouragement to keep writing.

*

By the time I saw Cantona's Exocet find the top corner of Arsenal's net to give us a vital win, I was getting a few decorating jobs and was also getting fit, playing football again: this with Westwood's own new fledglings, average age 19, the best set of players in the village since the days of the all-conquering Pye Hill Colliery team. I only joined in the 5-a-side training matches but I ran rings around them. Life in the old dog yet, and they started calling me 'twinkle toes' or 'Giggsy' (as I had on a United shirt and still had thick dark curly hair).

Now us back street amateur footballers enjoy and remember our best goals – be it just on the street as a kid or rec or only 5-a-side – nearly as much as our esteemed professional stars. I'd had a great 5-a-side match with the lads, scoring 2 class goals. For the first, I skipped past two challengers and curled the the ball round the keeper into the far corner – so good they applauded that one. Then for the second, turning past another challenge by throwing them a dummy and firing in a rocket from 15 yards, with my left foot! (I'm naturally right-footed, no bloody excuse that a professional can't use both I reckon). They were asking me to join the full Sunday morning 11-a-side team again. But, alas, I loved my Saturday days/nights going out and getting hammered too much (there's been many a truly great player from this village, who have had professional teams interested in them, but there downfall has been the local drinking culture they've been born and bred in to).

So I was full of myself when we went in a local pub after the match as usual. Newcastle had just beaten Leeds, Kevin Keegan was on the screen of the pub TV in the corner, giving his post-match interview. I could see his finger jabs, eyes wild but couldn't hear what he was saying. 'Turn it up,' I shouted. Then roared with laughter – 'I'd love it if we beat them, love it,' - Fergie had him.

Writing about United's 1977 Cup Final victory over Liverpool re-released that old strong feeling of being in love with United more than anything else in the book. Now here I was seeing history on repeat. It seemed to happen in slow-motion, rewinding my United life from kid to present day, flashing before my eyes, as Cantona connected with his destiny volley, past desperate Liverpool faces, bulging the back of the net, at Wembley, to seal the FA Cup for United. Their second Double and his, United's and my great comeback of 1995-96.

Inner-Village Life

When I'd not been having regular visits to see United and with little cash to go anywhere else, I'd turned to the myriad delights of Jacksdale for a social life. In other words I got pissed in the local pubs. These were the dens of iniquity. The Portland Arms, which used to be run by a South African and her cockney husband. Some of the punters took an interest in the literature of the BNP. On occasions there'd be a group of middle-aged musicians playing reggae and blues covers in the function room, competing with the sounds of the likes of Screwdriver performing at the skinhead bash upstairs. The Portland was the place to be Bank-holiday Mondays, which in Jacksdale is an excuse for an all day piss-up. After starting the day at other pubs in the village, many people would head to the Portland mid-afternoon. There, as the beer flowed, the tension would build, and I'd start taking bets on when the first fight would kick-off and who and what would cause it.

Two youths brawling over the same girl 2-1 fav.
Girlfight over the same boyfriend 3-1
Jacksdaliens v Selstoners 4-1
Jacksdaliens v Ironvillains (from the village of Ironville)
Jacksdaliens v Brinsley boot boys.
Man attacking another man for having an affair with his wife 7-1
Wife attacking husband for sneaking off to another part of the pub to chat up a younger female and trying to get her into the toilet for a quick shag 9-1
Skins v Bikers 9-1
Teenager who's had one shandy too many throwing up on the head of an older regular 11-1

260

Ironvillain trying to nick the laces out of someone's shoes 14-1
One man's dog fighting another man's dog 16-1
Some poor unsuspecting outsiders passing through the village and stopping off for a drink in what they thought was a nice country pub 25-1

From the Portland you go round the corner to the Social Club, a staunch Forest supporters' pub, infiltrated by the odd Derby County supporter. The Social Club is a drinking hole for more of your sensible Jacksdale born-and-bred regulars.

The sort of people you could set your clock by as they go to and from the pub at the same time every day. I'd look out of my flat window and, ah! there goes Irish Pete - it must be 12 p.m., time for dinner.

There's some great characters go in the Social, like Red Rum, so nicknamed because when pissed he recites the entire commentary from the 1977 Grand National, with the famous thoroughbred winning the race for a record third time. Some hopeless gamblers have been known to bet on a different outcome to the race.

Then there's my old mate Roger (one of the last of the Jacksdale cappers) with his dog Prince, which would sometimes escape from his master's grasp and get stuck up the bitch or dog (it's not fussy which) of another capper in the pub. There would be heated words between the two old fellas.

'If tha dunt get thee 'ound off, Is'll gie it some fist.' At which point Roger usually picks up his stick and starts knocking his poor mutt on the head with it, shouting, 'Gerr off, yuh dotty little bastard.'

Roger used to perform in the music halls, and if in the right mood will start a sing-a-long, covering everything from 'White Cliffs of Dover' to 'Sally' and, as James Cagney, 'Yankee Doodle Dandy'.

At the weekends there's live entertainment on at the Social, which is usually a pub singer who had either once appeared on *New Faces* or is going to appear on *Stars in Their Eyes*. Occasionally it's karaoke night, when it's guaranteed there'll be at least one Elvis impersonator and somebody will sing 'American Pie'. You can also get a late beer, hear the village gossip and indulge in a game of darts, dominoes or skittles. Fifty yards down the road from the Social is the Jacksdale Miners' Welfare, now, after the closure of the pits, imaginatively renamed the Dale Club. I'll regularly get a leaflet pushed through my letterbox, full of enticement:-

THE DALE CLUB
JACKSDALE
WHATS ON THIS WEEK
Monday - Prize BINGO
Tuesday - BINGO
Wednesday - Bar Night (come 'n' have some ale)
Thursday - Line Dancing (Beginners and competent classes -
YEE HA!)
Friday - BINGO with snowballs
Saturday - Entertainment and BINGO
Sunday - Dancing and BINGO

It was frowned upon if you went into the Welfare for a drink and you weren't a member. And you had to be very careful not to sit in a regular's seat. It's like with season tickets at United: they're passed down from generation to, generation, the same set of people have sat in the same seats for years. If someone had the audacity to park their bum on a regular's chair and refused to move, there'd be uproar. For such a heinous crime they could be summoned to appear before the committee and have their bingo book ripped up.

I preferred drinking in the Westwood end of the village, where there were three pubs in the space of 100 yards. First the Gate Inn, where occasionally its karaoke night and it's guaranteed there'll be at least one Elvis impersonator and somebody will sing 'American Pie'. You can get a late beer, hear the village gossip and indulge in a game of darts, dominoes or skittles.

On Sundays you can join the Westwood posse standing on the Gate Inn terrace in the tap side to watch the matches live on regional and Sky TV. The atmosphere is better than the Stretford End these days, with the Leighton brothers (Nigel, Stuart, and Phil) starting the chant of the Westwood anthem.

We like apple pie and we like Christmas pudding;
Watch out, watch out, watch out,
The Westwood Boys are coming

Many of the men in there play for one of the rival football teams in the village. In August, up on the rec, there's a pre- season (not so) friendly between the clubs. The night before the game players can be seen drinking into the early hours in order to ensure a hangover and be in the worst possible kick-ass mood for when they step on to the pitch. In 1998 the match lasted fifty minutes before being abandoned, after Dickie the goalkeeper raced sixty yards out of his goal to try to attack the referee, who'd failed to spot a handball before a goal was scored. The bemused match official (who had given up his Sunday morning to referee the match as a favour to one of the players) picked up the ball and marched off the pitch. Match over, friends again, the players went off for a drink together.

Forty yards up the road from the Gate Inn is the Royal Oak, the quiet pub, where occasionally it's karaoke night and it's guaranteed there'll be at least one Elvis impersonator and somebody will sing 'American Pie'. You can get a late I beer, hear the village gossip and indulge in a game of darts, dominoes, or skittles.

Another forty yards along Palmerston Street you come to the Corner Pin (my second home) run by Kath and Graham who sometimes sneaks out of his own pub to have a few whiskeys down at the Gate Inn or the Oak, returning an hour later, rat arsed, to face the wrath of his beloved.

'Where the bloody hell have you been?' Kath raged, one evening, hitting Graham over the head with the stiletto heel of her shoe. 'Get up them stairs to bed. You're in no fit state to run a pub.'

Graham went upstairs, opened a window, shinned down a drainpipe and staggered back for a drink at one his rival pubs.

There's no shortage of entertainment in the Pin. You can have a go on the meat raffle, play pool, watch OWL TV (Graham has set up a portable television in one room so people can observe the nocturnal birds in his aviary. I saw one's head move once). If you are feeling a bit peckish you can help yourself to the home-made pickled onions in a bowl on the bar, or sometimes a chestnut being roasted on the open fire.

Occasionally, it's karaoke night, when its guaranteed there'll be at least one Elvis impersonator and somebody will sing 'American Pie'. You can get a late beer, hear the village gossip and indulge in a game of darts, dominoes or skittles.

A Design for Life

My sister's ex-boyfriend Edward Barton came to the rescue with my season ticket, buying it off me for the 96-97 season. It kept it alive, in my name, and he kindly offered to let me go any game I liked (it would have been unfair and selfish on my part to cherry-pick these, so let Edward experience and go to any big match he wanted to...sort of).

I wish I could have gone with Edward, I enjoyed his company. Everyone did and this includes the likes of Mark Radcliffe - who described him as 'a general fantastic artistic person about town,' Tim Booth, Graham Massey and Shaun Ryder, as he's such a charismatic, creative, character. Apparently he caused quite a stir sat in East Lower at United: eccentric as ever, sometimes a strange hooded figure (for the duration of the match) looking around to reveal a Sir Patrick Moore vintage monocle covered eye. When his hood was down, it revealed a mop of unkempt ginger hair and long beard. I wasn't there to see what he was wearing but I guarantee it would have been something from a charity shop and not a sponsored megastore United shirt.

The wild ginger man of Chorlton, who saved a wild ginger and white collie dog, 'Osborne,' from a bad home in the back streets of Manchester. He took it everywhere with him (except to OT but would have sneaked the dog in if he had the chance). Even when Osborne went lame in his back legs Edward refused to give up on him, pushing him around in a 1970's pram. Edward would go jogging around the Mersey Valley area - at the back of Chorlton - composing songs in his head, then singing them aloud, Osborne on his shoulders. He was doing this late one night, when a potential mugger stepped out of the bushes about 50 yards ahead. Then on clapping eyes on a wild, ginger-haired and bearded urban caveman bearing down on him, giving a yodel scream, with a wild ginger dog on his head, he turned and legged it in terror.

My United mate Ed didn't know what to make of him at OT and his one-time uni mate Craig - a boring, square, in his Pringle cardigans, sensible side-parting and with a scouse accent that I could never warm to for a United fan - didn't like the 'weirdo' at all. Then Ed bought a book about MaDchester, *And God Created Manchester* by Sarah Champion - and excitedly showed it to me, then Craig, as Edward Barton had his own chapter in it. When I added that he used to play football with Ian Brown and co in a park in Chorlton too, they now looked at him in wonder, impressed, a lesser-known but brilliantly original and essential part of the MaDchester legend.

Funny how 'normal bloke' types like Craig can consider alternative characters 'weirdoes' until they find out they've had a brush with fame, then think they're 'cool.' The Manchester music scene has always been littered with them. None more so than Morrissey. I think it was Peter Hook who said he was the 'weirdo' in the club that everyone ignored until he suddenly appeared on stage with The Smiths and became one of the most 'coolest' cultural icons of our times. He's a one-time Stretford Ender too! Better to be weird than average Craig, you fickle scouse twat in Chickentown.

The first game of the 96-97 season that I told Edward I'd like to go to was the one against Forest in early September; I had to have the 'I was there,' piss-taking bragging rights in my local Notts pubs if United won.

266

I was shocked when I arrived in Manchester, a large area of the city centre was still in ruins: back in June the IRA had detonated the biggest ever bomb in peacetime UK there. The news had been shocking on the day and very worrying for our family. My sister, Elaine, was heading for the city centre that morning to catch the train from Oxford Road station to Nottingham to visit our parents. Similar to when the reports of the Hillsborough disaster began to filter through, no one knew if there were any casualties at first. In the event her taxi had been turned back. The IRA had sent coded warnings, the area was evacuated, but only just in time; there was still a few hundred injuries, such was the force of the blast, sending debris and glass into the air on a mushroom cloud. It doesn't bare thinking about how many would have been killed - a busy shopping area on a Saturday morning - without the warnings (at Warrington there had been warnings too, but not enough time given to clear the area; two children died and many were injured in the explosion).

From windows in the undamaged parts of the Arndale Centre you could see the bomb damage. A vast area of devastation, a post apocalyptic scene: broken buildings, streams of paper trailing from hollow windows, thousands upon thousands of pieces of shattered glass that so easily could have been symbols of thousands of shattered lives. Empty of humanity, a scene from a disaster movie, but in your face and chillingly real. It made your blood run cold, the hairs on the back of the neck stand up, a chill down the spine. A scene I would see again, but on TV and on a much larger scale on 9/11, when there weren't any warnings at all. My mate Feff and me stared at it in silence until I uttered: 'It would have been utter carnage.'

267

No lives were lost, however, and after the dust had settled, the rubble gathered up, windows boarded up and the glass and near horror of it swept away, the powers that be, in the corridors of corporate and council Manchester, looked upon it as an opportunity. The IRA had done them a favour, here was the chance to sweep away the 'Dirty Old Town' image (yes I know that song was written about Salford), to modernize Mancunia. While some of the redevelopment was great - i.e. the relocating of the old 15th century Shambles, freeing it from its 60/70's concrete prison – the rush to go up market and exterminate the flea markets left it all a bit soulless.

The biggest loss being the Corn Exchange: before the bomb full of Victorian charm. An alternative culture hub, a collection of old curiosity stall shops: second-hand records and clothes, comics and *Star Wars* toys, piercing booths, fortune tellers and many an oddball. All these were ordered out to the back streets in the northern area of the city centre, many floundered there. The Corn Exchange became The Triangle, a clinically clean, glitzy, upmarket mall full of designer shops, expensive clothes and jewellery for Manchester's new yuppie elite (so full of charm it gets 2 stars on TripAdvisor).

The interior of The Print Works - the former *Daily Mirror* building - looked like a Terry Gilliam or Ridley Scott film set and just as artificial as one. For a time, the still only half rebuilt area, with Times Square electronic displays, large screens, the sloping futuristic Urbis building (where the old packaged up real Manchester culture was put on display as museum exhibits) and constant mild winter Manchester rain, resembled *Blade Runner*.

There was certainly plenty of false replicants walking the sanitized city centre streets and sitting in the stands of Old Trafford – do androids dream of electronic strikers? Bring back the Bez Borg collective. The times were a changing, everyone's friends were becoming electric. Enemies - one time cowards, now brave trolls in cyber forums.

I think the IRA bomb signified the end of authenticity; the 90's big boom, a new false Utopia built on foundations of flimsy plastic. Even the Labour Party weren't genuine anymore (except the brilliant Dennis Skinner, forever). Not that we realised at the time. Tony Blair a grinning Cheshire cat, sat above us all, hypnotizing us, making us believe in his visions of tomorrow in Wonderland, then taking us into a hell.

Even Oasis were turning into false prophets with their overblown *Be Here Now* album. I thought about Richey Manic Edwards, who had now been missing nearly two years, was he one of the last genuine rock stars who gave blood for the cause? 4 REAL.

In the years to come I'd take the tram (or train from Oxford Road) to Old Trafford, passed all the old Victorian warehouses in Deansgate turned into luxury flats. As was the Hacienda (well a new building bearing that name sat on top of the flattened Manc music Mecca original). The gleaming office blocks of Salford Quays in the distance. And I'd think of the classic footage of this journey that accompanied John Cooper Clarke's 'Evidently Chickentown' when on *The Tube* (I believe it was): 80's Manchester, the gloom of an evening, dark leaden skies, the 4 REAL Hacienda visible down in the streets, smoke rising from chimneys. It may look dark and depressing to a Manc uncultured eye, but to me, like the rhythm of John Cooper Clarke's poem and delivery, it has a heartbeat, so alive and real in so many ways.

Yes the footage was used because it fitted Clarke's poem about the day to day monotony of downtrodden urban life. But those streets and environment also evidently created a great poem, and Clarke himself, and art, and Lowry himself, and writing, and Shelagh Delaney herself, and music, and Ian Curtis, Morrissey, Ian Brown, Shaun Ryder themselves. Several of the Busby Babes and Fergie's Fledglings (and those working-class football heroes not from Manchester came from similar environments i.e. Edwards, Charlton and Best). Some out there are violent, some are lost but many are found, the real *Coronation Street* characters, funny, salt of the earth, honest, true and genuine.

Morrissey was accused of romanticising that environment by some, but read his autobiography, he lived it. I could feel it and I've always thought you could have cut out 60's, 70's and 80's Jacksdale and drop it down in Manchester and it would fit (although the Forest and Derby fans would have to support a new local team. It would be City 'there's no United fans actually live in Manchester' myth). Give me that old village with its smoking chimneys, smoky bars (even though I don't smoke, it never bothered me, I liked it!), full of miners most days (clocking off from different shifts), a notorious music venue, the pit village bawdy humour and straight talking. Give me the Manchester of *Coronation Street* not Corporation Street, of a thriving underground music scene, oddballs and old curiosity shops. Give me a United with a drafty, old Stretford End, full of working-class kids who didn't need to break the bank or rob a bank for the privilege to be on the terrace; a wild-life terrace, with the pulse of real Manchester, United, the atmosphere, 4 REAL.

At least on this September Saturday in 96, the young lions on the pitch at United were the real deal. They'd carve 'United 4 REAL' on their hearts. They'd already stuffed Alan Hansen's words down his throat (and my doubts). A week before they'd beaten Leeds United 4-0 at Elland road – so sweet – and now at last they turned on the style at Old Trafford this season. A brilliant team display, beating Forest 4-0, with goals from Solksjaer, Giggs and two from Cantona. By the time the third goal went in my mate Feff was completely swept away by the excitement of the occasion. Football had never been his thing, this was his first ever match, he was here in memory of his United supporting brother who'd died of cancer. I'd feared he'd turn up with a rattle and wearing a 1970's rosette (actually that would have been pretty cool). Miserable Craig stared at him with contempt; he thought I'd let another imbecile sit with us. I must admit, though, I was red with embarrassment when, after United won a corner in front of us, Feff loudly asked who several of the players were, including Giggs and Beckham. I was laughing later in the match, he sat there clapping away like a little kid at a birthday party doing pat-a-cake pat-a-cake.

'Punk's don't like football,' he used to say, until I pointed out that *the* punk John Lydon loved it and was an Arsenal fan. Now that he was experiencing the thrill at being at a big match himself, his soul was ours.

I'd picked a good one for him, this was one of the real deal good days. Forest have always had good away support to help create an atmosphere. And the mix of experience and new blood in the United team was producing football to savour. Beckham was growing in confidence all the time, proving to be a stylish class act, possibly the best striker of the ball United had had since Bobby Charlton? Back in August he'd scored his famous goal against Wimbledon; lobbing the keeper from the halfway line. It wasn't just the football world that was now sitting up and taking notice; soon he'd be spicing up things off the pitch too. Cantona was at his majestic best, giving his swansong (not that we knew it at the time). Giggs was already established as one of the best players in the world and new signing Ole Gunner Solskjaer was well on his way to becoming the legendary 'baby faced assassin.'

All this United brilliance was on display that day, four special moments, make-believe magic, 4 REAL.

The Lucky Charm

If I've had a really lousy week or a couple of days leading up to a United game, then I know they're going to lose. Well, it always seems that way. So I didn't look on it as a mere coincidence that United's worst run of results for years intertwined with a personal run of bad luck.

This time, though, I discovered what was the cause of United's and my downfall. Beware of lucky charms. It started on the Saturday before United's game at Newcastle. Brian and his wife Jo returned from a holiday in America, bearing gifts. I was given a Native American lucky charm called a 'Mandella'.

'The Mandella symbolizes the Indian shield of good luck. With this shield they believed that the Gods would protect them and by having one in their homes, it would bring them prosperity, good health and happiness,' the accompanying card read.

272

I'll have some of that, I thought. I hung the lucky charm up on the wall, expecting to win the National Lottery, United to hammer Newcastle, and then meet the girl of my dreams. My luck changed all right, but not for the better. I didn't notice the danger signs on the Saturday.

Ten minutes after I'd stuck this Mandella on the wall I went out to the car to discover it had a flat tyre. Later that night I lost a tenner and fell out with a friend. Then came Sunday and United's 5-0 drubbing at Newcastle. After the game I prepared myself for the reception I would receive in the Portland. I knew the United haters had been waiting years for this day. It's different being a United supporter these days, the barracking has gone deeper than light-hearted piss-taking.

There's an intense jealousy or even hatred among non-United fans. Walking into a pub (even your local) wearing a United shirt, gets you looks like you'd walked into a mosque wearing a 'I LOVE SALMAN RUSHDIE' t-shirt.

I'd done well putting up with the verbal abuse all night without cracking. Even when the group of Leeds United season-ticket holders that go in the Portland started singing 'You're shit and you know you are'.

They'd already conveniently forgotten Leeds 4-0 home defeat to United earlier in the season. My bad luck continued. The landlord of the Portland had a pit bull terrier, that he took for a walk at the end of the night. This the Mike Tyson of dogs, it was kept upstairs and had to be brought down through the pub on its way for a walk. Everyone kept their distance from Tyson and the landlord kept him on a tight rein, the crazed mutt having gone for two people before. (There's a gym above the pub. One day a chap on his way up to the gym took a wrong turn and opened a door into the private quarters, and then just in time slammed it shut again as Tyson, frothing at the jaws, leapt towards him. This chap had to stand there for twenty minutes holding the door shut until someone heard his cries for help. Tyson, in a ferocious rage that anyone had dared to step foot on his territory, had been continually head-butting the door.)

So there I sat that Sunday night, feeling relieved that a bad weekend was coming to an end. I'd not noticed that the landlord had gone upstairs to fetch Tyson for a walk and had my back to the stairs door. Suddenly something gripped my arse. I didn't feel any pain, as I was too pissed. Turning around to see Tyson tucking into me for Sunday supper, I shot off the stool as quick as Linford Christie leaving his starting blocks. Moments later, right in the middle of the pub, the landlord was still trying to prise Tyson off me. He finally let go, tearing the back pocket from my Levi's and leaving two symmetrical bite marks on my bum. There was a lot of sympathy for me.

'Huh, huh, huh. I've never seen you move so fast. If only the United defence had been as quick today,' said a Forest supporter, roaring with laughter.

I was beginning to have suspicions about the Mandella. Was it the Native American's way of exacting revenge on the white man for all the years of persecution they suffered?

My bad luck continued. The dog bite became infected. I started vomiting. My joints ached, I felt weak and had the shivers. The doctor put me on antibiotics and Paracetamols, instructing me to take it easy for five days and not to drink alcohol. Just as I was starting to feel better, United lost 6-3 at Southampton. Then, on the Sunday, my cousin phoned to tell me Grandma's dog (that I usually took for a walk) had been run over by a car and killed.

And so it went on. I bought a second-hand video recorder that worked for one day, before chewing up my *United Champions '93* video. A few days later United lost their proud record of never losing a home tie in European competitions, with a pitiful display against Fenerbahce. That was followed by a home defeat against Chelsea.

I received a letter from an insurance company, trying to make out I had been involved in a car crash somewhere in London while driving a F-reg Vauxhall Cavalier, and that someone was claiming against me. I'd never driven in London in my life and owned a thirteen-year-old Ford Escort.

The gas, electric and telephone bills all arrived on the same day.

The final straw came on the day before United's home game against Arsenal. I was still sharing my season ticket with my sister's boyfriend and rang him to say I would like to go to this match, only for him to break the news that the season ticket had gone missing. He'd searched high and low for it but to no avail. That was it. I snapped. I snatched the Mandella from the wall, ripped the thing to pieces then set fire to it before emptying the charred remains into the dustbin. Ten minutes later the phone rang. It was Edward. He'd found the season ticket in his dog's basket.

On Saturday United beat Arsenal. I won forty quid on the lottery, and ended up in bed with a lovely blonde lass.

Baby You Can Drive My Car

By the spring I'd got enough cash together to buy back my United season ticket as soon as the current football season

275

was over. Then Claire came around to see me. We'd been close friends for ages. She's small, blonde and pretty with gorgeous blue eyes (except when bloodshot) and I think the world of her. We decided to go for a drink at a pub called the Hole In The Wall (a few hours later that would be an apt name for the place). We were just getting into my car when Claire asked, 'Can I drive?'

A chill ran down my spine at this suggestion. She'd not passed her test and I'd taken her for driving lessons before (I have the grey hairs to prove it. Forget the white-knuckle rides at Alton Towers, the ultimate experience is to take Claire for a driving lesson.) On one occasion I was sure I was going to be the victim of a road-rage incident when Claire, driving on the wrong side of the road, narrowly missed a Ford Fiesta XR2 coming in the opposite direction, driven by a youth so big that the top of his head stuck out of the sun roof.

There was also the time she failed to turn the corner at a T-Junction, leaving us heading for the front garden of the house opposite. A chap peacefully mowing his lawn had to dive into his hydrangeas, before running up the street after us, wielding a pitch fork.

'It's all right, I've improved. I'll be taking my test soon,' Claire assured me.

She was right, her driving had improved. I can get used to this, I was thinking, as we drove along. If Claire drives, I can have a few drinks. My mood brightened, but I started to get nervous as she pulled into the Hole in the Wall car park. There was only one free parking space left. And that was between a Jaguar and a sparkling P-Reg Rover. But before I could suggest that I take over, Claire had successfully manoeuvred between the two vehicles. I relaxed.

Then Claire slammed down her foot, not on the brake, but on the accelerator. The car smashed through the wooden fence in front of us and plunged down the 10-foot drop on the other side. The last words I thought I would ever hear were Claire saying, 'I'm sorry, Tony.'

At the same time I was thinking that my book was going to be published posthumously. The car landed upside down on its roof. Miraculously, we were both uninjured, but appeared to be trapped in the car. The buckled doors couldn't be opened. My immediate fear was of the car bursting into flames. I quickly turned off the ignition. I managed to smash the window on the driver's side with a steering lock, and we crawled out.

Within minutes three fire engines, two ambulances, and a host of police cars had turned up. It looked like a scene from the TV series *999*.

The firemen jumped down with hosepipes and steel cutters; the paramedics jumped down wanting to know where the injured were. And when they'd checked us over in the ambulance they sat there shaking their heads in disbelief, telling us how lucky we were.

There's a restaurant at the rear of the pub that overlooked the scene of the crash. The majority of the diners in there had carried on tucking into their meals while we were trapped upside down in the car. What did they think it was, some kind of free stunt show put on by the pub for their entertainment? I told the manageress of the Hole In The Wall that if the payment was right, we could crash a car at the same time every week if it was good for custom.

The car was a write-off, and I only had third-party insurance, so couldn't claim a penny. The police instructed me that it was my responsibility to pay to have the wreck shifted (within seven days). And it was going to cost me several hundred pounds to get another car on the road. Claire offered to pay me back. But I told her to forget about it. So now I was back in the red financially, with little chance of buying back my season ticket.

The strange thing was, though, it didn't bother me as much as it should have. Apart from watching United win the European Cup, I felt I'd seen more than everything I ever wanted to see in football. And sometimes, sat in the false, orchestrated atmosphere of late nineties Old Trafford, I felt I might as well be sat in an armchair back home. (Too many times it takes a lone youth to get up out of his seat, yell 'SSINNGGG' to everyone, then like a nursery school teacher showing infants how to sing 'pat-a-cake, pat-a-cake, bakers man', he starts slowly clapping his hands encouraging supporters to sing 'Alex Ferguson's Red and White Army' in an attempt to create an atmosphere. Maybe it's because I was a part of the last generation of terrace supporters and I miss those days. It all went tragically wrong at Heysel and Hillsborough, but it shouldn't have been that way.

The Hillsborough disaster was caused by a set of avoidable factors converging on the same day. But terraces could still exist. Recently, nuclear scientists, no less, announced that they'd developed safe terracing. But there's no way the big clubs are going to rip up the seats. They no longer want cheap sections of the ground filled with young, noisy working-class people, singing their nasty little songs. Ooh, noo, we don't want to go upsetting our £800-a-season Club Class members, do we?

I don't want to see the reintroduction of terraces for selfish reasons. I'm at an age now that even if terraces did still exist I would be moving to a seated area. There's always been, though, a new generation of young supporters to fill the shoes of the older ones and be stood together in one section of the ground to give vocal support to the team and create that special atmosphere unique to football. Now those days are gone.

Several weeks after the car crash, United, er, crashed out of the European Cup with a semi-final defeat by eventual winners of the trophy Borussia Dortmund. We didn't cry about it, though. We were certain United would be back for another shot at Europe's major club prize the following season.

The tears were on Tyneside, as Kevin Keegan's £60-million ensemble were being eclipsed in the title run-in by Ferguson's home-grown fledglings, marshalled on the pitch by Monsieur Cantona, who sadly had announced his premature retirement from football at the end of the season.

With only a week left to the season-ticket-renewal deadline, the panic set in: If I let it go now I'll never get it back, and there's not much hope of getting in to see United without one . . . what if the atmosphere returns and another star descends from the heavens to replace Cantona, and I'm not there? I'd had a trial separation from United and now I was missing them. You can never totally break away from a major love of your life. My Technics stereo had to go and I bought the cheapest roadworthy car I could find, a rusty old Austin Metro (the colour of which was red, of course). Leaving me with just enough cash to renew my season ticket with a day to spare. And so I looked forward to the new season.

Bitter Sweet Symphony

'I have found nothing - neither religion nor philosophy, to ease my troubled soul. But I would go mad were it not for music. Music is heaven's best gift to humanity.' A great quote from Tchaikovsky. Manchester United had been my religion for years, but at times I'd lost faith, along with thousands of other troubled Stretford Ender forever souls. At other times however I'd felt divine rapture and thankful that on the seventh day God had created Manchester United. In seventh heaven as United's seventh goal went in against Barnsley during a great run in the 97-98 season. The sacred No.7: Best, Coppell, Robson, Cantona (Beckham and Ronaldo in the future). Were it not for United I would have gone mad, but they often sent me mad too. In 92 I thought Cantona was seventh heaven's best gift to humanity, I was a disciple, but his philosophy puzzled my soul.

Yet did music now mean more to me? I agree with Tchaikovsky in that a world without music would be unbearable. In summertime there was no United to ease my troubled soul, and although I did have withdrawal symptoms I just about managed to find other things to keep my sanity intact. I couldn't go long without listening to music, and I'm not one of those people whose record collection stopped having any new sounds added to it after the age of about 22. I've always needed an injection of new bands and singers (even if, sometimes, it's music and bands from before my time that I've discovered, so are 'new' to me).

Music is powerful on the emotions, there's nothing like it for triggering the nostalgia and memory switches; listening to a track - or whole album – capture's a moment in time and your feelings at that moment, then transports you back there on hearing it again. For example, I can tell you that on my first visit to Old Trafford in 1977, they were playing The Tom Robinson Band's '2-4-6-8 Motorway,' and Chicago's 'If You Need Me Now,' before the kick-off. And if I hear them now I don't think about the song's real meanings: Tom Robinson driving down the motorway with a verse based on a gay chant in his head. No, I'm peering through the bars at Old Trafford, first in awe at the Stretford End and the noise they were making, then feeling their pain when silenced by Clough's Forest scoring 2, then 4 and it could have been 6 or 8. I'm not lamenting Chicago's lost love but that of Red Manchester, worried that we're missing Tommy Docherty and need him now.

One of my favourite ever band t-shirts was that of one of my favourite ever bands, The Verve. Under their name was a picture of a neon cross and the words: 'Music Saves' (I bought this at their gig at Manchester Academy on the *A Northern Soul* tour in the summer of 95). Even though I'd been into them ever since John Peel played 'She's a Superstar,' (I still think their early material – like 'Gravity Grave,' 'All in the Mind' and the debut album *A Storm in Heaven* - find them at their best), the masses didn't tune in until their breakthrough album *Urban Hymns*, and listening to this now transports me straight back to 1997.

The single 'Bitter Sweet Symphony,' was definitely the soundtrack of my roller-coaster life and United's season of wonderful highs and crushing lows. But this was an upbeat track, a surging anthem on a hypnotic hook. A two-fingered fuck you kiss, to fate, authority and the bastards that tried to drag you down. It struck a chord with everyone and reached No.2 in the charts. The follow up single, 'The Drugs

Don't Work,' was just as brilliant, but released other emotions: sadness, a mood of melancholy, it pulled at the heart-strings; will we see your face again? So it was fitting that the song was No.1 in the charts the end of the first week in September 1997.

I'd started the previous weekend on a high. I'd finished a lucrative decorating job, so had a money in my bank account for the first time in ages. I'd completed the second draft of this book, and been up to United to see them continue their fine start to the season, with a thrilling 3-1 victory over Coventry.

That night I treated Claire to a night on the town in Nottingham. Things were going my way, my luck was in, time to open up my heart to Claire. I loved her, time I told her, this was my chance. The double-whammy left me reeling – 'it's not you, it's me' – 'you're more like a brother to me,' (ha, brother? what about the times when…everyone is inbred in our area so no problem there) – then she announced she was joining the navy.

There remained an awkward tension for the rest of the night, intensified by the consumption of alcohol and jealously. When in a Nottingham nightclub, possibly to emphasize her point, maybe trying to be cruel to be kind, Claire starting dancing, then heavily flirting with a guy on the dance floor, his hands were all over her, the green-eyed monster bit. We fell out, Claire told me to 'fuck off home.' The guy sneered at me, his three mates glared at me; I didn't trust any of them and certainly wasn't going to let Claire stay in the city with four men that were strangers. Narrowly escaping a beating I insisted she leave with me. The only words spoken on the taxi drive home were me wanting her to look in my eyes and tell me it meant nothing the times we broke through the 'just friend's' barrier, and her insisting she regretted doing so now. She asked to be dropped off at her parent's home and I went home alone, there drowning my sorrows with several whiskies.

I'd fallen asleep on the settee; the TV was still on when I woke in the grey morning light, with a mixture of a hangover, depression and regret. On the screen a news reporter was talking to a tearful elderly couple about Princess Diana. My head wasn't tuned in to catch what they were saying. I just thought, oh what the fuck's gone off in the Royal soap opera now? I don't need this sentimental crap. I went into to the kitchen to make a mug of coffee; carrying it back into the living room I saw the face of a sombre newsreader. In the background was a picture of Princess Diana and the years 1961 – 1997. To 1997? They then gave more details of the car crash that had killed her, truly shocking news. My parents had always said that everyone can remember where they where and what they were doing on hearing the news of JFK's assassination.

The reaction of the realm, the grief, was unprecedented for stiff upper lip Britain. It became almost unbearable for the duration of the week of mourning that followed. It was like my hangover, depression and heartbreak didn't leave me, such was the dense fog of despair that seeped into every corner of the UK. It was if everyone's feelings were exposed or people's personal sorrow was released by Diana's death and became a collective despondency, a form of hysteria. Ironically, some of you may feel, I found listening to Radiohead's *OK Computer* (also recently released) an escape and calming sedative.

By the day of the funeral – the following Saturday – I couldn't stand it. Half way through the service I turned off the TV and left the house. Not because I wasn't sorry for Diana and her family (Harry and William following the coffin gave heartbreaking echoes of JFK's children on the day of his funeral), or found it moving, that was the point, it was overwhelming. The streets were empty and silent, like a scene in a *28 Days Later* type film. I first called in at my parent's house, but they were dead souls too, and when Elton John came on singing a newly crafted 'Candle in the Wind,' it finished everyone. I quickly left and went down the pub, and stayed there all day.

The Diana mourning dragged on until the following Wednesday and into Wembley before England's must-win World Cup qualifier against Moldova: the minutes silence, the crowd singing 'Candle in the Wind,' holding lit candles and pictures of Diana. Until the 28th minute when Beckham crossed for Scholes to fire home, and a pressure cooker of emotion was released. We could breathe again, we could cheer. It wasn't disrespectful or confirmation of football being more important than life and death (Hillsborough had made Shankly's words facile), it was just time for us all to move on, they'd given us a United hope.

'Man does not change, his winter dreams live on' (the last line in Derek Hodgson's great 1977 book *The Manchester United Story*). Broken hearts can be mended; especially when Claire came around to see me, when on leave from her training to join the Navy. She was hating it, she missed me. We went for a drink, then back at mine, she at first asked me if I'd give her back a massage, then pulled my hand onto her breast (nothing like brotherly love!) I'd found one of the top literary agents in the country (based in Mayfair) who loved my book - 'we much enjoyed the freshness and spontaneity of your style' and were confident enough to show it to

Mainstream Publishing and Victor Gollancz. I couldn't believe it, the latter were publishers of *Fever Pitch*!

And United - most notably 'Fergie's fledglings' - were absolutely flying in the Premier League: they scored an incredible 28 goals in 6 games between October and early December. Including a 3-1 away victory over Liverpool and a 6-1 home win against Sheffield Wednesday. The run had started with a 7-0 thrashing of Barnsley at Old Trafford. I was totally ecstatic and in a great frame of mind after this game. So found it hard to rein in my ego when I found the only seat free on the train home was next to a Barnsley supporter. I tried my best though, as he was a real nice guy when we started chatting. At first I felt sorry for him, Barnsley had already suffered a 0-6 home thrashing to Chelsea and a 0-5 defeat at Arsenal, yet the man was completely content. 'I've supported Barnsley all my life (he was about in his mid 40's), been hoping all my life that we'd make it into the top league. Despite the results it's a dream come true to go to places like Old Trafford and Anfield to watch my team, I'm savouring it. It'll probably never happen again in my life,' he told me, quite calm. I was humbled, shook his hand to acknowledge he was a special breed of supporter.

But I have suffered too, I'll have you know. In the stands at Luton on a Wednesday night, watching them thrash Mansfield Town (my local team, not Forest you glory hunting Nottinghamshire bastards who point the accusing finger at me but live near the old coal town and go to the City Ground instead) 7-0 in the League Cup, yet we never stopped singing.

These few months in my life, and United's performances, had restored my faith....for a while. The only defeat in the great run was a 2-3 defeat to Arsenal. This would come back to haunt us at the end of the season. The first real setback in United's season came in a fifth round FA Cup tie...against Barnsley, going out in the replay 2-3. By which time Claire had passed out her Navy training and was off sailing the seven seas for 4 years (where she'd meet her future husband). We're all running on Boethius's wheel.

Red Van Winkle

United Review 97-98:
'Shoot, Sheringham, yer cockney twat.' Cantona's replacement wasn't going down too well with the United faithful. It was never going to be easy for him to follow in the footsteps of lost legends Hughes and King Eric. Especially when we were expecting the new striker to be Ronaldo (the Brazilian one), Weah, or Batistuta. At least someone younger, with a little more verve and je ne sais quoi (he'd soon gain our respect and end up with our love forever for his Champions League Final equalizer against Bayern Munich in 99, of course). I sat sulkily in my seat in East Stand, Lower, and looked at the discontent on the faces of the Reds around me, as United struggled to find a way through an average West Ham defence.

We've become a spoilt lot at United. We expect the winning of a trophy, an annual visit to Wembley and the thrashing of all opposition with a majestic display of football. This a prerequisite of owning a season ticket.

It wasn't just the loss of a loved one or the drop in the standard of football that troubled the mind of many a supporter. There was also the frustration of not being allowed to stand and get behind the team 'other than momentarily at times of great excitement'. If you did

286

persistently stand the stewards/SPS (Special Projects Security) had the power to evict you from the stadium and confiscate your season ticket.

Maybe it's just because I'm getting older, but I was beginning to think I'd never again feel the buzz that I used to get when watching United at Old Trafford. Then came the match against Juventus in the Champions League. I must admit I was expecting United (now without the inspirational Roy Keane for the season) to get hammered. And Del Piero putting the Italians ahead within the first minute did nothing to allay my fears.

Well, change my name to Tony Doubting Thomas. That night 'Fergie's Fledglings' came of age. A group of young men not accustomed to defeat, pounded Juventus into submission. Giggs looked the worldbeater that everyone who'd watched him frequently since he was a seventeen-year-old knew he could be. Sheringham gave an international-class performance. And the crowd (free from harassment by SPS) stood for the entire ninety minutes and created an atmosphere akin to the terrace days, as United won 3-2.

'The Manchester fans won it for them, they were incessant for the whole match. Their supporters could inspire a team of mad cows [say what?],' said Marcello Lippi after the game. For the next three months Old Trafford was, at times, a magical place to be. The team cruised into the quarter-finals of the European Cup. And the opposition in the Premiership were nothing but fodder for the 'mad cows' (as mentioned Barnsley beaten 7-0; Sheffield Wednesday 6-1, on consecutive Saturdays).

Andy Cole, in particular, was on fire. He's one of the few strikers who've signed for United and not frozen on the stage of one of the grandest football theatres, in front of the most demanding of audiences. Cole has been unjustifiably criticized by some people who claim he misses too many chances. Andy Cole, through ability and effort, gets himself into more goal-scoring positions than any striker I've seen in my time watching football, and as a result has the best strike rate at United since Denis Law - and that speaks for itself.

United had the Championship won by January, so thought a Manchester bookie who paid out over £40,000 in winnings to punters who'd backed them for the title. And although the atmosphere was far from what it should have been, there was a backlash against the actions of the SPS. A growing number of United loyalists in the East Lower section were prepared to stand up for their cause and refused to sit at games.

The inevitable confrontation took place on Boxing Day during a match against Everton. United secretary, General Ken Merrett, fearing defeat for the PLC, sent his troops storming into East Lower to quell the uprising. United supporters were forcibly evicted from Old Trafford and banned by the club, not for violent conduct or throwing an object, not for chanting racial abuse or using foul language, but for standing and giving vocal support to their own team in their own stadium.

The events that day brought the standing issue to the attention of the national press. Everyone waited in anticipation for the next home game, against Spurs. How would the crowd in East Lower behave . . .

'Can you hear United sing? No-ooooo,' came the all-too-familiar chant from the away fans, breaking the silence and the monotony of a dull game. There was no response from the United fans. It was all quiet on the Eastern front.

After meetings with IMUSA (Independent Manchester United Supporters' Association) the club had agreed to a ceasefire and pull out the SPS for the Spurs match. But Reds, with threats of bans hanging over their heads if they stood up, sat subdued and apathetic. There was a feeling of 'this is what you want; 'this is what you'll get' towards the board. Several minutes later a long loud snoring sound came from several rows behind us. There were fits of laughter as we all turned around to see a chap slumped in his chair fast asleep. Brilliant, that sums up Old Trafford, the Theatre Of Dreams, these days.

Thank God the press photographers or *Match of the Day* cameras didn't get a shot of him. You can imagine the headlines: 'THE STANDING DEBATE - UNITED FANS SLEEP ON IT'.

The main complaint, though, is that the United supporters want some consistency from the club in addressing the standing issue. If they're going to force supporters to sit down, then they've got to do it at every game, not one in three (usually the games when the opposition are not our greatest rivals, i.e., Southampton or Wimbledon). This results in the ludicrous situation of the SPS taking several minutes getting everyone to sit down in East Lower. Just as they've done so, the team attack again and the crowds are up out of their seats. Then the process begins again.

But when United were playing Juventus, Liverpool, or Arsenal, the SPS were nowhere to be seen. That's because they knew there wasn't a chance of getting people to sit at those games.

The board use the same two excuses every time. Firstly that Trafford Borough Council are threatening to close sections of the ground if supporters continue to infringe safety regulations by persistently standing at matches. (Can anyone explain to us what's so unsafe about standing up to sing? People do it at church every Sunday. When *Songs of Praise* was held in Old Trafford I didn't see stewards storming in to banish the sinners and confiscate their Bibles.)

The second excuse is that there have been complaints from people whose view is obstructed by those who stand. Well, I don't know what it's like in other sections of the ground, but certainly in East Lower I've never heard one United supporter tell anyone to sit down. This is because the majority of supporters in there are ex-Stretford Enders who had no choice but to transfer to a different area of the ground when the old terrace was demolished.

The club has to start to seriously consider the views put forward by the IMUSA: an organization set up to look after the interests and give voice to disillusioned United supporters fed up at being treated with contempt by the board. With United's own chairman Martin Edwards expressing an opinion (one shared by a large percentage of football supporters) that he would like to see the reintroduction of terraces, it's an issue that can no longer be disregarded.

Alex Ferguson knows the importance of a passionate atmosphere. In his diary of the season he said: 'Recently, Old Trafford has not been the same daunting place for visitors that it once was. There certainly isn't the kind of atmosphere that made the stadium quiver with excitement and tension when we played Barcelona here. It doesn't seem as vibrant as in the it old days when Liverpool, then the dominant force in the game, found the atmosphere so frightening that they couldn't handle it. Whatever the reasons for this, I would like to see a return to a more hostile stadium.'

Crowd participation is as integral to the football experience as it is at rock concerts. Some years ago I went with friends to see a Siouxsie and the Banshees concert. I'd seen them several times before and they'd always been excellent live. But that had been in smaller, atmospheric venues, where the majority of the crowd stood. This time we were going to see them play in the new multi-million pound, all-seater, cavernous, acoustically perfect, Royal Concert Hall in Nottingham.

Several songs into the set - sat in our shiny, cream-coloured plastic seats - something was amiss. The group were giving it their all, but to the obvious annoyance of lead singer Siouxsie there was a feeling of detachment from the crowd, with just a quick cheer and applause at the end of each song. Halfway through the next song she stopped the group playing and yelled into the mike at the audience: 'Don't sit there like fucking dummies; get up, get involved.'

Everyone cheered and got up out of their seats, with many moving down to the front of the stage (in fact several Jacksdale ex-Topper punks came hurtling down to the front causing rows of seats to collapse). Now, with group, music and crowd merged, the concert took off.Old Trafford doesn't rock any more. These days it's akin to a Barry Manilow concert. Maybe supporters could wave their cigarette lighters in the air as the players come out.

The United team peaked with their 5-3 demolition of Chelsea at Stamford Bridge in the FA Cup third round. It could have been overconfidence from the young players leading to complacency, but after that performance the season began to fall apart. Three defeats in four League games (against Coventry, Southampton and Leicester) started the alarm bells ringing. Roy Keane's experience and drive missing from midfield became more evident. United looked a couple of world class players short of their European dream.

By April they were out of the FA Cup, out of the European Cup and I knew the Championship was slipping away the moment Pallister and Schmeichel started doing their Chuckle Brothers routine against Liverpool - 'To me, to you, to me, to you,' and Michael Owen sneaked in to score. Arsenal's foreign legion swept past us on their way to the Double.

So It Goes

Sat with the suits on the train home from London. The one to the right of me was nervously picking his nose, making little crow balls and placing them in a neat pile in the corner of the table as he scrutinized the pages of the *Financial Times*. 'Bastard!' he muttered, occasionally banging his head sideways against the window. Twenty minutes later he opened up his briefcase and took out a copy of the *Manchester UNITED* magazine.

The suit across from me was engrossed in *The Times* crossword. 'Oh yes, of course,' he said to himself every five minutes, as he filled in the answer to another clue.

I was thinking about the day I'd had, my life, the future. I'd been to London to meet the people from the publishers Gollancz. A coincidence: my editor originally came from Nottingham and was also at the same Jesus And Mary Chain concert at Rock City in Nottingham, early in 1985, when they were a little known group and only a few hundred people were present. That was back in my Goth days.

All those years I spent when I was younger, trying to find an identity. At the end of the day (I had to get in one last football cliché), it's not about the clothes you wear or the way you look. It's about personality, being yourself, the outlook you have on life. The singer-song writers and musicians I most admire are natural talents, not manufactured by the record industry. The greatest footballers were born gifted. Their skill can't be taught.

You could put a thousand kids through an FA school of excellence and you may produce a few international class players, but you'll never create a Best, Maradona or Cantona. Flawed geniuses some might say, but their temperamental character was an essential part of their footballing ability. And anyway, as Neil Young once sang, 'It's better to burn out than fade away.' Yeah, Neil Young: my musical tastes have broadened and mellowed out in my late twenties and early thirties. I've come to appreciate the sounds and influences of music pre-1977. The Sex Pistols are rubbing shoulders in my CD collection with John Lee Hooker, Tim Buckley, The Velvet Underground, Jimi Hendrix and Des O'Connor, alongside current favourites Spiritualized, Beck, Super Furry Animals, Travis and Embrace. Sometimes I even dip into Dad's record collection and stick on a Dave Brubeck or Billie Holiday album.

And when I find myself listening to *Dream Letter* by Tim Buckley, while reading Gabriel García Márquez's *One Hundred Years of Solitude* and inhaling the uplifting aromas drifting from an oil burner, I think I may be a hippy at heart. I've become environmentally friendly, I stop and hug a tree from time to time and piss on my plants when I get home from the pub instead of flushing it down the toilet. I enjoy taking Mam and Dad's dog for long walks in the countryside. Not Benny Hill, alas. Another decade, another dog; this one's a West Highland terrier called Whisky. I get some looks when I walk down the street shouting,

'Whisky, Whisky!'

'Oh, listen to the sad drunk shouting for his bottle,' two old women once said, while stood gossiping.

I start to feel a wee bit broody when I hold my baby nephew Christopher in my arms. So, yeah, in some ways I've changed. And in my time on the planet so too has society, and with it football.

Jacksdale's no longer the flat-cap populated mining village it was when I was a kid. Because of cheaper house prices and the proximity to the M1 motorway, an increasing number of townies are moving into the area. The once spit-and-sawdust backstreet pubs have now been lavishly refurbished (well, the Royal Oak has laid a new carpet and re-upholstered the seats), and you can now find yourself drinking with a variety of people: computer programmers, school teachers and drug dealers.

Jacksdale still has plenty of council houses, and the diluted social problems of rougher areas of Britain. The crime rate has gone up. I was once stuck in the Portland until the early hours of the morning (no, I wasn't complaining), as a youth prowled about outside with a pump-action shotgun, threatening to shoot people ('E's only gone an got a bladdy shooter,' said the cockney landlord, rushing back in), joyriders burn out stolen cars. Someone nicked a couple of cabbages from old Bill's allotment.

Dad (now retired) is keeping up the flat-cap tradition. He's started wearing Grandad's old headgear, which further enhances his resemblance to Victor Meldrew (he's got good cause to shout 'I don't believe it' when reading about the salaries of today's top footballers, who earn in a few weeks what he earned in a lifetime). Mam (still a secretary at the creosote firm) is content to knit woollen animals and clothes for her grandson. Jacksdale is still a football-mad village. There's no shortage of kids on the rec - their £40 Umbro training tops for goalposts - kicking a ball about. The other day I heard one of them shout a phrase I've not heard for a long time: 'Yuh nowt but a bloody goal-hanger.'

But, hey, everyone loves good old football these days. The stock market, sportswear manufacturers, sponsors, businesses wanting a nice bit of corporate hospitality to impress clients with, ad agencies, football agents, touts, television and video production companies, female TV and radio celebrities who bring out books and videos about which hunk of a footballer has the biggest bounciest bollocks. Even the royal family, in their efforts to be more in touch with the common people, are using football and starting to turn up at more games. It'll not be long before the Queen appears on television on Christmas Day for her annual speech wearing a blue-and-white bobble hat and scarf, giving her half-season analysis and views on the game.

Everyone's cashing in on the three-hundred billion dollars a year industry. And it's norr'as though ah dunt know owt about football. So I thought I'd have my say with this three-minute pop-single of a book. I'm going to get the publishers to rip-off readers by changing the colour and design of the cover of the book twice a season. Then by bringing out limited editions of *If the Kids Are United* with different authors doing their own mixes of selected chapters....

The train pulled into Nottingham station, and the last of the suits departed. The one who'd sat across from me had left his copy of *The Times* on the table. I noticed the crossword had one blank space. Curiosity got the better of me. Nine across 'same again (5)'. G something P something. . .hmmm... 'same again . . .' I gave up after five minutes. So OK, I thought, I can't do *The Times* crossword. Then I noticed the answers he'd put to other clues: 2 down, 'comfortably placed (7, 6)' — bapples pratty; 1 down 'cumulative, an extra put in (8)' — anglenot. The bogger, the majority of his answers were gobbledegook.

I peered out of the carriage window into the darkness. I knew that in a few minutes' time the train would pass by Jacksdale, a few hundred yards from my house before it reached Alfreton station, where I'd get off. Ah! there it was, the landmark I was looking for. The bright blue illuminated letters of Jacksdale Co-op in the middle of the village, with the war memorial in front. Who needs Trafalgar Square?

A few months later, I decided to watch the World Cup Final 98 with Dad.

I'm settled into an armchair. Dad and the dog are on the settee. Mam can't go out shopping - it's Sunday night - she's knitting in the kitchen.

Refreshments are sorted; Dad with his bottles of brown ale, a pork pie and cheese and pickle sandwiches. Me with bottles of brown ale, a pork pie and cheese and pickle sandwiches. And the dog with a bowl of water and three Boneos.

Epilogue
Comeback to What You Know

2011:

If the Kids are United was published in April 1999. Off on trips down London to see the publishers Victor Gollancz – George Orwell's! Nick Hornby's! They gave me a copy of Hornby's new book *About A Boy* (which I read on the train home and was great) and informed me he'd been in the day before, had been sat in the very seat I was sat in. Wish I'd have met him. I'd have told him that I thought the bit in the film of his book *Fever Pitch* – when his girlfriend turns to him and asks what he's thinking about, which is football but he says 'D.H. Lawrence,' was raight pretentious mi duck. As I actually live in the middle of D.H. Lawrence country, walk my dog in the countryside where he used to wander and set several of his novels, that he used to come dancing in my village, knew my sister-in-law's great grandad, but I've never said to a girlfriend I was thinking of D.H. Lawrence instead of football.

They also told me he said Arsenal wouldn't win the championship (this was on the first visit to them in April 98 and United were top), I replied that on the evidence of United's current form Arsenal would catch United and win the league. Unfortunately I was right.

The book came out and – as you can now see at the beginning of this version of the book – received great reviews, including the 5 star book of the month in *Four Four Two*, the top football magazine in the country. Some considered *If the Kids are United* the 'working-class *Fever Pitch*.' But no film deal has been struck yet, damn. I had visions of a scene where I'm showing a girlfriend around the D.H. Lawrence birthplace museum, up t'rowd in Eastwood – my dream girl, who supports Manchester United and likes every track on the CD compilation I've put together for her (I'm still searching for that combination) and when I ask her what's she's thinking about she doesn't reply with: 'Sons and Lovers,' but 'Giggs winning goal in the FA Cup semi-final in 99,' instead and I know I'm in love.

A few publications and local people inevitably had a go at me for being a 'glory hunting Judas' for not supporting a local team. And I reckon that when I did an interview and photo session for a local paper a subtle revenge was exacted on me. Perhaps it was just United supporter paranoia that everyone hates us?

Whilst the journalist – a Newcastle fan – did the interview, on a tour of my *If the Kids are United* world, the photographer – a Forest fan who was usually to be found behind the goal of the City Ground on match days, capturing action of the local team – took snaps of me, holding, kicking or playing keepy uppy with a football. Now it was a muddy March, so I don't know whose idea it was to go out into the D.H. Lawrence countryside - where I walk the dog - to take a few pictures there. But guess it must have been me showing off as they didn't know this fact. As we trekked up a path - under grey skies and drizzle - the photographer halted us.

'That would be a good shot, if you kicked the football up in front of those trees over there,' he said pointing to a line of 4 trees – each separated by a gap of about 30ft – that stretched across a muddy ploughed field.

I looked down at my trainers, new ones bought with some of the book advance, then at the churned up mud 'Would it?'

'Yes,' he replied with a hypnotic stare.

Now if you've ever done a photo shoot with a professional photographer you'll realise what power they wield. You feel like you'd do almost anything they say. So I have to be thankful that I got away with just the following really for a being a 'glory hunting Judas.'

I picked up the football and gamely trudged out across the field. It was like walking on the moon and there was so much mud caked on my trainers that they resembled an astronauts boots by the time the photographer shouted 'there' to indicate I'd reached the desired spot.

'Now kick the ball into the air,' he instructed, zooming his lens in on me.

I tried, the ball rotated into the air, I attempted to connect with it with my trusty right foot, but it was like I was wearing a Jules Verne era diving suit. Slowly I tipped backwards until I was lying on my back in the mud, the ball landed with a thud and splat at the side of me like an unexploded bomb in the Somme. I slowly looked back to the journo and photographer to catch them laughing, one patting the other on the back, before trying to hide their mirth from me.

'Got it,' said the photographer with a thumbs up.

Ah well, at least I now looked like the dirty scruffy oik from my childhood days, which was apt as the next location we were off up to was my grandparent's old end terrace house in Selston. This place still looks more *Coronation Street* than *Coronation Street*. And has been used for the location for several films. The latest being Meera Syal's *Anita and Me*. Several scenes were actually shot in the house that had once belonged my grandparents (the one mentioned earlier in this book). One scene made my sister cry her eyes out (in the cinema where she saw it in Manchester) as it showed Anita's friend waving her away down the same lane we used to wave goodbye to our grandparents.

I chatted to Sanjeev Bhaskar - a real friendly guy - on set and gave him a copy of *If the Kids are United*, wishing to get a call a few months down the line with Bhaskar saying he'd loved it and wanted to make a film of it, even if this was only a Bollywood version.

On the day I took the journo and photographer there, we did a more appropriate shot of me – down a back brick alley, me leaning against a brick wall, football tucked under my arm, trying to do my best Albert Finney *Saturday Night Sunday Morning* smouldering look (being featured alongside Alan Sillitoe - and Sue Townsend and a little-known Hilary Mantel, whatever became of her I wonder? - in a book about East Midland writers and swapping a few letters with the great man was also one of the highlights of getting published) and failing; David *Kes* Bradley maybe. As these snaps were being taken a woman I knew came walking down the alley.

'What you on wi?' she asked.

'Publicity for my book.'

'Yeah right, like you've wrote a book. What's it called *Peter and Jane* goo for a piss up?' She replied walking off laughing.

A month later United won the league, the FA Cup and then the European Cup for the historic treble. This was great, of course, and it would have been fitting for this epilogue to tell you I was there in the Nou Camp to witness United's dramatic late comeback against Bayern Munich to win the European Cup. Alas I wasn't. Perhaps it's more fitting for this book that I wasn't. I'd forked out for a season ticket, not missed a home Champions League game – including the quarter final and semi final victories against Inter Milan and Juventus. But missed a few League Cup and FA Cup games and United's' allocation for the final wasn't big enough to fit me in, even in a stadium as big as the Nou Camp.

I was gutted, but the way I have to look at it is: if I had have been there that night then nothing ever would top it as a United supporter, nothing. So still not having seen United in a European Cup Final keeps a dream to be achieved alive, and you need things like that to keep you going in life, the desire for something.

Maybe, just maybe, I'll be there when United win the European Cup in style in the final. They still haven't done this since the extra-time period of the 68 final at Wembley. In 99 I'd sat there totally miserable for over 80 minutes as Bayern Munich completely outplayed us, and they were desperately unlucky, going 1-0 up, hitting the woodwork twice. Yes those last 5 minutes are never to be forgotten, but wouldn't it be great to see United win in the final in the fast attacking United football style we're famous for? This didn't happen in Moscow either (no, I didn't have a ticket for that one too), a boring 1-1 draw, again United lucky in the second-half, then a penalty shoot out. So I'm still dreaming of being there the night United thrash Barcelona (or City or Liverpool) 4-0 to be crowned kings of Europe.

The good thing about watching the 99 final on television was seeing the shell-shocked face of Bayern's Lothar Matthaus at the end; he'd looked so smug sat on the bench a few minutes earlier. And guess I didn't feel as bad as George Best, who was there, but with United 0-1 down he left early to head to the nearest bar to beat the crowds and get the beers in. Bless his troubled soul.

Best is one of the people and things mentioned in *If the Kids are United* that are sadly no longer with us. Dad and me shared one last great sporting occasion together: watching (on TV, of course, with refreshments sorted and the dog with Boneos) England win the Rugby Union World Cup, with Jonny Wilkinson crushing Australia with his last minute drop goal (I would have liked it to have been the England football team winning the World Cup, but we both would have had to have the life expectancy of an Oak tree to live to see that), before he passed away, dying from cancer in 2007.

The night Dad died was the same night United really did turn on the style in Europe, crushing Roma 7-1 (they'd lost the first leg 1-2). I've heard this was one of United's best ever performances, but I've never seen the match or highlights and probably never will. There was a glimpse of it, in Nottingham City Hospital, you could say meaningless in the sad circumstances for our family, but Dad and me always had a connection via United, as you've read.

I'd had to rush back to my car to top up the exorbitant hospital parking fees, in case I got clamped. We thought Dad would be make it through this night at the time. He'd been in and out of hospital since being diagnosed with cancer. However it was terminal pancreatic cancer, and we knew we had little time left with him. On the way back I passed a ward where a television was on, the match, Man Utd were winning 6-1. At Dad's bedside I held his hand and told him the latest score, as a way of saying 'Come on Dad United are making a comeback you can too.' His eyes widened 'Six one!' he replied, and a smile appeared on his face. He then told me to take my sister and leave him with Mum. He passed away shortly afterwards. We sat with him, his shell, for a while. Somewhere in the ward Radio 4 was on, the shipping forecast followed by 'Sailing By.' Whisky dog went to have walks with him - wherever he maybe - a year later.

The great John Peel and last of Jacksdale's flat cappers - musical hall singing Roger - are other lost heroes. Many favourite pubs have been shut down and old Wembley pulled down.

When I wrote *If the Kids are United* I criticized Wembley and called it 'the biggest public toilet in the world.' With hindsight I regret that now. At least the old stadium had soul, now it has been replaced by yet another lifeless bowl. I'd love to splash through the Wembley piss waterfall and make my way to a cheap seat to watch another final there now. They didn't even keep the twin towers, the most iconic structures in world football. It's like Christians demolishing St Paul's dome and replacing it with a Meccano arch.

I recently saw Sex Pistol John Lydon interviewed on *The One Show*, and he talked about his trip to the new Wembley to watch his team Arsenal in the League Cup final.

'Talking of basic civil freedoms, I went to Arsenal v Birmingham yesterday and I was constantly harassed by stewards, telling us we should sit down, we're spoiling the game. Football is now a sit down sport? I need to come back to this country more and put things right, it sucks.'

Well said Johnny, you should, but although you've always been ahead of the game, you're over ten years behind me, I wrote about this in *If the Kids are United* in 1998.

I'd urge West Ham fans to fight tooth and nail and hammers, not to leave their spiritual home for the Olympic Stadium. You won't realise what you had until it's gone.

The money from the book enabled me to keep my season ticket at United for several more years and experience some great moments. Even though I wasn't at the European Cup final, the 99 Treble year had many more special memories for me: beating Forest 8-1 at the City Ground; never have I been more unpopular in my Notts local pubs than that night, especially as I walked in taking the piss by quoting Michael Palin's *Ripping Yarns: Golden Gordon*: 'Eight one, eight bloody one.' Needing to win the last match of the season at Old Trafford to secure the title, but being 0-1 down until Beckham equalised with a screamer into the top corner; Cole scored the winner. Losing 0-1 to Liverpool at Old Trafford in the FA Cup 4th round, with only 2 minutes of normal time left, the red Scousers celebrating, singing 'You'll Never Walk Alone.' Until Yorke equalised and then Solskjaer - doing a dress rehearsal for his Treble winning climax to the season - scoring the winner in the 2nd minute of injury time. After the game, outside Old Trafford, there was a few Walkers Crisps lorries doing a promotion for their new 'Max' crisps by giving box loads of them away to United fans. They were chucked at the Liverpool fans instead with chants of 'Feed the Scousers let them know it's Christmas time.'

Demolishing Arsenal and their title hopes in February 2001 at Old Trafford with United going 5-0 up in 38 minutes (winning 6-1 in the end), and going on to win a third consecutive title.

Ruud van Nistelrooy scoring 17 goals in 16 games as United rose from 10th place and eight points behind leaders Arsenal to win the 2003 Premier League title.

The debut of Ronaldo, coming off the bench and getting us off our sorry seats by performing his first trick: dropping his shoulder to skip past a defender and signal a new great United winger and No.7 had arrived on the scene.

'The Battle of the Buffet,' - United ending an arrogant Arsenal's 49 match unbeaten run in the league (their players had '50 Not Out' t-shirts on under their team shirts ready to reveal them). Rooney won a penalty (scored by Van Nistelrooy to avenge his miss in 'The First Battle of Old Trafford' the season before) and scored the second himself; his first league goal for United on his 19th birthday. Then Rooney's wonder volley against Newcastle shortly afterwards. These were the standout highlights, then shortly afterwards.....

...the Glazer family took over the club. An American business family with little, if any, interest in English football, Manchester United as a football club and its proud history, its supporters and Manchester. Financial jugglers, acrobats and illusionists that would put Billy Smart's Circus to shame. Loading the club with their own £500 million debt, incurring huge annual interest payments, to pay off their other debts, and pocket the profit from the sale of shares. Milking us loyal supporters by increasing season ticket prices then bringing in new conditions that you had to purchase all cup games in advance on top, taking the upfront price to over £1000 for a season, for what? A lifeless bowl most of the time, for a stand that it used to cost me £2.50 to stand in a real atmosphere, a real experience, to pay your debts and see little investment in the team and club, other than by 'restructuring the composition of our stadium,' with 'a particular emphasis on developing premium seating and hospitality facilities to enhance our overall match-day profitability.' I sold my soul to the Red Devils, not to a group of American businessmen to play poker with for financial gain, I fold!

I'd already been thinking that it was time to Stretford End it all. The atmosphere at Old Trafford is all but dead, most of the time. But a ludicrous sight that sums up the modern day state of what was once the most fearsome, vociferous football 'ends' in the game, the noise of which was once described as being like the sound of an aircraft taking off, pushed me near the edge: during one game, the lame pantomime sing-a-long atmosphere spluttered into life. In front of us a line of 50-somethings and pensioner season ticket holders sat. Several of them often complained if any younger fans stood up in front of them. One woman, a Molly Sugden a-like with purple rinse hair – who could usually be heard (yes it was quiet enough to hear the conversation of the row of people in front of you most of the time) between munches on tuna sandwiches from their packed lunch (so ok at least not prawns) chatting away with her husband about getting a few more marigolds for the garden, started – still sat in her seat but excitedly clapping her hands above her head, swinging her head from side to side - to sing the old 1970's Red army hooligan song:

'My old man said be a City fan,

And I said bollocks you're a cunt,

I'd rather shag a bucket with a big hole in it,

Than be a City fan for just one minute,

With hammers and hatchets, Stanley knives and spanners,

We'll show the City bastards how to fight (how to fight),

I'd rather shag a bucket with a big hole in it,

Than be a City fan,

Altogether now...'

To use a modern day abbreviation FFS. I bet the away fans were cowering in their £45 seats, their team's players trembling so much they can barely kick a ball. I shook my head with dismay and looked to my left and saw the grumpy grey haired guy (whose scouse accent never seemed right in there), who usually wore Ronnie Corbett jumpers but had just graduated to Val Doonican ones, was also joining in, gingerly punching the air with as much power as his arthritic limbs could muster.

I was 39 at the time and thought that's it, I'm out of here, I'm not going to end up like that, time to bow out. It has always been my belief that no one over the age of 40 or 35 even should be in the Stretford End. That's how it used to be, becoming a Stretford Ender was a rights of passage for a United fan when a kid/teenager, your time had arrived to step up to the mark and become part of the engine room that generated the mighty red cauldron's energy and atmosphere. At the same time men in their thirties, who've given twenty years loyal service, make way for the new generation and move to the seats (yes I know there used to be seats at the back of the old Stretford End, but you know what I mean, well should do).

Recently two guys in their 50's, who go in my local, long time armchair United fans, have only just started actually going to Old Trafford to support United. Where do they sit? Yep, the Stretford End. One asked me if I went to any matches and when I said 'no' he replied with 'Huh I've been to more matches than you' (he's 52 and been to 6). He was a bit taken aback when I told him I'd been there, done that, bought the t-shirt and team shirts and wrote the bloody book. My days as a real Stretford Ender queuing in the rain outside for over an hour to get in and stand on the terrace, all those years as a season ticket holder.

The Glazer take over was the final straw.

I'd seen other genuine Stretford Enders and hardcore United fans disappear after the Glazer take over. A line of them had sat in the same row as us. Members of IMUSA. They used to give us leaflets giving voice to the genuine working-class Reds and warning about the changing face of the club; prominent voices and protesters in fending off the Murdoch take-over. But when they failed to do the same with the Glazers – and had little support from influential people from the inner corridors at Old Trafford – they were out of there, helping the breakaway club F.C. United get off the ground.

There was only Alex Ferguson and Ryan Giggs (to think - standing on the Stretford End - I saw him make his Old Trafford debut back in the MaDchester days of 1991, when I was 25 going on 19 and he's still playing! Makes me feel old, but what a legend, what a great example of how to be a professional footballer) keeping the pulse alive of the United I love. And it can beat stronger than any other club with those two involved as it did last night. Fergie's shrewd team selection and another tireless, timeless Giggs performance ripped their opponents Schalke apart 'Giggs, Giggs will tear you apart again and again and again..' to all but secure another European Cup final appearance.

Even though United totally dominated, my heart still thumped with danger every time Schalke attacked. Not as fast and powerful as when I was a 10-year-old United nut, listening to the transistor in the kitchen, when the tension and excitement nearly gave me a heart attack. Good job too, it would kill me now.

Part of me did feel sorry for Schalke. There's a club to envy in its running and structure. No one person owns the club, its thousands of supporters all do. Ticket prices are kept low and even though the stadium is a modern one it has terraces - like many in the German Bundesliga - so great atmosphere too. These have to be converted into seats for European games, but this is a simple process, the terraces simply lift back to reveal seats underneath.

I'd love to see this type of terracing at Premiership grounds. It won't happen in this nanny state, where conker trees are cut down by councils less one fall on someone's head, (ouch the pain, the pain! They'd be rolling down the street in agony like the modern day footballer who's had the merest contact with an opposing team player). Or someone may pick them up and revert to gladiatorial savagery by attaching the conker to strings and fighting with them. Where my nephew was given a yellow card in his junior school playground for gathering snow into a ball shape, he didn't even throw it! If he had it would have been red and a 3 month playground ban.

Yes but what about Hillsborough, surely you don't want to go back to those days? I hear you say. Of course not. Following Germany's lead there's no danger of a disaster like that happening again. Their terraces are designed, planned and incorporated into modern purpose built stadiums. Barriers separate every row and every supporter stands on an allocated spot. It's actually more dangerous at Premiership stadiums as many supporters stand anyway (and those who don't and moan wouldn't be in a 'standing' section) but with the obstacle of seats that don't fold away. At one United match I saw one frustrated fan - after a dodgy refereeing decision - stamp down his foot accidentally on a seat, this shattered and he was also sent tumbling over the rows of people in front.

I hope Fergie keeps the fires burning and the Red flag flying high for as long as he feels fit enough to do so. Long enough to thwart Jose Mourinho's apparent desire to become the next United manager anyway. His type of tactics and football are not in keeping with the United spirit. Last night (this epilogue is ongoing over a week or so) his Real Madrid played Barcelona in the other semi-final of the European Cup.

Now I know this is one of the biggest rivalries and derbies in world football, so would be highly charged, especially as a European Cup final appearance was at stake, but these two teams usually let their football do the talking. Mourinho knew he couldn't win this way, fairly, so the tactics he employed were to bully and kick the beautiful game out of one of the best purveyors of it the game has ever seen. And everyone knows bullying is really cowardice and it will always fail in the end.

For an hour it worked, Mourinho looked on with an evil, knowing grin. Then a modern day George Best took over, things got Messi. His second goal, a mazy run leaving desperate defenders lunging in his wake, keeping his balance beautifully before slipping the ball past the goalkeeper into the net, was reminiscent (dare I say it, perhaps even better?) of George Best in his prime, leaving Chopper Harris and the goalkeeper on their backsides to score.

Messi, his team-mates (nurtured as a flowing skilful team since being brought together as youngsters ala Busby Babes) and the club owned by the supporters are a great example of how United could go back to the future.

I've been back to the future myself this week. First for writing this epilogue and going through *If the Kids are United* again. Then last Sunday on BBC 2 was an excellent TV film called *United* about the Munich air disaster and its aftermath, centred around Jimmy Murphy (played by David Tennant) and Bobby Charlton. This prompted me to dig out BBC's 1980's video on the history of Manchester United that ends at the dawn of Fergie's era. And then one of my favourite books from childhood, Derek Hodgson's *The Manchester United Story*, still one of the best. This ends in 1977 and was given to me as a present the Christmas of that year, a week after my first visit to Old Trafford, Dad's best ever Christmas present to me (even though they lost 0-4 to Clough's rampant champions to be, Forest).

So two things happened that week that shaped my life: my devotion to the United religion was secured after the pilgrimage and I discovered the beauty of storytelling (thinking about it, you have to add other essential life shaping elements from Christmas 77. I was listening to my sister and brother play punk records, loving the sounds and just months away from starting my own record collection. And the magic of my Christmases as a kid has never left me and 77 was one of the best).

The great on-going documentary series *7 Up* starts with the phrase 'show me a boy at seven and I'll show you the man.' For me you could say 'show me Tony Hill in December 1977 and I'll show you the man.' As, when you fast forward to this week, I'm watching Manchester United reach another European Cup final, dreaming of getting a ticket for the final, which is at Wembley but doubt I will (I still have my lucky 1977 Cup winners scarf and no doubt will be clutching that tightly on the big day) and checking Amazon daily for my new book *The Palace and the Punks* to be listed, and putting the finishing touches to a side project – a photo book about the Glastonbury Festival.

Finally making it to Glastonbury was the music equivalent of getting an FA Cup final ticket. Even though I wished to go there right back to my 1980's indie days, for several reasons I never made it (probably because money was short in those days and getting to United was top of the list, and later the festival became so big that tickets sold out fast and I never managed to get one), until ticking it off my bucket list in 2009 and returning in 2010.

All good things come to those who wait. Both years were great – and hot and sunny! But my first in 2009 was part of one of the most magical weeks of my life. Unforgettable spirit, many new friends, fantastic music, ending with Blur's comeback gig. I cried along (this was a release from a couple of tough years, my spirit reborn) with Damon as they ended with 'Universal' – 'it really really can happen.' After the festival I chilled out with friends down in Devon, then crashed at Bristol with mate Jamie (who's originally from Jacksdale) and girlfriend Naomi. A visit to the Banksy exhibition before Jamie took me out on the streets at night looking for Banky's in their right environment, both of us stoned, listening to dub-step on pirate radio.

I was so enchanted by it all that I started writing a collection of fairytales – the first of which *The Curse of the*

Crooked Spire I'm waiting for a brilliant artist to illustrate. Or was that those magic mushrooms?

I still love United, but it's no longer an obsession, I like football but it's no longer a passion, I can take it or leave it most of the time. Music, that's my drug, I'm still addicted to it.

Manchester United reached the FA Cup final again in 2004 - the opponents were Millwall - but it fell on the same day Morrissey was making his Manchester comeback gig (he'd not played there for 10 years and it was his birthday too). Me and my music mates (James and the lads) had tickets for the gig and I've got to admit – and this might seem hard to believe, coming from the same person that dreamed of barely nothing else but seeing United in the Cup final for 25 years – but I wouldn't have swapped it for a FA Cup final ticket, these days. In fact I didn't even watch the entire match, just the first half in the pub, before we set off for Manchester and the Morrissey gig. Those friends I was going with weren't into football, so I didn't have the cheek to ask them to turn off The Smiths classics (I wouldn't have dared more like) to put the Cup Final second half commentary on. I only found out United had won when I spotted United fans in jubilant mood in Manchester pubs when we got there.

And you know what? Seeing United win the cup (at the Millennium Stadium at the time) would not have been a more treasured memory than that Morrissey gig (Franz Ferdinand supported him too). He did four The Smiths songs, including the timeless 'There Is a Light That Never Goes Out.' Grown men, tough looking Manc bastards, cried as they sang-a-long, I tell you! The moment was spoilt a little when I looked down and saw a lad about 13, a Franz

Ferdinand fan, a mini Alex Kapranos look-a-like, his back to the stage, arms folded with disdain, scowling at his dad and the rest of us.

Glastonbury 2010 fell when the World Cup was underway, I watched a woeful England scrape to a needed victory against Slovenia on big screens in the Pyramid Stage field, stood in baking sunshine on the Wednesday (this before the music had begun).

This set up a knockout showdown with old rivals Germany...on Sunday teatime, by which time I'm full of the Glastonbury spirit, and there's nothing to enhance the soul as much as Glastonbury. I'm winding down after 5 glorious sun soaked days full of wonderful sights and sounds, chilling with friends in the gathering tent at our camping area up on the hill overlooking the Pyramid Stage.

Down there thousands are gathered as Slash rips through his set. But thousands - maybe 10,000 to 30,000 - have gone to fields at the edge of the festival to watch England versus Germany on big screens. I was torn, I'd never missed an England game in the World Cup in my life. I have the mental scars, and that was the problem, did I really want to wreck the blissful Glastonbury state I was in? But if they won? I'd be in a perfect state of mind.

I decided to leave it until half-time then wander over there, see how they were doing (which I didn't know, no radio or TV of course. You rarely hear any news from the outside World at Glasto, the death of Michael Jackson during the 2009 festival being the major exception).

So I told my friends I'd catch up with them later and started walking down the farm road at the back of the camping hill that lead to the fields where the match was being shown. I'd only walked 100 yards when Slash's guitar screamed out the intro to 'Sweet Child O Mine,' grabbed me by the scruff of the neck and dragged me back up the road. There was no way I was missing that. And anyway I knew the England World Cup script too well. I wasn't in the mood for a nightmare. Slash it was, and up next was Ray Davies; chilling with friends on a sunny Sunday afternoon at Glastonbury, listening to 'Waterloo Sunset' is just about the most spiritualized I've ever felt.

I knew I'd made the right decision, especially as - in unplugged moments between Slash and Ray Davies - groans could be heard drifting from thousands of people stood in a field at the edge of the festival watching England. Their long faces on their return confirmed it, England had yet again gone out of the World Cup in a painful manner.

Yep I love live music more than live football now. You still get great atmosphere at festivals and gigs and can stand. The nearest I've come to that old football terrace days feeling was seeing Oasis live at Old Trafford (the cricket ground that is, there was never any prospect of the City diehard Gallagher's doing a gig at United's ground.) I was full of boasts after that gig, about being a hardened gig goer and terrace survivor; as I made it near to the front of the 50,000 crowd just in time for 'Live Forever,' whilst another young lad in our crowd - all 6ft 2 and 14 stone or so of him - went down, was dragged out and given oxygen by medics.

And on one memorable night I could dream I was a 'Rock 'N' Roll Star.' I went with a couple of mates to see Killing Joke at Rock City; we stood up on the balcony there. Then 'Purple Star' (that's the nickname that I've thought of her as ever since) sort of singled me out for spiritual healing at the gig. She shows up - a Courtney Love look about her - and starts pushing these tables back, saying she needs space to dance, telling me how she's being following the Killing Joke for years and the night before she'd got up on stage with them wearing this purple sequined dress.

'I'd like to have seen that,' I commented.

'Well I was going to wear it tonight,' she replied.

'You should have,' I said with that cheeky old smile of mine.

Then she tells me it's in her hotel room (next to Rock City) and would I go back with her so she can put it on. Of course I was only too eager to oblige. You should have seen the look on my mates faces as she took me by the hand and led me out of Rock City via a stage door – stopping to chat with the support group, who'd just come off stage and she seemed to know. Turned out she was sharing a hotel room with the manager of Killing Joke (but he wasn't there at the time).

She plonked me down on her bed, takes out the purple dress and starts stripping in front of me, casually chatting away, asking me what my star sign is. I tell her Scorpio and said she knew I was because she is and so was her ex.

'That caused fireworks in our relationship and he wanted to shag me all the time as well. You shagged another Scorpio?' she asks stood there in her sexy underwear. I couldn't believe my luck.

She gets up from the bed, puts on this purple dress, grabs a set of keys and takes me by the hand again. The keys are for Killing Joke's tour bus. We have it to ourselves - at the rear of Rock City - whilst the group are inside the venue ready to go on stage. Purple Star pours me a drink, shows me a framed picture of her (taken some years back by the looks of it) that's in there and tells me she'd travelled with them down from a concert in Manchester. Tonight I can

316

believe I'm a rock 'n' roll star. Until an enormous roadie (he looked like an extra from *Mad Max 2*) who knew I wasn't, came aboard.

I'm thinking, fuck he's going to kill me, but what a way to go. But no, Purple Star – who obviously knew him as well – disarmed him straight away with her sharp, streetwise Manc humour. Hearing Killing Joke are on stage we head back to the gig.

The stage door was now locked so we had to walk around to the front entrance. She took me by the hand again, held it tight and said: 'Glad I met you, I feel safe with you already, I can see your aura, it's so like mine.' Then she stops to point out a shimmering star - just visible through the light pollution - 'that star is me.'

Back on the balcony, at the gig, she danced up and down like she was possessed, spiralling around, flinging her arms out, knocking people out of the way. She looked like a purple super nova. We kept in touch for a while, met up in Manchester, but we were just star sailing spaced ships passing in the Rock City night, that had briefly docked in a port in a solar wind storm.

I wasn't so full of myself (several years later) when I nearly suffered the same fate as the fallen lad at the Oasis gig – and then realised that my days in the mosh pit could be over too – when we went to see the White Stripes at the Empress Ballroom, Blackpool on my 40th birthday (the best live performance I've ever seen). We were half way back to start with, but midway through their set they moved to a side stage to do a few quieter acoustic numbers. A guy told me to move to the front of the main stage whilst I had the chance, as he'd seen them the night before and they came back on that one for the encore.

So I did and soon regretted it. Maybe it was too many birthday tipples and not age I told myself. But the crush of bodies was too much for me. During a slow number the lights were slowly going out in my head, I was fading away, passing out and there was nothing I could do about it. I did momentarily, but the amount of bodies pushing into my back kept me on my feet and luckily next up was 'Blue Orchid.' This not only brought me around, but had me pogoing up and down punching the air like the teenager again.

At the gigs end, though, I decided it best to retreat from being on the front line ever again. And when we went to an indie club afterwards and I threw myself about to the Artic Monkeys 'I Bet You Look Good On The Dance Floor,' and I didn't, I noticed, when catching a glimpse of myself in mirrored tiles. So decided to quit doing that too. I could never dance anyway, but then again neither could George Best and he had the balance of a ballerina on a football pitch.

At least I can't see any danger of me becoming as sad as another group of 'gig goers' we saw outside the Winter Gardens before the White Stripes gig. Sat in deck chairs, wrapped up in sleeping bags in the storm force winds and driving rain was masses of Daniel O'Donnell fans; securing their place in the queue for the mad stampeded for when the wet crooners tickets went on sale the following morning. Yes if I get that sad, fucking shoot me!

But as I finish writing this epilogue it's the Monday after United have lost in the European Cup final. Not just lost, totally outclassed, and I am gutted. I wasn't there of course, celebrities got a ticket, even people I know who are not really football fans but are connected through business so ended up with corporate seats were there.

At least United lost to a great side, Barcelona, so no complaints about that. Beaten by one of the best teams ever, with one of the best ever players. This Barcelona play the game the right way, don't cheat or roll down the pitch if tapped on the ankle. The beautiful game on show, they restored my faith in football so thumbs up for the short arses. Yep the average size of their midfield and forwards is 5ft 8. I could have been a contender.

By chance, a guy who knew me as a kid was in the pub the following day with his wife and friends. He pointed to me and told them: 'You know him he was the best footballer I've ever seen as a kid, you couldn't get the ball off him, he should have been a professional, you should have been,' he said turning to me.

'Yeah, maybe,' I said looking down at my pint, 'but they said I was too small to make it, Barcelona proved them wrong yesterday, maybe.' I laughed.

So no I didn't become a professional footballer, but if you go back to December 1977, see that boy and I'll show you the man. And I'd like to sign off with a quote from Derek Hodgson's great book *The Manchester United Story* that I received as a Christmas present that year, the final lines in the book are: 'Man does not change and his winter dreams live on.'

Not Nineteen Forever

June 2012:

Reasons not to be cheerful, Elizabeth my dear:

The Queen may have long reigned over us, for 60 years, it's her Diamond Jubilee celebrations. She looked radiant in her sunny bright yellow dress and hat, but had a painted on twisted Rolf Harris portrait smile on her face as she looked to the heavens, stood on the Royal barge travelling down the Thames; although God may be saving her, the almighty one was pissing on her parade, refusing to part the clouds and send long sun rays over her majesty and subjects. This day it long rained over us – Atlantis street parties, stubborn fuckers determined to do their patriotic duty, sat out there in sodden clothes, waving sagging Union Jacks, eating soggy salmon paste and cucumber sandwiches, with Vera Lynn on in the background – as it had for most of the last 60 days of what was becoming one of the wettest summers on record.

The constant downpours began as soon as the authorities and meteorologists had issued the accursed words: 'drought, hosepipe ban, barbecue summer ahead.' But I'm sure the constant days of damp blues was brought on by that moment, the one us Reds try not to recall but are haunted by....

...'AGUEROOOOOOOO .....'

And so it continued, like some horrible *Groundhog Day*, day after day, a relentless rhythm, week after week: being woken by rain beating on the window, beating up our sun starved souls. Out walking the dog again, through a swampland, ambushed by clouds of midges, once bitten, a thousand times, bitter blues now the only fuckers happy.

'Down, down, you bring me down, I hear you knocking at my door when I can't sleep at night.'

I developed the worst cold I've had in years, in June, then had a vomiting stomach virus; I was already sick to my stomach. What chance did the United fans have of being cheered up by England in the European Championships? None of course, Groundhog International Duty Day, inevitably they went out on penalties. Another Blue

Monday, except for the blues of Manchester, full of the joys of summer, even this one, forever…

…'AGUEROOOOOOOO…..'

So you wouldn't have thought that the best place to be heading for during one of the wettest spells since Noah considered building an ark would be a Manchester full of blues, even in the red half. Yet here I was, on route there, halfway across the Peak District, having driven through some of the worst conditions I've ever encountered on the road: not one, but two thunderstorms of Biblical proportions. The first just a few miles out of Jacksdale. Rainwater – several inches deep – overflowing from drains and cascading down Somercotes hill; it was like driving up a waterfall (queue 'Waterfall' on my iPod coming out of my car stereo). There was some comic relief here: a woman emerged from the front door of her terraced house (only about 10ft from the road) and was engulfed by a wave caused by a lorry speeding through the flooded road.

But come rain or shine, monsoon or a thousand piss-taking Bertie blue nose Magoo's, I wasn't going to miss the following day's event. The biggest music event of the year, of many a year, many of us had waited, many, many years for it and thought it would never happen (like City winning the league). The Stone Roses were back, tomorrow would be their first homecoming gig at Heaton Park, Manchester.

The second storm over the Peak District was spectacular in the setting. I paused here in my usual spot - off the main road up a little lane to a lay-by with a beautiful view. There a wonderful thing happened, the rain stopped and - off in the direction of Manchester - the clouds briefly parted, sun rays touched down, a strip of blue sky, hmm Man City blue, was this another new 'Welcome to

321

Manchester' sign, like the huge one in town that had ex United player Carlos Tevez now wearing a City shirt?

...'AGUEROOOOOOOO.....'

On that fateful last day of the 2011-12 season, I was in the back room of a local pub, watching United's match at Sunderland, sat with a few other Reds and several unbiased locals. The next room in the pub was the lounge, then at the front of the pub the tap room. In the latter they were showing the City game, loads of United haters were in there.

'Fuck em, it's in the bag,' I said smugly, full of confidence. There was just minutes left, United 1-0 up at Sunderland and City fucking it up; Sparky Hughes was getting his revenge on them, forever a United warrior, his Q.P.R. team 2-1 up.

A cheer went up in the tap room, so what, too late. 'It'll hurt them even more getting so close.' The ref blew the final whistle at Sunderland. The United players and Fergie began to celebrate the winning of the championship, for the 20th time. Full of myself I knocked back my pint and headed for the bar in the lounge to get another and a celebratory whisky in - to do a toast to the tap room City glory hunters. I froze in the doorway, excited chants arose: 'Go on City, go on City...'

Balotelli toe-poked it to....

...'AGUEROOOOOOOO.....'

My pint pot shattered on the floor, all the heads in the tap room turned on me, the chants, the piss taking, several ran across the room to playfully wrestle me to the floor, 'pile on.'

I wriggled free, escaped (there'd be no escape, not all summer) to the back room. In frustration I kicked the pub dog's ball (a rubber toy one, not the dog's bollocks), it flew across the room, knocking a pint out of the hand of Spike, a 18st Leeds fan. I had to get him a new one in. I remember little of the rest of the bottom of a glass day of blues.

I try to shake off that memory, The Stone Roses 'I am the Resurrection' is on the stereo, United will be back. And the weather improves by the mile on the drive down into Manchester.

I arrived at my sister, Elaine's home in Chorlton, and later went for a few beers in what I consider my local pubs up there, around Chorlton Green. Then was astonished to learn, next morning – when reading the latest news about The Stone Roses comeback online – that these very pubs are the places the Roses used to drink in around the time they were recording their classic debut album. I'd never knew that until this day (then again I recall that my sister's ex, singer/songwriter Edward Barton, used to play football with Ian Brown and co in a park in Chorlton back in the day), and I was going to see them live, at last. Not only that, 'Mersey Paradise' was written about Chorlton Water Park, we often went there too. I'm buzzing now, the time to head off to Heaton Park draws near. Even though they'd been forecasting rain for this day, another miracle of the Roses third coming happens, there's no rain in sight, the clouds are parting, the sun shines.

I took the tram into town and when I stepped off in the city centre I feel like a 20-something again: loads of people in their old MaDchester gear, smiles on t-shirts, smiles on faces. Many shops are playing The Stone Roses and other Republic of Mancunia rave revolution sounds. There's a real great vibe, I'm filled with nostalgia, and head for Affleck's Palace for more of a trip back in time. On the wall there I see a classic old The Stone Roses poster, hung next to a Wedding Present, *George Best* album one, the United legend in classic pose, the Roses and Best, a perfect United Manchester combination.

I catch another tram off down to Heaton Park, and realise it's not just us old Roses fans looking forward to this day, there's loads of teenagers wearing Roses and MaDchester t-shirts also heading to the BIG event; a couple of teenage girls start loudly singing Roses songs, and everyone joins in, a beautiful moment. In the queue outside Heaton Park there are people who have travelled far and wide to be here. I start talking to a couple from America, who tell me they've never been to England before but just had to be here for the Roses comeback.

Then the gates open and we pour in. There are still hours to go yet before the Roses make their entrance, but no one cares, we're here, the lucky ones, and the sun still shines. There are lovely views back to the Peak District from here – I think of the couple in a *Love on the Dole* sat on those hills looking back over Manchester.

There are several support acts to look forward to: the Wailers, The Vaccines and Primal Scream. Mani had been in the latter until now, of course, and it was whilst he was with them that I'd met him on the platform of Oxford Road station - where he was with his lad, taking him to watch United. A real friendly guy, but I thought it best not to ask about a Stone Roses reunion as I was sure he was asked that all the time. So just talked United and told him how much I loved what he'd done with Primal Scream and that I saw them support the Jesus and Mary Chain in the 80's (when Bobby Gillespie played a drum for them).

In Heaton Park I meet up with Roses loving mates from back in Westwood/Jacksdale. We're in time to get wrist bands to be in the inner circle in front of the stage. We get beers in, watch the support acts (all great) then the moment has arrived.

As the Roses walk on stage the roar of the crowd is as loud as being at Old Trafford if Best, Law, Robson and Cantona all somehow came out of the tunnel to play at the same time. Remi on drums as wild and brilliant as Keith Moon (ok not quite, but who could be?), Mani a wild eyed possessed Manc wizard, John Squire proving he's one of the best guitarist ever, and Ian Brown Manc strutting around, he's lost none of his swagger and unique vocal delivery.

A setlist of all the classic songs with a psychedelic Squire art inspired light show behind. The highlights are definitely 'Fool's Gold' – that goes on for about 20 minutes, building all the time, Squire's guitar playing stunning, and they sign off with a barnstorming delivery of 'I Am the Resurrection.' We all feel our soggy souls have been resurrected. The Roses line up, arms around each other, take their bows to loud cheers and then a spectacular firework display finishes off the show. Walking out we see Bez just in front of us. Mad fer it all, sorted and buzzing again.

The resurrection had begun, the mood of the year changed and by the time of the London Olympics, the whole country was bathed in golden sunshine and on a collective high as Team GB's gold haul mounted (this after a brilliant 'leftie' Danny Boyle opening ceremony – the music of the Sex Pistols, PiL, then Glastonbury Tor, coal miners, British countryside - my life flashing before my eyes). Now for United's resurrection.

2012-13:

If I only could have been that optimistic about United's prospects for the 2012-13 season, I feared Fergie's potential farewell party could turn into a wake. To me the team he now was left with looked average by United's standards; the new generation of Fergie's Fledglings looked nowhere near on par with the class of 92. I wasn't even one hundred percent sure they were good enough to finish in the top 4 (which of course would prove to be true at United A.F. – After Ferguson). So I consider it one of Ferguson's greatest achievements and a demonstration of the genius of his management that he turned a mediocre team into Champions. The £24 million signing of Van Persie was the key factor, though; an ever present in the team, scoring 26 league goals (many of which proved to be the winner in close fought matches), with a sublime hat-trick against Aston Villa to snatch back the Premiership crown from Bertie Magoo.

As United cruised to the title there came the expected announcement that Sir Alex Ferguson was to retire, a fitting fairytale ending as he lifted the Premiership Trophy, United's 20th league title. New Manc music heroes (and United fans) The Courteeners had provided the perfect anthem, 'Not Nineteen Forever.'

And to think I was not much more than 19 when Fergie's reign began, just about all my adult life he'd been at United. I still thought I was 19 in my head, still trying to live that lifestyle - going to Glastonbury for the first time in my 40's, a free spirit, no commitments, still going to Rock City for gigs, even still wearing band t-shirts and black Converse boots - until I looked in the bathroom mirror and saw my Dad looking back at me (well, elements of, Dad was far

326

more handsome than me; there's a photo of him from the 1950's looking very much the Albert Finney as Arthur Seaton type). I'm developing his later years characteristics, like Victor Meldrew moaning about the state of modern football in Dad's language. I used to cringe when Dad called people 'duck,' even men, and I've started doing the same, uncontrollably, like I've developed some kind of local dialect Tourettes.

I was in the Woodstock pub in Didsbury, Manchester. A big pub and I wasn't sure where the toilets were located, so I asked a young Irish woman, serving behind the bar: 'Where's your toilet duck?'

She looked at me a little nonplussed at first, then disappeared and returned with the Toilet Duck cleaning fluid. I reckon she thought I was from environmental health doing a spot check.

Another 19 forever nostalgia trip in the summer (a proper one, the sun never stops shining now United have replaced City as champions). Transmission 5, live from Jodrell Bank (where we watch Andy Murray win Wimbledon on big screens in the afternoon in baking sunshine), Johnny Marr performing several of The Smith songs in his set, including 'There Is A Light That Never Goes Out' and 'Hand in Glove.' Then headliners New Order – 'Ceremony', 'Blue Monday', '586', 'True Faith.' All fantastic, especially with images projected onto the giant Lovell Telescope; we're space tripping out.

The best track of the night and one of the best live track moments I've ever experienced (which includes the following live: Radiohead doing 'Creep,' PiL 'Public Image' 83, the Jesus and Mary Chain 'Never Understand' 85, The Cult 'She Sells Sanctuary' 85, SLF 'Alternative Ulster,' Echo and the Bunnymen 'Killing Moon' 85, Siouxsie and the Banshees performing 'Fireworks' on Nov 5th, The Verve 'This is Music' 95, Neil Young 'Cinnamon Girl,' U2 'Where the Streets Have No Name,' Oasis 'Liver Forever,' Blur 'Park Life' with Phil Daniels, Gorillaz with The Clash's Paul Simonon and Mick Jones and soul legend Bobby Womack doing 'Stylo,' Killing Joke 'Requiem,' Motorhead 'Ace of Spades,' The White Stripes 'Seven Nation Amy,' Morrissey singing 'There is a Light That Never Goes Out,' Stevie Wonder 'Superstition,' Laura Marling 'Rambling Man' in York Minster, the Sex Pistols 'Anarchy in the UK,' Black Rebel Motorcycle Club 'Love Spreads,' Arcade Fire 'Wake Up,' PJ Harvey 'Pocket Knife,' Muse 'Supermassive Black Hole,' UK Subs Charlie Harper dedicating 'Warhead' to me as I put the concert on, The Stone Roses 'Fools Gold,' being on the guest list – thanks to Manc singer/songwriter Jo Rose – to see an early, intimate gig of First Aid Kit at Manchester Deaf Institute for 'Hard Believer' beauty, and Spinal Tap turning it up to 11 with 'Big Bottom Girls') was a mind blowing version of 'Temptation.' To accompany this they pulled out all the extra terrestrial wizardry for the telescope display; giant lasers zapped us, but with a life giving force rather than death beams, a visual and aural mind fuck. Then the telescope turns into a giant 250ft in diameter spinning mirror ball, unbelievable, as the music spins on and out there.

They end with my favourite song of all time, 'Love Will Tear Us Apart' – 'Giggs, Giggs will tear you apart again.' At the end of the song the Lovell Telescope turns into a giant blue moon, 'you started singing too soon,' tranquillity base.

Then it's the drive back to Manchester through the countryside, miles from light pollution with stars shining down, pulsars pulsing, my head pulsing, 19 again in my head, but happy United are not 19 forever.

I'm staying at my sister, Elaine's, for the night, she now lives just a mile and a 5 minute drive from Manchester United Football Club (football club, football club, it's a fuckin' football club!). So on my way back from the New Order, Jodrell Bank gig I can't resist stopping off at Old Trafford. It's 1.30 am on a Monday, all is quiet at the Theatre of Dreams, the red neon Manchester United lettering up on the stand, a light that never goes out. The statue of Sir Matt Busby below, the man who lit the eternal flame. The bronze figures of Charlton, Law and Best looking up at him and the stadium. The Munich air disaster memorial plaque just round the corner to the left. All legends that shaped United's and my destiny.

My head's still nostalgia spinning to the sounds of Joy Division, New Order and The Smiths from Transmission 5 at Jodrell Bank. The never to be forgotten image of the giant mirror ball still spinning to 'Temptation' flashing into my head, like a giant looking glass back into the past, triggering my memory projector, reeling out my United and Manchester history. I now see Old Trafford as it was when I first came here with Dad in 1977, stood on this very spot with him (the entrance for away fans was here back then), saying I wanted to stand on the Stretford End, Dad having none of that.

The music now drifts away and I can hear the roar of the crowd. The mirror ball time machine on fast forward, stopping when I was a teenager, getting off the bus and walking down to the ground to finally become a Stretford Ender, on to the rise of 'Alex Ferguson's red and white army.' Flashes of great players, matches and goals, the night so long waited for, when United were crowned champions for the first time in 26 years, thousands of flags flying, boy to man.

I walk round the corner of the stadium to pay respects to the man who made some of my dreams come true, pause at his statue, Sir Alex Ferguson, in front of the enormous stand named in his honour. Like a Caesar at the coliseum, where his elite gladiators defeated all-comers. I take bow, 'thanks Fergie.'

The last twelve months – from The Stones Roses resurrection, the Olympics, United winning the 20th League Title, this night of 19 forever nostalgia Transmissions and Old Trafford pilgrimage – has been another memorable passage of time, but the mirror ball is spinning on, Boethius's wheel is turning, another chapter is to be written in the history of Manchester United and my life.

2013-14:

Embarrassment! My knees are definitely not 19 forever. I took my nephew Alex down onto the rec with a football to demonstrate the art of a Giggs shimmy and Rooney scissor kick, and ended up tearing a knee ligament.

'Ha, you're about fit to be in the United team now, not exactly the Artful Dodger are ya,' was Alex's response to my United Red faced antics.

He was about to appear in a school play version of *Oliver*, so I mentioned the 1960's musical film.

'Are the men who played Oliver and the Artful Dodger still alive?' He asked

I told him the one who played the Artful Dodger is dead but Mark Lester (Oliver) is still around, and in fact was good friends with Michael Jackson and that it's rumoured (in the papers, mind) that he is the real dad of Jacko's kids. Then I was worried I was going to have to explain this, but Alex was ahead of me:

'When he was in bed with the mother did he ask "can I have some more," was his reply.

Humiliation! United lose 1-4 to City at Old Trafford, it could have been 8 to them, and even more of my own family are taking the piss now: Mam loved telling me how she phoned our Elaine in south Manchester on Sunday tea-time and my sister says to her: 'Hold up, listen to this,' putting the phone to an open window. Loud cheers could clearly be heard down the line from all the surrounding pubs, 'sounds like another City goal has gone in, our Tony will be happy ha ha ha.'

I reckon the spirit of Dad is living on through Mam: I called in at the old house for Sunday dinner, and put the football on; Mam stared at the TV screen with a mixture of bemusement, amusement and disgust.

'What the bloody hell, they're all wearing coloured boots, and him, HIM, he's wearing pink ones. Then she spotted the football. 'Oh my god they're playing with a pink ball n'all, what a load of pampered pansies.'

I stepped - metaphorically speaking – into her pink slippers (that were not as pink as those boots of professional footballers on screen) and looked through her spectacles, saw her vision and laughed, she was right how did we get here?

Can you imagine Norman - bite-your-legs - Hunter putting on pink football boots to tiptoe through the tulip coloured boots of other players on the pitch to kick a pink football that is as heavy as a balloon, with the same trajectory as one when the knot is untied and you let it go.

331

I recently saw a great series of photos posted in a Facebook football group: the great 1960's teams of Manchester United and Leeds (there's only one United), the middle of a soggy English football season. A pitch like a ploughed field, George Best lying prostrate in this, Bremner, Crerand, Hunter, Giles and Stiles in a punch up with United players, Law's shirt torn to shreads by Jack Charlton, who has his fists clenched, and even his supposedly mild mannered gentlemen brother Bobby is striding into the fray.

Now I'm not saying modern football should be the equivalent of cage fighting football, at the expense of flowing skill.....wait a minute, that's not a bad concept, has anyone else come up with that idea? I'll patent it and take a mini version into the *Dragon's Den*.....but we don't want a non-contact sport. You want your players to battle – and be allowed to – for your team. A captain like Bryan Robson or Roy Keane, who'll go in with a crunching tackle in midfield and come away with the ball at their feet (not a limb), lionhearted, to show us they have passion and know what it means to pull on your team's shirt, know your club's history, give 110% in effort to inspire your team to victory. When they get paid £100,000 to £300,000 a week that's all we ask for starters.

The absorbing contest between a skilful winger or striker and a seasoned, solid defender. George Best may have been lying in the mud having come off worst in the photo, but you can guarantee he wasn't faking it. Best would never get a mere clip on his heel and start resembling Jack rolling down the hill after Jill, or lie there crying. He'd get up, brush the dirt off of him, a mischievous, but steely look in those twinkling eyes, an emerald isle tough heart, from the same rough back-streets as his fans on the terraces;

he knew what it meant to them. Minutes later his foe would be the one lying in the shit after Best had humiliated him with a piece of mesmerising balletic skill (not a Swan Lake death), David defeats Goliath. I saw Giggs flattened by Vinnie Jones and get up and do the same to him with skill as Best before him, cut from the same working-class cloth.

I loved the battles between Fergie's United and Wenger's Arsenal - Keane Vs Vieira, giants of the modern game, Giggs against Keown or Dixon (most memorably in the 99 FA Cup semi-final).

By mid season 2013-14 United were showing no fight, no passion, no clue at all under the management of Moyes. I had felt sorry for him from day one; we knew he was taking on a near impossible task, following Ferguson, with only an average team at his disposal. It was similar to when Frank O'Farrell and Tommy Docherty had to try and step into Sir Matt Busby's footsteps, with the added enormous challenge of rebuilding the entire team. In Docherty's first full season he had to deal with the loss of three European Footballers of the Year legends – Law, Chartlon and Best (but Docherty was given time…until he made a fuck up, 'knees up Mother Brown'). By the time Moyes became United manager, Giggs was only playing a bit part, ready to finally hang up his boots, Scholes retirement had left a gaping hole and the failure to find another midfielder and captain in Keane's mould was showing more than ever.

Moyes only real signing was a late panic buy of Marouane Fellaini, who was out of his depth in the Premiership at United. In the Champions League he was drowning: not one forward pass, lost the ball just about every time and to say how tall he is (and has more hair than the *Hair Bear Bunch*) why the feck couldn't he win a header?

Bad signing, just my opinion. It was like replacing the engine of a Ferrari with a simple dynamo, it'll keep the car running but with no power. United were a Red machine with the sat-nav removed, trying to follow Moyes's road map, going nowhere fast, Fellaini running around in ever decreasing circles. You might as well put a huge perm wig and United kit on Mo Farah, at least when he's running around in circles he knows where his goal and gold are and has the ability and determination to get there.

The lack of fight at United under Moyes was shaming us Reds the most, not just the defeat, the manner of it. After a woeful performance in Europe they interviewed Carrick after the match, and I wanted to kick the TV screen in he was so dispassionate. Roy Keane was steaming too.

'That interview reflected United's performance tonight, flat, no urgency, keeps saying the next game, for some there won't be a next game, that's the reality.' Another thing was irritating him too: 'All this hugging in the tunnel, lets just cut that nonsense out.'

*

I'd been watching a repeat of *Dr Who* on BBC 3, when the Time Lord was in the incarnation of Christopher Eccleston travelling the space-time continuum. The best Doctor in my opinion, but maybe I'm influenced by the fact he's a United fan. Years before he was in *Dr Who*, we saw him outside Old Trafford, during the glorious 1993-94 season and he was wearing the exact same attire as he did as the Doctor – black leather jacket, jeans and black boots. A no nonsense Stretford Ender Manc Time Lord. Perhaps he'd used the Tardis to travel back in time to the pick of United's glory years and great games?

Wouldn't that be great, to have a Tardis. Then I saw one, when I took my nephews Chris and Alex to Crich Tramway Museum. We pretended it was real and imagined the places we could go to if we were time travelling. Well I used my imagination to, my nephews explained that they could go anywhere and anytime in any universe they wanted to via their Xbox's (I owned a PS2 for a short while, but couldn't make it round the first few bends of Gran Turismo without crashing and was getting passed by every other car. I had a *Star Wars* game too but was stuck in the docking bay of a huge Empire spaceship for weeks, until I slapped myself around the face and said 'what the fuck are you doing? Take the dog a walk, have a shave and wash, do some writing.' I sold it on Ebay a few weeks later. My nephews were seemingly born knowing how to live long and prosper in these worlds).

I'd take the Tardis to all United's glory games too of course: the Busby Babe's final league game – the 5-4 victory over Arsenal, the 68 European Cup Final (and England World Cup 66), all those bloody FA Cup finals I missed out on and Barcelona 99 - where I'd make sure I sat next to George Best and talk him into staying until the end. I'd go back and find out what Stonehenge was all about; were the standing stones nothing more than goals in some primitive game of football? To the Battle of Agincourt and find out if a distant relative actually fought there. To Dickens's London. United had travelled back in time, they were playing like it was 1974.

Still disillusioned with United, modern football, the state of the nation, *Question Time* with vomit inducing, rage against the machine intensifying 3-headed Eton monsters, wearing three different coloured ties but from the same background, saying the same bullshit that doesn't answer any questions honestly,*.....

(*Stop press: just as this book was about to go to print, old style, left wing socialist, 4REAL Labour politician, Jeremy Corbyn, was elected Labour leader. I'd rather have the party deemed 'unelectable,' but sticks to the core values that created it and represents the people it was created for than a party that has take on Tory policies so they can get in power, that's not an alternative choice, it's false, people are sick to the back teeth of false politicians that's why so many didn't vote last time.)

.....the nanny state, the loss of English identity and traditions (even a group of Nottinghamshire Morris Dancers have had to end a 900 year old procession because of red tape, health and safety, mountains of paperwork and costs – madness!), I discover my car can be a Tardis for the day. Just 20 miles down the road but 500 years (at least) back in time is the Royal Shrovetide Football Match at Ashbourne, Derbyshire (well I've seen everything else in the English game so thought I'd check out its origins).

This is more like it, I'm thinking shortly after stepping out of my Tardis. A buzz missing from many a modern plastic bowl football stadium, it's like I'm on terracing; in the huge car park in the centre of town, the starting point for the game. Like in the Stretford End paddock days I'm there early and see it slowly fill up, the atmosphere build, until thousands are packed in there. Songs and chants start to break out, either for the 'Up'Ards' or Down'Ards.'

I've a mad Norwegian commentator (being filmed) at my side, rattling on in Scandinavian Motson-esque tones into a huge old Wolstenholme microphone, wearing a 1970's purple tracksuit, shin pads on the outside of these, hobnail boots and outlandish woolly hat on head.

The origins of the Ashbourne game are not known (records were destroyed in a fire in the 1890's) but rumour has it that it started when a severed head, of someone executed, was tossed into the crowd. There are only 6 rules including do not commit murder or manslaughter. A goal is scored when a player from one of the opposing teams, the Up'Ards or Down'Ards, taps the ball (these are bigger than a modern football and elaborately decorated) three times on one of the two millstone scoring posts, situated at the either end of the town. Bruises, black eyes and broken bones are common.

The game even continued to be played through both World Wars. Men from the town, fighting on the front, insisted it went ahead, saying this was one of the things they were fighting for, old England and its traditions.

Large cheers erupt as the first of the teams, the Up'Ards, arrives on the scene – after pouring out of town centre bars, where they've been fuelling up for battle. A long line of them march down through an archway into the square, wearing rugby and football shirts, t-shirts, hoodies and fleeces in their colours of yellow and blue. Soon the Down'Ards – in mainly red and blue – pour in too. More cheers as a dignitary is carried shoulder high through the crowd holding the ball above his head, he's the one who gets the game underway. Many a VIP and well-known person has had this honour: football legends Sir Stanley Matthews and Brian Clough and two future Kings of England - Prince Edward in 1928 and Prince Charles in 2003.

The whole crowd and both teams sing 'Abide With Me,' with a passion I've not heard at a Cup Final since about 1985, followed by 'God Save the Queen.' The atmosphere is now at real fever pitch, as the dignitary – up on a 10ft high plinth – 'turns up the ball,' by chucking it into the fray.

The ball stays in the midst of the largest scrum in the world for a good twenty minutes, until the Up'Ards finally wrestle it free. Chaos engulfs us all as the mass of bodies is on the move following the break out; a 'runner' now has the ball and makes a dash in the direction of one of the millstone goals. He doesn't get far, the mob hunts him down. Both teams tussle for the ball all the way down a street and all around a large block of flats (those in the executive boxes, the ones living in the flats sat out on their balconies, enjoy this moment) and ends up just behind the high wall I've been sitting on to view the action so far.

I jump down there and quickly realise I've made a tactical error. In an instant, the pyroclastic flow of bodies is heading my way, I'm pinned up against a wall, fearing my bones won't remain intact as the crush is on me. Then manage to pull myself up into a tree and back up onto the wall. It's utter unrestrained madness and I'm loving it, full of adrenalin and excitement. How long before health and safety, councils and insurance companies kills this old tradition too? I'm thinking. I love this England on days like this. 'Tis a glorious game, deny it who can, that tries the pluck of an English man,' is the chorus of the 'Shrovetide Song.' Both teams here are showing more fight, guts, passion and desire to win than I've seen on the pitch at United all season. But these men won't shrug off the disappointment of a loss and pick up a cheque for £200,000. The losers will go back to their everyday jobs and be smarting about it for a year, counting down the days to get the chance to comeback victorious.

The ball breaks out again and a series of Up'Ards runners make it several hundred yards towards their goal. We all have to run to keep up with them, the thrill of the chase, the slight worry that the wave will suddenly come back in and engulf you. The game soon gets bogged down in a small muddy field, the ball lost in the throng, who are squashed up against a grass bank. I stand near a group of elderly locals, veterans of the game, and listen to their expert knowledge and memories.

'I kicked the ball once, the highlight of my Ashbourne life,' says one.

Another can top that boast.

'I've scored a goal, of course, still have the ball [all scorers get to keep the ball], it's up there with the birth of my son,' he says proudly, chest out, eyes glazed at the memory of it.

They nudge each other and nod in the direction of another veteran, but one who still gets involved. He's red faced, eyes bulging and is spinning around like a whirling dervish. 'He's had a jar full of energy sweets,' one explains, laughing.

The ball makes slow progress towards the town's park, before that is the River Henmore. I'm quite close to the action now and get some good pictures, even getting a glimpse of the ball as it is thrown up into the air, before it quickly disappears into the midst of the mob again.

Then....it momentarily breaks out and is spinning towards me. A nano-second of thoughts flash into my head: the chance of glory at last in my amateur football career – it's just yards away – if I can give the ball a kick or just a toe-poke, it will be the standout line in my obituary. Better than winning my street's Subbuteo World Cup as a kid....until, on the low wooden bridge behind me, I hear a noise akin to the galloping horses of a posse of cowboys on a bounty hunt. I look up and see a fearsome band of men, like a heard of buffalos, bearing down on me; barn doors and brick shithouses, painted in coloured stripes, tattoos on arms and on the shaven heads of several, eyes ablaze, smoke coming out of their noses, rising above their heads and billowing behind them like a steam train.

'Get out of the fuckin' way,' one shouts.

Too late, I'm knocked out of the way like a juggernaut hitting a road cone and sent spiralling down into the river, up to my knees. Bomb splashes all around me as the ball and the mob go in the river too.

'Head em off, jump the river,' a senior player orders a young rookie in his squad.

'I'm not a fuckin' gazelle,' protests the lad.

So he's shoved in instead. 'Get in there.'

Fergie would love to manage one of these teams for a day.

I feel like I've been initiated now too, as a spectator, and with my jeans drenched and muddy, sodden boots, I happily wade across the river as the ball pops back out on the far side. Then the biggest break out of the day so far occurs, this time in favour of the Down'Ards. A spring heeled runner for them is off across the playing fields, ball in hands, dodging Up'Ards like Gareth Edwards in his prime, over the park and into the streets of the town centre for the first time. It takes several of the Up'Ards youngest and quickest runners to hunt him down. Most of the rest of the teams and thousands of us spectators are racing across the parklands to catch up. I've not run like this to watch a football match since my car broke down on the way to United in 92, and the AA got me near Old Trafford minutes before the gates would shut.

The mass wrestle for the ball is now on the main street through town. A lorry from abroad is surrounded; the driver looks petrified, like he's ended up in England as a new English Civil War has broken out. A policeman wanders over to put him in the picture but I'm thinking about how he's going to explain this to his firm. 'Ok boss, I know I'm late but it went like this, believe me. I went through this town and was surrounded by a frenzied mediaeval mob trying to get a ball to a stone goal. Stuck there for an hour I was, fer sure.'

Soon the Up'Ards take control again, and for a time the game is stuck on a muddy modern football pitch, the other side of the park; it resembles a match between Derby County and Leeds on the notoriously muddy Baseball Ground pitch in the 70's. The ball and teams end up back in the river, then a big lake. Here several strong swimmers get hold of the ball and try to leave the rest in their wake, they're headed off.

I see another film crew, an American one, but the presenter is an English Bear Grylls type, someone who could have been in the Special Forces by the looks of him; the local girls are shouting suggestive remarks in his direction. He continues with his update report. 'This is incredible, I've never seen anything like it, they've been at it for nearly five hours and the match is at a crucial point, just a mile from the Up'Ards goal at last.'

Five hours? I look at the time on my mobile and am astonished, he's right, the time has flown by in all the excitement. The sun is going down, and there's stunning moment, all the crowd are looking across fields towards where the ball is lost in another stalemate, but stood at the back of them it looks like they're all out watching the magnificent sunset like it's the last one on Earth.

By about 7.30 pm I've been in the same field, in the pitch dark, freezing and wet, for about an hour; the ball and mob have been at stalemate for all that time down in a muddy, barb-wire fenced in, ditch, in the middle of high, dense hawthorn bushes.

'Looks like it's going to end goalless today' says a local observer.*

*the match goes on over two days, if a goal is scored before 5.00 pm another ball is thrown up, if no one has scored by 10.00 pm they call it a day.

So, fearing trench foot and pneumonia, I head on back to my car, I'm ashamed to say (I want my pancakes). Just as I'm getting in my car (barefoot, having removed my soaking socks and sodden mud caked boots and put them in the boot) loud cheers go up. Never leave a game early, especially one that's already been going on for over 6 hours and 500 years. I read later that the Up'Ards had scored (they end up winning 2-0 over the two days). Still I'd had a great day, a great tonic and pick-me-up to heal United wounds.

It may have been a good tonic for the yellow-bellied troops for Moyes to have taken the United squad to Ashbourne for a training session. Made them leave their expensive cars behind at Carrington, leave useless tactics behind, it was a fighting spirit they needed. Put them onto an open topped charabanc for their journey into Derbyshire, and shoved them on the Ashbourne front-line for 6 hours. As United's next home game was the most pitiful performance yet, a 0-3 defeat to Liverpool. A total capitulation, the manner of it, the dispassion, was something Reds couldn't forgive. Moyes's management could never recover from it and many of the players proved once and for all that they didn't have a long term future wearing the Red Devil shirt.

Inevitably Moyes was shown the door and Giggs installed as interim manager. The moment Giggs emerged from the tunnel (in his new role, already established as a United legend) and the salute from the Red Army for the man who'd given his career and soul to United, was probably the highlight of the season, especially as he inspired United to a 4-0 victory over Norwich. Both Giggs and the Reds knew he's not yet ready for the job full-time, but he's forever a bright light that never goes out amongst dim bulbs.

ITV made a documentary about Giggs final days as a player – now manager, *The Life of Ryan*. At the final whistle at Old Trafford, the final match of the season, Giggs's last ever match as a player, the camera zoomed into his face on the pitch. In agonizing slow motion, the haunting sound of Brian Eno's 'An Ending' as a soundtrack, to fit Giggs's haunted look, as he glanced around the Theatre of Dreams. Realising it's over as a United player, his eyes glazed black marbles, a black hole time-tunnel back into United's last two decades. He's shaking with emotion, broken-hearted, the look of a man saying goodbye to a loved one at a funeral.

'Giggs, Giggs will tear you apart again,' sing the Stretford End.

Then Giggs spots the camera, forces a smile, and raises a defiant fist, saying he's United forever; my playing days may be at an end but I'll always be there for you, fight for you. It's painful to watch, beautiful to watch. Compacted into that brief moment, etched onto that face, is everything it should mean to be a United player, a hero, a legend.

Although it seemed he always would be, not even Giggs can be 19 forever, except in the memory, on film and illuminated in Man U scripts as a Red star, a Red giant, forever.

2014-15:

So Louis Van Gaal is appointed the new Manchester United manager. A good appointment in my opinion. He has the experience and is a big enough character for the job, to live in Ferguson's presence. He's been given the financial backing to rebuild United, £150 million so far (let's hope it's from the Glazers seemingly bottomless magicians top hat pit and they're not taking more gold reserves out of Old Trafford's foundations), and wisely invested in some class signings: Herrera, Blind, Rojo, Falcao and Di Maria Angel (even if Moyes had that amount to spend he couldn't have attracted this quality, especially as United are not in the Champions League). The last one for a British record of £59.5 million and he's going to be on £200,000 a week.

Yes it's obscene, but, despite all my gripes and groans and lamentations in these pages about the state of the modern game and the United experience, I'm just as fickle as any football fan. We're all living on borrowed money and time, observing the hypocrites and being hypocrites. As I've just watched the new United hammer Q.P.R. 4-0 and felt that old buzz and excitement, that forever Red Devil blood pump through my veins. Yes the younger fans, who know no difference, think it was a great atmosphere, and it wasn't anywhere near the mighty red cauldron's days. It never will be until sections of cheap terracing for young fans is reintroduced (both subjects are all over the football news again and of course I was writing about that in the 90's). No, what brought out the United kid in me was the style of play, the United traditional style of play; fast paced, attack attack ATTACK. The most joyous thing to see, for any true United fan, is a new flying winger in the sacred No.7 shirt (and there's talk of the return of Ronaldo!)

*

Luddite as ever (I've only just been thinking of upgrading my iPod nano to iPod classic and heard the news that the latter is to be discontinued as it's out-of-date. My mobile phone is an old one that is just that, no apps that you can talk to that tell you exactly where you are in the world at that moment and where the nearest Wetherspoons is), I still have a VCR, well it's sort of traditional to have one: when I was, erm about 19 again, I started recording my favourite music and videos off of TV. This started with the, post whispering Bob, *Whistle Test* and the first appearance of the Jesus and Mary Chain and spangle makers The Cocteau Twins in the studio. There's also recordings of *The Tube, Max Headroom*, Nirvana shocking Jonathan Ross on his show by doing 'Territorial Pissings' (instead of 'In Bloom') and trashing their kit, *The Word, The Chart Show* (mainly MaDchester sounds), The Stone Roses and The Verve on *Snub TV*, Oasis on *The White Room*, Jools Holland's *Later* from then until now (I still need new music, though, and listen to BBC 6 Music all the time).

So looking at this book again - in readiness for a re-write, additions and update - I thought it would be good to dig out the BBC's brilliant 1987 video about the history of Manchester United (narrated by John Motson, class), it ends with the appointment of Alex Ferguson. This is treasure enough, but I found real gold amongst the box of videos.

Some years before Dad died I spent an afternoon with him on our landing, going through old cine film (the curtains closed, in silence, apart from the whir of the projector) that he'd shot of our family growing up and now needed to be converted to video (now needs converting to DVD).

None of us had watched any of it since his passing, it would have been too upsetting. But now, for me, as time has healed and I just remember Dad in the good times, great times, funny and magical times (regrets, we all have a few in hindsight, unnecessary arguments), with a smile on my face. So couldn't wait to watch the video of the cine films again.

Oh my, it's brilliant. From the late 1950's, Author Seaton types and Terrence Davies family gatherings. Black pit hills in the background, 60's flowered wallpaper and flowered skirts. Apollo 11 landing on the moon filmed off the TV screen live. To 70's fake stone wallpaper, orange settee, green carpet, red swivel chair (me spinning around in this, for the love of being dizzy or imaging it's the gun turret of a WW2 bomber), silver tinsel Christmas tree. Loads of our Christmas Days, and dogs and cats, and arrival of the unwanted 3rd devil child, Damien me (later imprisoned behind said orange settee – pushed into a corner – when I wouldn't behave). Growing into a kid as cheeky as they come. Footage of me, about 8, at Blackpool, smoking a fake toyshop cigarette, a woman passing by with a disgusted look on her face (nowadays CCTV would alert the authorities and Dad and Mam would be in shackles by the time we'd reached the end of the promenade and I'd be dragged off t'work'us). The 1977 Silver Jubilee street party in Jacksdale. The best footage of me as a little kid – I must be only about 5 – is in our back garden: 'Fluff' the cat watching on, pigeon lofts in the background, as I kick the ball into the air three times without it touching the ground (my new record then, I'd eventually be our estate keepy uppy champion by doing 1000, I'll have you know). Big toothless grin on my face (the tooth fairy was on her way). *If the Kids are United* the movie, and I wonder what my life would have been like if that kid hadn't been United, it doesn't bare thinking about, does it Giggsy, you know.

At least some things never change, elements of Jacksdale/Westwood are 1919 forever. Dr Who could pick up D.H. Lawrence from back then and drop him in the present around here and he'd still hear the same dialect and snatches of priceless speech to note down.

Westwood, the real *Coronation Street*, a conversation in a local pub:

Man 1 – 'Where's ya mate Bob?' [a 60 something]

Man 2 – 'Oh ah reckon he's up to no good, he bought a new hat.'

Man 1 – 'Ah appen then.'

Man 2 – 'Not with Lighthouse Lil, he's done with her, he's seeing Coalhouse Carol nah - been mekin out he's painting coal'us but meeting her there, put about 8 bloody coats on place.'

Then there was Spike being asked how he was getting on with his new mattress – a dodgy one bought from a lad selling them from a back of a van. It's a 'memory foam' mattress that's supposed to mould to the body and be extremely comfortable, a bargain at £100 when they retail for about £500. 'Mine's forgotten me already,' he moaned. 'I reckon he's sold me one suffering from amnesia.'

And Jon Pertwee's *Dr Who* could land his Tardis in Jacksdale Welfare today and find it's still 'Life on Mars' in 1974. It's typical of them to have bonfire night in October and Halloween in November (chalked on the notice board). Don't miss the Christmas party in February. All the dates of historic events, pagan and Christian festivals can be altered if they clash with BINGO night.

Stop press: I'm in these pubs (me with a pint of bitter and a pack of pork scratchings and my Collie dog, Flossy, with a bowl of water and 3 Boneos), back to boasting about United after their impressive 4-0 win over Q.P.R. the weekend before. Full of my old Red Devil self as United cruise to a 3-1 lead at Leicester. Loving the jealous hatred of the Forest and Derby fans. Until given a blue - pool chalk – nose by one of them, as United crash 5-3 in the end. 'Nah who's got a blue moon nose fer singing t'soon?'

Guffaws all around, and my turmoil isn't over yet: my brother's old mate Steve Hall is originally from Leicester and is a season ticket holder at the Foxes, with his son. It's not long before they're back from the match. I'm hiding my head under a coat, but they're pointed in my direction. An hour before my head had been as big as the Elephant Man's, now it's like the scene when the crowd surrounds him at the station and whip off his cloak to mock him.

Ah well I'm convinced United are on their way back to the top, I'll bide my time and not let the bastards grind me down. So I stay out and endure with good humour. You never know I might get lucky this night yet. I've heard 'Lighthouse Lil' is free, I need some kind of light that'll not go out. Born a punk rocker die a punk rocker, Stretford Ender forever.

What happened next
New (major chapter in Tony Hill's life)

Even Everest Shook
Caught in the Nepal Earthquake 2015

Looking for adventure Tony Hill made the spontaneous decision to trek to Everest Base Camp in April 2015. After visiting the ancient temples and squares of Kathmandu, he flew into 'the most dangerous airport in the world,' Lukla, and with a group of fellow travellers from around the world set off up the Himalayan valleys Everest bound. Only 3 days into the trek they were in a mountain village when the devastating Nepal Earthquake struck. Lucky to escape uninjured - buildings crumbled at their side, boulders crashed through the ceiling of their teahouse - they find themselves stranded. Journey with Tony Hill, before, during and in the aftermath of the earthquake (and many aftershocks), and through his writing and eyes (via a series of stunning and haunting photographs) experience breathtaking beauty, the bonding and humour of a diverse set of characters, then overwhelming tragedy, and the fragility, resilience and spirituality of the human condition, as he slowly makes his way out of a disaster zone and home.

One of his Sherpa guides was a Manchester United fan (his team play the in the highest football tournament in the world, wearing United shirts and walk 3 days to get there!), they became friends and Tony Hill turned to the help of Stretford Enders to raise money for Phurba Sherpa, his family and community after their village was badly damaged in the second big earthquake on May 12th 2015.

www.manutdbooks.com